VIRTUALITIES

VIRTUALITIES: TELEVISION, MEDIA ART, AND CYBERCULTURE

IS VOLUME 21 IN THE SERIES

THEORIES OF CONTEMPORARY CULTURE

CENTER FOR TWENTIETH CENTURY STUDIES

UNIVERSITY OF WISCONSIN–MILWAUKEE

GENERAL EDITOR, KATHLEEN WOODWARD

VIRTUALITIES

TELEVISION, MEDIA ART, AND CYBERCULTURE

Margaret Morse

INDIANA UNIVERSITY PRESS / BLOOMINGTON AND INDIANAPOLIS

This book is a publication of

Indiana University Press
601 North Morton Street
Bloomington, Indiana 47404-3797 USA

http://www.indiana.edu/~iupress

Telephone orders   800-842-6796
Fax orders   812-855-7931
Orders by email   iuporder@indiana.edu

The paper used in this publication meets the minimum requirements of American National Standard for Information Sciences—Permanence of Paper for Printed Library Materials, ANSI Z39.48-1984.

Manufactured in the United States of America

Library of Congress Cataloging-in-Publication Data

Morse, Margaret.
Virtualities : television, media art, and cyberculture / Margaret Morse.
p.   cm. — (Theories of contemporary culture ; v. 21)
Includes bibliographical references and index.
ISBN 0-253-33382-2 (cloth : alk. paper). — ISBN 0-253-21177-8 (pbk. : alk. paper)
1. Virtual reality—Social aspects. 2. Communication—Social aspects. 3. Television broadcasting—Social aspects. 4. Mass media—Social aspects. 5. Social interaction. 6. Computers and civilization.   I. Title.   II. Series.
HM258.M689   1998
302.23—dc21   97-40901

1   2   3   4   5   03   02   01   00   99   98

For **Janet and Jonathan,** my parents,
with love and gratitude
and for
Melinda and Mary,
my heroes and my sisters

Susan Kozel (*right*) is about to experience the virtual touch of Andrea Zapp
in Paul Sermon's "Telematic Dreaming" (1993). (See chapter 1, fig. 3.)
By courtesy of Paul Sermon.

CONTENTS

Acknowledgments   ix

PART ONE: VIRTUALITIES AS FICTIONS OF PRESENCE

ONE
Virtualities: A Conceptual Framework

3

TWO
The News As Performance: The Image As Event

36

PART TWO: IMMERSION IN IMAGE WORLDS: VIRTUALITY AND EVERYDAY LIFE

THREE
Television Graphics and the Virtual Body: Words on the Move

71

FOUR
An Ontology of Everyday Distraction: The Freeway, the Mall, and Television

99

Contents

FIVE

What Do Cyborgs Eat? Oral Logic in an Information Society

125

PART THREE: MEDIA ART AND VIRTUAL ENVIRONMENTS

SIX

The Body, the Image, and the Space-in-Between: Video Installation Art

155

SEVEN

Cyberscapes, Control, and Transcendence: The Aesthetics of the Virtual

178

Notes   213

Works Cited   243

Index   257

Acknowledgments

This book draws on conference papers, public lectures, and previously published material, as well as the help and expertise of the following people, listed chapter by chapter. The presses and journals who have previously published material drawn on or reprinted in this book are gratefully acknowledged here.

Parts of chapter 1 draw on a paper delivered in London at the 1984 International Television Conference, later published as "Talk, Talk, Talk: The Space of Discourse in TV News, Sportcasts, Talk Shows and Advertising," *Screen* 26, no. 2 (March-April 1985), 1–11; and on "The End of the Television Receiver" in *From Receiver to Remote Control: The TV Set,* ed. Reese Williams and Matthew Geller (New York: New Museum of Contemporary Art, 1990), 139–41. The discussion of the Gulf War is based on an interview given to Fran Dyson and aired as "Highways to Virtuality," the Listening Room, ABC Radio, Australia, 1991, and printed in Frances Dyson and Douglas Kahn, *Telesthesia,* Walter / McBean Gallery, SFAI, 1991; and on the papers "Three Machines of Vision," SCS, 1991, "Television, Virtual Reality and the Gulf War," San Francisco Art Institute, 1991, and "Virtual War" for the Symposium "Television Studies," Taiwan, 1992. These papers have been previously published in Finnish ("Persianlahden sota, televisio ja virtuaalitodellisuus," *Lahikuva* 2–3, 1991, ed. Erkki Huhtamo, 72–84) and in Chinese.

Chapter 2 incorporates ideas developed at greater length in "The News Personality," delivered at the Center for Twentieth Century Studies, 1984, published as "The Television News Personality and Credibility: Reflections on the News in Transition" in *Studies in Entertainment: Critical Approaches to Mass Culture* (Bloomington: Indiana University Press, 1986), 55–79; and as a longer monograph, *Working Paper No. 5,* Fall 1985, Center for Twentieth Century Studies, University of Wisconsin. The discussion of the Romanian Revolution draws on the papers

"The Romanian Revolution on American Television," delivered in Budapest, and "Social Revolution and the Electronic Revolution" at the International Communications Asssociation in Dublin in 1990, published in part as "Das US-Fernsehen berichtet über die rumänische Revolution," in *Von der Bürokratie zur Telekratie: Rumänien im Fernsehen,* ed. Peter Weibel and Keiko Sei (Berlin: Merve Verlag, 1990), 28–42.

Chapter 3 came out of the papers "Television Graphics and the Body," SCS, Montreal, 1987, and "Immersive Media and Architecture," Media Research Institute, Universität-Gesamt Hochschule Siegen, 1992. Pacific Data Images has generously helped me keep abreast of trends in high-end computer imaging through tours of its facilities over the years. Thanks to CEO Carl Rosendahl and his staff, including Judy Conner, for discussing ideas in the chapter with me and for permission to use images from their archives. Louis Dorfsman also generously made time in 1987 to talk to me about his career in design and television graphics.

Chapter 4 grew out of a paper, "Chronotopes of Television," delivered at the Center for Twentieth Century Studies conference on television, 1988. It was published previously as "An Ontology of Everyday Distraction: The Freeway, the Mall and Television," in *Logics of Television: Essays in Cultural Criticism,* ed. Patricia Mellencamp (Bloomington: Indiana University Press and London: BFI, 1990), 193–221.

Chapter 5 developed out of the papers "Telefood and Culinary Postmodernism," SCS, Bozeman, 1988, "The Body and Virtual Reality," The DIA Foundation, New York, 1992, and the public lecture "What Do Cyborgs Eat?," Concordia University, Montreal, 1993. It was previously published as "What Do Cyborgs Eat? Oral Logic in an Information Society," *Discourse* 16, no. 3 (Spring 1994), 86–123; and in *Culture on the Brink: Ideologies of Technology,* ed. Gretchen Bender and Timothy Druckrey (Seattle: Bay Press, 1994), 157–89, 198–204. The section on the "fresh" in the above publications, reprinted as "Fresh Failures: Tourisma and Frankenfood," in *Zyzzyva X,* no. 3 (Fall 1994), 55–57, was omitted here for reasons of thematic coherence. I wish to thank Jude Milhon (St. Jude of *Mondo 2000*), Mark Rennie of Smart Products, Jack Walsh, Steve Fagin, Danielle Escalera, and Alisa Steddom for insights and suggestions on smart cuisine and oral logic, without implying that they approve of my conclusions.

Chapter 6 draws on the unpublished paper, "Surveillance: Closed Circuits and Fragmented Egos," delivered at the Society for Photographic Education panel on "Surveillance," Rochester, 1989, chaired by Julia Scher; and incorporates the publication "Video Installation Art:

The Body, the Image and the Space-in-Between," in *Illuminating Video*, ed. Doug Hall and Sally Fifer (New York: Aperture Press / BAVC, 1991), 153–67. Thanks to John Hanhardt, at the time Curator of Film and Video at the Whitney Museum of American Art, and his staff, Lucinda Furlong and Matthew Yokobowsky; JoAnn Hanley, then Curator of Video and Performance at the American Museum of the Moving Image; and to the installation artists who discussed the video installation art with me in meetings over February 1989: Judith Barry, Dara Birnbaum, Ken Feingold, Dieter Froese, Doug Hall, Jean Jonas, Beryl Korot, Shigeko Kubota, Mary Lucier, Antonio Muntadas, Rita Myers, Curt Royston, Julia Scher, and Francesc Torres. While I cannot presume they share or endorse any or all of my conclusions, I could not have arrived at this construction of the form without the insights gained in conversation with each of them.

Parts of chapter 7 draw on a paper for the Fifth International Symposium on Electronic Art Catalogue published as "Enthralling Spaces: The Aesthetics of Virtual Environments" (Helsinki: UIAH, 1994), 83–89. The chapter includes portions of a review of a show at Siggraph curated by Simon Penny in 1993, "Art in Cyberspace: Interacting with Machines as Art at Siggraph's 'Machine-Culture—The Virtual Frontier'," *Video Networks* 17, no. 5, 1993, 19–23, as well as parts of "¿Ciberia o comunidad virtual? Arte y ciberespacio" (Spanish translation of "Cyberia or the Virtual Community? Art and Cyberspace"), *Revista de Occidente* no. 193 (February 1994), 73–90, and incorporates much of "Nature Morte: Landscape and Narrative in Virtual Environments," *Immersed in Technology*, ed. Mary Anne Moser (Cambridge: MIT Press, 1995), 195–232.

Research was supported at various stages by a Rockefeller Research Fellowship in Residency at the Whitney Museum, and by research and travel grants from the Vanderbilt Research Council, the Committee on Research plus the Arts Division at the University of California at Santa Cruz, the DAAD, and Critical Studies in Cinema-Television at the University of Southern California. Thanks are due to the archives and the generously helpful staff at the Vanderbilt Television News Archive, the University of California at Los Angeles Film and Television Archive, and the Pacific Film Archive.

Since the number of persons who have been influential and supportive of working out the ideas in this book is far too large to encompass in this acknowledgment, I wish to recognize those who were the first to get me started or who created the first forum, or gave me my first assignment in, or access to, various areas of research in film, television, media, and cyberculture, among them the discussion group at the Pacific Film Archive, including Sandy Flitterman and Bob Stam and mentors Bertrand Augst and Christian Metz; E. Ann Kaplan for television theory; Steve Fagin for video art criticism; Christine Tamblyn for performance art; Keiko Sei and Suzanne Meszoly for art in Eastern Europe; Allucquère Roseanne Stone and Jaron Lanier for virtual reality; and Lisa Goldman and Simon Penny for interactivity. Among those on whom I have relied for ready consultation and feedback are Judith Barry, Ann Bray, Anne-Marie Duguet, Fran Dyson, Steve Fagin, Sharon Grace, Bill Horrigan, Erkki Huhtamo, Douglas Kahn, Marsha Kinder, Chip Lord, Pat Mellencamp, Steve Seid, Vivian Sobchack, and Dorothy Wako.

Note that the "Works Cited" is a pale reflection of the works consulted. To the many colleagues and students who have shared ideas and conversations and to the public who have heard my papers given on the subjects of *Virtualities,* your responses have been invaluable. To the artists who are my subject and my inspiration, my sincerest appreciation.

The very demanding work of preparing the book manuscript was performed by Nigel Rothfels of the Center for Twentieth Century Studies, assisted by Eric Hayot and other affiliates of the Center. My spouse, Joseph Petulla, advised me on the manuscript, provided ongoing moral support over the decade that this book took shape, and put up with me while I was glued to my computer. Meanwhile, senior sponsoring editor Joan Catapano of Indiana University Press waited most patiently and supportively; she deserves special thanks. The manuscript was graciously handled and expeditiously prepared for publication by Grace Profatilov, Terry Cagle, and Dorian Gossy at Indiana University Press. Most of all, I would like to thank Kathleen Woodward, Director of the Center for Twentieth Century Studies at the University of Wisconsin–Milwaukee, editor of this book and of the series in which it appears. She has been a mentor year after year and an editor who has been unstinting in her encouragement and support. It is impossible to imagine *Virtualities* without her.

PART ONE

PART ONE

VIRTUALITIES
AS
FICTIONS
OF
PRESENCE

ONE

Virtualities: A Conceptual Framework

The future lies with dealing with information in real time.

—Andy Grove, CEO of Intel

THE RISE OF CYBERCULTURE

Why do we need cyberculture? One might as well ask why modernizing postwar cultures needed television. Raymond Williams offers the most compelling logic for understanding the social processes that generated television. He was concerned with the long-term and incremental change in the way cultural discourse is mediated and culture itself is transmitted and maintained. For Williams, television as a means of social control and communication is a response to the need for a mechanism of cultural integration created by the development of an industrial economy that uprooted much of the population, divided work from home, and isolated one person from another in privatized forms of living, such as the separate dwellings of suburbia. Highways may link home to work and commerce, but they do not overcome the isolation of what he called "mobile privatization." Television broadcasting, on the other hand, offers culturally unified experiences and can even substitute relations to itself for some aspects of human interaction. The allure of television has deep roots in the need for human contact and the maintenance of identity and for a sense of belonging to a shared culture, the very aspects of life that socioeconomic processes were undermining.

VIRTUALITIES AS FICTIONS OF PRESENCE

Before information, television was a prime shifter of value from one ontological state to another, in the socioeconomic and cultural circulation of material objects and bodies, money, and other symbols by means of images. The computer-based electronic networks into which television itself is being integrated serve the far greater complexities of a postindustrial and postnational sociopolitical information economy. This economy is now the excuse or the occasion for a wrenching restructuring of the workforce that both displaces some people and brings others together electronically—but only as they are separated from each other in physical space. Today, virtual sex on an electronic chatline or the arrival by overnight mail of a cubic zirconia ring ordered by phone from a home shopping channel are complex chains of exchange between images, symbols, bodies, objects, and money that are ultimately based on the instant transportability and the ease of processing images and digital information. Information itself acquires the instrumental or exchange-value of a kind of virtual money. Ultimately, as the matrix of electronic culture, banks of data have the potential to take on the value of the symbolic system itself, much as a library is the storehouse of culture in print, and the archive of visual and aural mechanical and electronic recordings amount to our cultural memory. However, this memory is activated, not as information, but as images that seem to virtually share a temporal and spatial realm and interact with the human beings that are engaged with and in them. Cultural forms from television graphics and shopping malls to the apparatus of virtual reality, as well as practices from driving to conducting war to making art employ various forms of engagement to construct a *virtual relationship* between subjects in a here-and-now.

Seen from the point of view of a developed electronic culture of human-machine relations, television is an interim phase in a process in which only part of the burden for the discursive maintenance and transmission of culture has been delegated to machines. Television has yet to master a full complement of pronouns in relation to the viewer: it is versed in addressing the viewer with *we* and *you*, and it is good at the present subjunctive mode of a fictively shared present, but it is left to the genres of cyberculture to develop the full implications of the impression of being immersed *inside* a virtual world—what amounts to appearing to enter inside the box and the screen. The interactive user is an *I* or a player in discursive space and time.

If we consider the crucial role of storytelling in cultural maintenance, then it is useful to consider the different modes of narration as phases of enculturation. The anthropologist Greg Urban conceptualizes the process of identification with a social role as a passage of narration through degrees of embodiment, from third-person narration of a story that happened to protagonists elsewhere in another scene, to what amounts to a kind of possession by the spirit of a character in the story. Urban stresses the enormous importance of the "dequotative 'I'" or speaking the words of another as if one were present in a social role, not merely identifying but embodying and inhabiting it, in effect transmitting culture itself. While interactivity is often understood as "control" over machines, it could also be considered a way of inhabiting the "you" produced by the virtual address of television. Then, post-televisual machines are charged with the production of "dequotative 'I'" and, hence, with the full range of subjectivity in cultural transmission.

The paradox of the development of the media generally in this century is that as *impersonal* relations with machines and/or physically removed strangers characterize ever-larger areas of work and private life, more and more *personal* and subjective means of expression and ways of virtually interacting with machines and/or distant strangers are elaborated. An information society will not be experienced by most users at the level of its technological foundation or as algorithms and abstract symbols in an imperceptible realm of data. The very impersonality and lack of context that are fundamental to information are far too sterile a basis on which to build the human relations that data is designed to disavow.

Information is impersonal and imperceptible, knowledge stripped of its context in order to be transformed into digital data. It is at once a means of production and a currency of exchange that can be accumulated and stored as virtual wealth that is also cultural capital. Just as the computer is a "universal" machine that can emulate any other, information is a freely convertible currency between material and symbolic orders and reservoirs of value. Bodies and goods, as well as images, money, and other symbols can be exchanged once they have been replicated as digital abstractions, programmed and processed.

Therefore, whether business or entertainment, in order to support a culture based on more than just the economic exchange-value of data, information that has been *disengaged* from the context of the subjects, time, and place in which it is enunciated must be *reengaged* with personality and the imagination. That is, an information society inevitably calls forth a *cyberculture* that enjoys far different characteristics—much like alphabets and phonemes can be articulated at higher levels of language. Cyberculture is personal rather than impersonal, irrational rather than rational, perceptually elaborated rather than abstract, and so on. The logic of this argument or hypothesis on the relation between socioeconomic and cultural forms in the computer age suggests that the more abstract and removed information has become from everyday life and the perceptual field, the more *virtual* the substitute context of subjectivity in a here-and-now at the foundation of cyberculture will be. While objects and images can be virtual, the *virtual relationships* that people in physical reality have with machines and images of various types are the primary focus of this book.

Machine Subjects/Subject Machines

Seen in the temporal framework of over a century, the shift from print and recorded media to television and electronic networks is an evolution that not only depends on subjectivizing machines with more and more symbolic functions, but on granting machines more and more of the process of creating cultural subjects out of human beings. Thus, regarding changes in subjectivity supported by different media beginning with television, machines not only mediate stories, but they also simulate the act of personally narrating them in a shared virtual space. Television's "interaction" with the viewer is a legacy from the hosts and announcers of radio. Sound media like the telephone and radio, in which subjects as conversation partners are separated spatially if not temporally from each other, depend on the imagination of the auditor to construct personas and environments of the broadcast situation and of the world in the stories being told. Paralinguistic cues such as tone and pitch of the voice as well as noises that are coded as signifiers of objects and environments are clues as to the personalities and events involved. It is television that first raises the problem of constructing full-fledged parallel visible worlds and then linking them with our own, via speaking subjects, proxemically "near" to and addressing the viewer with some degree of intimacy. (Proxemics is the study of body language in social interaction, especially the meaning conveyed by the spatial distance between interlocutors.) Your television (via the intermediaries of hosts, anchors, and spokespersons of all kinds) cajoles, instructs, and directs you incessantly, "you" being a virtual position in space about equivalent to the position of your couch or bed, or possibly your aerobics mat or kitchen counter. You may not actually be in that position;

you may in fact have clicked the television off or onto another channel. Monitor-human relations are thus bubbles or pockets of virtuality in the midst of the material world.

More completely interactive and immersive technologies are not different in kind—they are simply better informed about where *you* physically are in material space and, we might add, social space, as might be available as data from the trail you have left of personal credit transactions, tax and income records, as well as rental and housing prices in your zip code and the record of World Wide Web sites you have visited. The agency responsible for a television ad for a luxury automobile implicitly addressed to a male head-of-household with significant discretionary spending is using ratings and demographics as conjectures about who is watching, when, where, and what, to place its spot to target a select *you*. The Web on-line ad may even be specifically constructed for a specific user according to data available about his or her prior "hits" (site visits) and purchases. Ongoing surveillance by machines is then a corollary of the feedback of data from interaction with machines.

However, machine-human relations are not restricted to the space of the monitor, for a material artifact and even a physical space itself can be "cyberized," or granted agency by programming it to simulate some form of human interaction, in the process ultimately lending it uncanny qualities associated with human personality. Unlike prior modes of culturally controlled and contained fiction, virtual environments or cyberspaces can enchant spheres of everyday reality. As Jay David Bolter explains in *Writing Space: The Computer, Hypertext and the History of Writing*, "Artificial intelligence leads almost inexorably to a kind of animism, in which every technological device (computers, telephones, wristwatches, automobiles, washing machines) writes and in which everything that reads and writes also has a mind" (182). One futuristic vision of the personified or "smart" home proclaims, "Once your house can talk to you, you may never feel alone again" (Roszak 35, quoted in Bolter 183), suggesting this animism and a quasisubjecthood can extend to even physical space, once it has been "cyberized." A utopia of ubiquitous computing would enchant the entire world, distributing magical powers to the most mundane aspects of existence.

Any realistic assessment of the foreseeable development of computing power would dismiss a totally cyberized physical world as utter fantasy. Enchanted spaces and animated appliances are likely to remain a spotty and localized experience. Yet this very unevenness, this mixture of the virtual and the material and of this distribution of agency and personality to machines and computer programs is itself disturbing to a sense of control over what the reality-status of any one instance or sector of the world may be: to whom or what is one a *you*?

When to type a computer command brings a graphic world to virtual life as an immersive environment and when human qualities of subjectivity and agency can be granted to objects or even distributed over space itself, we have entered a realm for which we have little vocabulary and few reference points except the language of magic tricks or the linguistics of speech-acts or *performatives*, a category of words that bring the very situation they describe into being. As Julian Dibbell explains:

> After all, anyone the least bit familiar with the working of the new era's definitive technology, the computer, knows that it operates on a principle impracticably difficult to distinguish from the pre-Enlightenment principle of the magic word: the commands you type into a computer are a kind of speech that doesn't so much communicate as *make things happen*, directly and ineluctably, the same way pulling a trigger does. They are incantations, in other words, and anyone at all attuned to the technosocial megatrends of the moment—from the growing dependence of economies on the global flow of intensely fetishized words and numbers to the burgeoning ability of bioengineers to speak the spells written in the four-letter text DNA—knows that the logical of the incantation is rapidly permeating the fabric of our lives. (42)

If the future promises to be an "augmented reality," an animistic, artificial world supported by ubiquitous computing, in which the material and virtual are distributed indeterminately in mixed environments and in which we interact with undecidably human and/or machine agents in what only appears to be "real time," and in which virtual space itself is a surveillance agent, then this will be a world that television has prepared for us by pretending to be talking *to you*. It is this physicality mixed with human agency and language using capacities that even utterly uncomputerized television anticipates as a machine subject, addressing the viewer directly, or more accurately, virtually.

But television is not only a machine subject. It is also a subject machine—that is, a machine of enculturation. In the process of the expansion of the fictions of present tense, "soft" social control has become industrialized and delegated to impersonal machines capable of simulating intimate and primary relations of social reality. Social institutions of family, education, politics, religion, and the economy—once the matrix for enunciating, conveying, interpreting, and enacting narratives stored in print or in local and familial memory—have converged to some degree or other with the media. The television is virtual baby-sitter, matchmaker, educator, (non)site of electoral, legislative, and executive political events, a judicial body, a church, and a mall. Electronic neighbors, hosts, announcers, instructors, performers, and communicators of all kinds now share the interpersonal tasks of presenting and narrating culture with "real" parents, teachers, actors, politicians, ministers, and, most of all, considering the commercial foundation of television, salespeople. For the most part such electronic personas are conveyed secondarily by the images of human beings framed with the machine, though at times we hear, for example, the voice of a network or "the voice of the Olympics" emanating from the body of the television itself.

The logic of such an automation of cultural exchange suggests that machines will come to employ "I" and "you" with greater ease, speaking in personal modes of address that, according to Émile Benveniste, construct subjectivity in a primary way. In Benveniste's linguistics, subjectivity is based in discourse between subjects in a here-and-now. "Discourse is every utterance assuming a speaker and a hearer, and in the speaker, the intention of influencing the other in some way. [It comprises] all the genres in which someone proclaims himself as the speaker and organizes what he says in the category of person" (*Problems* 209). From that standpoint, "he," "she" and "it" are nonpersons, whereas subjectivity is characterized by the reversiblity of "I" and "you," as shifters or empty positions. "I" can be "filled" by any speaker who refers to her- or himself, including what Benveniste might have considered ridiculous—machines.

Of course, the notion of the subject in a face-to-face conversation as real and full has become highly problematic in contemporary linguistics and philosophy. The sense of presence in a here-and-now that "imposes itself upon consciousness in the most massive, urgent and intense manner" is what Peter Berger and Thomas Luckmann call "paramount reality." This is not to say that "paramount reality" is truth or reality itself. It is rather a problematic social construction that is contingent and historical. In *The Social Construction of Reality*, Peter Berger and Thomas Luckmann explain how "reality," however monolithic it may appear to us, is a constructed, relative, and fragile objectification with which a subject precariously and incompletely identifies. Furthermore, there are different levels of this "reality." "The most important experience of others takes place in the face-to-face situation, which is the prototypical case of social interaction" and also the primary means of "reality maintenance" (21). "In the face-to-face situation the other is fully real. This reality is part of the overall reality of everyday life, and as such massive and compelling. . . . Indeed, it may be argued that the other in the face-to-face situation is more real to me than I myself" (29).

Note how a sense of unreality haunts the self in Berger and Luckmann's variable and constructed "paramount reality" in its reliance on the other that is, after all, "imaginary"[1] (Lacan, "The Mirror Stage"; Metz, *Imaginary Signifier*). This paramount reality has undergone great mutations since the advent of electronic culture, particularly since that other in the face-to-face situation is likely to be a television or a computer.

A face-to-face encounter can seem to possess spiritual resources, participating in the realm of what the theologian Martin Buber calls the "I-Thou." We might speculate that the news personality, as a transparent soul addressing the viewer face-to-face, draws upon a powerful cultural potential for a reality of spiritual communion. However, this differs from the face-to-face I-Thou situation that occurs in a shared place and time, for one thing, in that the viewer's own subjectivity is inhibited. (He or she is a "you," but in this one-way situation, not an "I.") To appear on television is then to achieve a level of authority and validation as a subject that is not fully reciprocal. This suggests that the subject who speaks to the viewer face-to-face on television may even seem more "real" than the viewer seems to him- or herself.

One of the fundamental assumptions underlying this book is that there is a basic human need for reciprocity and the reversibility of "I" and "you" in discourse—seeing and being seen, recognizing others and being recognized, speaking, listening and being listened to. Though this need for recognition and self-expression is not well met in contemporary culture's weak public sphere, it still prevails. The following section will take the risk of using specialized terminology in order to propose another species of fiction, called virtuality, with a different relation to social reality. The claim is not that television and a computer-supported cyberculture are less authentic than "real" discursive exchange between human beings. It is rather that socially constructed reality is already fictional and that virtuality is an aspect of that fictionality that has come to be more and more supported and maintained by machines, especially television and the computer.

Two Fallacies about the Relation between Language and the World and Two Species of Fiction

Subjectivity can never be real or full, as it is always based on simulation or what Algirdas Julien Greimas calls the "enunciative fallacy." That is, "I" and "you," "here" and "now" are *not* the subjects, place and time of the act of enunciation: these linguistic forms are "shifters" and "simulacra" within the discourse that *imitate* the act of enunciation within the utterance. In the ordinary use of simulation, language approximates the world through the *concomitance* of subjects, space, and time, that is, personal proximity, spatial contiguity, and temporal simultaneity. Perhaps that is why "discourse" is so often, albeit fallaciously, equated with reality itself. (On the other hand, enunciation is a form of action and part and parcel of the world of material reality.) Using linguistic and semiotic tools, the following explores the rupture or gap that must be bridged to produce "reality."

The first questions we ask about a *representational* image or document are referential. What is this an image of? Is it realistic? Is it true? Our questions are an attempt to reach beyond the image as the utterance now in front of us to the totally distinct exteriority of a world in which there was an object there and then. Our attempts to close the gap between the world and language and other symbols are ultimately successful only in producing what Greimas calls the *referential fallacy.* Photographic technology is quite if not utterly successful in fostering the illusion of access to an "indexical reality" or what Roland Barthes called the sense of someone "having been there" that haunts the image with an ineluctable sense of the past and its loss ("Rhetoric" 44).

However, with the dominance of digital image production that William J. Mitchell dates from 1989, "the connection of images to solid substance has become tenuous. . . . images are no longer guaranteed as visual truth" (Mitchell 57). Once the "postphotographic era" in which we live began, the adherence of the referent (indexicality or "the trace of the real") was set in question. The rupture between the image and world it represents makes objectivity and the closure of possessing the final or true image always illusory. Once photographic realism is no guarantee of "having been there," then the credibility the photograph nevertheless possesses is undermined. "A digital image may be part scanned photograph, part computer-synthesized shaded perspective, and part electronic 'painting'—all smoothly melded into an apparently coherent whole. It may be fabricated from found files, disk litter, the detritus of cyberspace" (78). It will probably take some time for faith in the evidential value of images to erode, in the meantime granting a reprieve to older forms of journalism.

The credibility of television news has, however, long been tacitly based on subjective rather than objective sources. It depends on a different fallacy fostered by electronic media: that the subject or "I" in the utterance or image is the one who actually enunciates it, here and now, or what Greimas calls the *enunciative fallacy*. Even the body we see in physical space, lips moving, voice sounding, belongs to another order of reality than the subject "I" in the linguistic utterance, despite the "identification between the subject of the utterance and the subject of the enunciation" (Greimas 100). In fact, the engaged forms of "I" and "here" and "now" (as opposed to the disengaged or impersonal forms of "he," "she," and "it" in a "there" and "then")[2] are first-order *simulations* of the speaking subject, and the time and place of enunciation. Any "I" in such an utterance that aims to return to the source that enunciated it is condemned to futility: "Engagement is both a goal of the domain of the enunciation and it is a sort of failure, an impossibility of reaching that goal" (Greimas and Courtés 102).

Disengagement refers to "the constitutive aspects of the primordial language act" that "appears as a split which creates on the one hand, the subject, the place, and the time of the enunciation and, on the other, the actantial, spatial, and temporal representation of the utterance" (Greimas and Courtés 88). "Engagement logically presupposes disengagement, for it is the return of forms already disengaged to the enunciator" (89). To call oneself "I," for instance, has to begin from the basis of a not-I and its negation. Thus, a rupture or break is and remains at the heart of subjectivity in the Greimas and Courtés model.

Nor need the subject, space, and time in the utterance be a unified or coherent whole; they can be simulated independently and are capable of being disengaged or engaged separately. In addition, an utterance can undergo further internal disengagement. For example, a narrative may disengage a second-order narrative, and then install a third-order dialogue and so on. Even apparently simple cultural forms such as television news can have many orders of complexity. See "engagement" (Greimas and Courtés 100–102) and "disengagement" (87–90) for a description of these two planes of language.

Once uttered, the breach between an utterance and its enunciator widens, set adrift, beyond the intention and out of the control of subjects who enunciate, quote, and transform it in ever new contexts, setting the "authority that is supposed to spring directly from the voice-consciousness of the self-present speaker" in question (Spivak 214). In his critique of logocentrism, Jacques Derrida deconstructs "presence" and the primacy of speech and the speaking subject over writing. In his critique of Anglo-American speech-act theory in *Limited Inc.*, Derrida stresses the absence at the origin of written utterances: the absence of the sender from the message made known later to persons absent from the scene of writing is but one aspect of the original absence of writing itself. Once a message is sent, it is disengaged from context and intention, free to be read, quoted and iterated endlessly in other contexts, generating semantic meanings that are particular, secondary, and supplementary each time. Derrida prefers the notion of dissemination to communication or polysemy for this widening gap. The written sign is not exhausted by the context of its inscription; once ruptured from that context in an act of enunciation, it is free to drift, separated forever from the chain of present reference, never to be identical with itself.

Hence, what Austin regarded as "infelicities" and accidents—speech-acts which do not achieve their intention—are what Derrida presupposes as the very condition of possibility of speech-acts. While intentionality and meaning do not disappear, they are not central in a structure of rupture and iteration in which the intention animating an utterance will never be through and through present to itself and its content. Consider also that simulation and *dissimulation* rely equally on the enunciative fallacy. The gap between enunciation and utterance that makes meaning possible is also what makes it possible to lie. (The "I" in the utterance does not ever equal the "I" that enunciates it.) Therefore, Austin's notion of felicity could be amended in the light of Jacques Derrida's critique of John Searle to include the intention to persuade, to lie, or to otherwise attempt to control the perlocutionary force (or effect on the interlocutor or speech partner) of a speech-act in a way favorable to the ends of the utterer.

Consider also that whatever the sincerity or authenticity of its intention (Trilling), a speech-act is also an event or performance, the outcome and meaning of which cannot be completely foreordained, even when the intention of a speech-act is to lie. Shoshona Felman's *The Literary Speech Act* deals with promising as the act of bequeathing what the seducers in question do not have: "their word, their authority, their promise." Such a speech-act does not require belief, nor is it ever satisfied. Yet the speaking subjects are "the scandalous authors of the infelicity that never ceases to make history" (150).

This raises the thorny problem of belief in relation to machine subjects or the metapsychology of the viewer in relation to television or the user in relation to the computer. The argument to be made here is *not* that once there was something sincere and unmediated called face-to-face conversation of which exchanges mediated by television and the computer are inherently inauthentic or debased simulations. If anything, machine subjects are made possible by the fundamental gap that has always existed between language and the world and between *utterances*—be they subjective or impersonal—and the act of *enunciation*—whether it is produced by a human subject or has been delegated to machines. An article of faith or fundamental assumption of this book is that there is a human need for and pleasure in being recognized as a partner in discourse, even when the relation is based on a simulation that is mediated by or exchanged with machines.

Such language-using, or more precisely, language-simulating machine subjects, insofar as they are embodied, belong to the category of "intelligent" robots. Insofar as they reside within the virtual world of computers and networks, they could be the agents roaming the databases, assembling and digesting individually targeted news, like a descendant of Walter Cronkite and Max Headroom on whom one can double-click.

Raymond Williams observed in *Television: Technology and Cultural Form* that "since the spread of television, there has been a scale and intensity of dramatic performance that is without precedent in the history of human culture" (53). When he wrote that "watching dramatic simulation of a wide range of experiences is now an essential part of our modern cultural pattern," he could not have anticipated the role in the process of machines invested with personality and agency in a virtual scene. However, since enculturation is a process that passes through a range of persons and positions in language, automating this process would require just such an expansion of "personhood" to machines.

Features of Cyberculture

The "cyber" in *cyberculture* is appropriately built on the analogy of Norbert Wiener's cybernetics, from the Greek *cyber* for steersman and, by extension, feedback, as the study of feedback systems of communication and control. However, as a prefix for the imaginative subculture associated with the computer, it is popular rather than scientific. *Feedback* in the broadest sense (not just as noise or interference produced by a system itself) is a capacity of a machine to signal or seem to respond to input instantaneously. A machine that thus "interacts" with the user even at this minimal level can produce a feeling of "liveness" and a sense of the machine's agency and—because it exchanges symbols— even of a subjective encounter with a persona. In computers, feedback is elaborated into a programmed responsiveness which Sherry Turkle has noted can captivate the user as a kind of "second self."

Furthermore, feedback is a rich substrate for amplifying and morphing echoes and image fragments of one time, one space, and one voice into multiple personalities and overlapping machine-produced subjects. Cyberculture is built upon such a proliferation of *nows* in diverse modalities and inflections and *heres* that are not single, material, and contiguous but multiple, discontinuous, and virtual.

What media-machines responsible for discursive maintenance— "live" television, radio, the telephone and before that, the telegraph— share in common, in contrast to print and cinema, is "liveness" (Feuer) as concomitance, the simultaneous emission and reception of messages—or far more importantly, the impression thereof. Even when the mythical simultaneity of "liveness" that is at the heart of the enunciative fallacy on television is actually or technically achieved—as if the concomitance of production, transmission, and reception meant that these instances are indeed the same event—a problematic feedback loop arises between news and its reception. The news becomes the immediate or apparent cause rather than the report of events. Furthermore, the very notion of "liveness" is more and more compromised by algorithmic image processing that erases the difference between *having been there then* and *being here now*.

The fundamental difference of the use of simulation in ordinary language and in television is that the relation between the sender and receiver is *virtual*: the utterance in direct address of television subject to the viewer disavows the camera lens and the monitor glass, the distance between the speaker and receiver in space and possibly time. Furthermore, as already discussed, the addressee or "you" that is specific and personal in everyday conversation, is a generic and impersonal "you" of anyone in that virtual place, or rather, the population segment targeted as a commodity in the economic exchange that supports television as an American institution. This virtual relation to "you" is expressed ubiquitously in television news, sports, talk and how-to shows, and "reality" programming of all kinds, as well as advertising and the introductory or sponsorship sequences that accompany every dramatic production, every movie or other narrative form on television. Because the image has an x-, y-, and z-axis—width, height, and depth—motion into or out of depth toward the viewer may be called a z-axis move. Even without a "host," or talking head, television space becomes a virtually shared and interactive space whenever logos, openers, title sequences, and bumpers move objects on-screen on the z-axis toward or away from the viewer, or for that matter, appear to move the viewer into the depths of the world on-screen, inducting the viewer as if into the set and the simulation of a parallel world.

"Interactivity" is thus a kind of "suture" between ourselves and our machines. Film theory adopted this medical metaphor to describe the way in which shots or film segments were joined together by vectors such as eye-line or direction matches and shot-reverse-shot techniques to form a coherent fictional world that is separate from our own. Another series of actual and invisible barriers inscribes the divide between the world of the spectator and of the film story (or *diegesis*)—the stage, the proscenium, the curtain, the screen, the invisible or fourth wall, and the 180° line that the camera doesn't cross.

Television discourse, on the other hand, ignores the glass or screen that divides a material and an immaterial world of story. And unlike film, rather than folding representations on the screen back over onto themselves, as if sewing a world together, the z-axis of television is like a skewer or pin on which many layers or different levels and stances of discourse can be stacked deep within screen space and, by extension, virtually beyond the glass into viewing space. This "interaction" underlines television's role as a transitional cultural form, one stage, if perhaps the most historically important one, in the development and consolidation of fundamentally fictitious close personal relations with as well as via machines. In network television, a series of conventions have evolved which segregate the news into different virtual planes within screen space that also are invested with different degrees of subjectivity. These planes or layers are arranged hierarchically, according to a virtual "nearness" to the viewer or "you" that also marks power into the image. Today, such strategies of discursive engagement or interaction with the viewer extend beyond the set to include the remote control and the VCR, telephone calls to 800 and 900 numbers and to computer interfaces, networks, and multimedia links.

These virtual relations or what I think of as fictions of presence have become increasingly elaborated in the shift to utterly artificial realms of *cyberspace* (coined by the science fiction novelist William Gibson, also on the analogy of Wiener's cybernetics). *Cyberspace*, defined as the noplace in which, for instance, two people talking by telephone meet,[3] is the most inclusive term for the imagined, as well as the completely or partially "realized" virtual environments which are capable of *interacting* with users to some extent or other and/or within which, to varying degrees, users feel *immersed*, and, by extension, for the subcultural discourse loosely concerned with the future and technology. Whether we call the noplace in which exchanges on electronic networks occur or the scene of an immersive computer graphic "world" a *virtual environment*, *artificial reality*, or *cyberspace*, the gathering places and sites of experience in electronic culture are increasingly situated in what amounts to *nonspace* and in which humans not only interact with human agents but also with the semiautonomous agency of machines.

The contemporary notion of *virtual reality* as a subset of cyberspace is an extreme example of the substitution of the material world for an immaterial and symbolic one.[4] In virtual reality, the user electronically wraps him- or herself in symbols by means of electronic clothing—the head-mounted display that tracks the head position (that is, the direction of gaze) and covers the eyes with small display monitors, datagloves for tracking hand gestures or the data suits that track the disposition of the whole body—producing the illusion of inhabiting the virtual world displayed inside the fold. It is as if one were capable of moving around inside a drawing that responds to one's changing point of view—or for that matter, as if one were able to climb into a monitor and experience the symbols inside without apparent mediation.

Another heavily promoted, albeit embattled metaphor for this realm is the "information superhighway," modeled on a built environment which is already a protocyberspace or partly derealized and enclosed realm of distraction, as explained further in chapter 4. In any case, the gathering places of culture promise increasingly to be in *nonspace*, taking on a variety of metaphoric shapes and offering different kinds of allure. In fact, once one has factored in the physical machinery of computers and cables plus the machine languages which process digital data, what else is cyberspace but *metaphors* made virtually perceivable by means of a display system? And what are the devices which permit human-machine communication (for example, a keyboard, mouse, joystick, touch screen, et cetera) but metaphoric ways of interfacing via machine with a symbolic world? Those symbols, in turn, have the uncanny ability to answer back.

Fiction and Disavowal in Cyberculture

This is not to say that virtualities or fictions of presence dupe or fool anyone into believing that, for instance, a television anchor is actually speaking to them. Nor, despite its very name, is something like virtual reality, which requires a great deal of cumbersome equipment, likely to make us forget where and who we are. The membrane between virtual and material reality is an actual and easily verifiable second skin. The very commodity status of theme park worlds of present-tense experiences provides them with well-policed boundaries separate from everyday life. Television, on the other hand, cultivates a far thinner membrane between itself and everyday life (see Gardner), since its very function is to link the symbolic and immaterial world on the monitor with an actual and material situation of reception. Yet, while viewers may waver as to the reality status or degree of fictionality to accord live disaster coverage, a reenactment or a docudrama on television, to assume that anyone in the audience is actually deluded into forgetting "this is television" would be to misunderstand the work of disavowal and willing collusion in rituals and conventions, even when these conventions operate contrary to fact or contradict brute physical reality. The present and past subjunctive and its various degrees of fictionality—what might or could have been and could or might or never could be—manifest and sustain cultural values and meanings that are intangible and invisible or otherwise absent in the object world and physical space (see Mannoni).

Nevertheless, while most viewers offer television their divided attention and largely treat it as a thing to which one owes no mark of recognition or politeness, a few viewers (including Elvis Presley) have been known to break the set when angered by the quasireality and its quasisubjects on screen. Other television viewers have been known to go so far as to return the salutations and valediction of the newscaster as if he or she were physically present, in what is known as "parasocial behavior." Parasociality may blur the distinction between primary and secondary experience (Mark Levy 69), but saying goodnight to the television news anchor may also be a classic example of *disavowal* or split-belief familiar from the theater and fiction film: "I know (it's just television, a movie, etc.), but nevertheless. . . . " Note that disavowal cuts both ways. Not only can images and objects be subjectivized, when persons are celebrities, American mass culture may treat them as if they were not feeling subjects but "semifictions," objects available to un- bridled curiosity and free game for imaginative fabrication in the ser- vice of play with cultural values (see Gamson).[5]

Contemporary virtualities or fictions of presence as well as the fic- tions of the past tense to which we have been acculturated over centu- ries in oral narrative, stage, print, and the cinema employ the subjunc- tive mood "to denote an action or a state as conceived (and not as fact) and therefore used to express a wish, command, exhortation or a con- tingent, hypothetical or prospective event" (*Oxford English Dictionary*). The purpose of staging fictions of the past or of what is otherwise absent was to create a liminal zone outside of the demands of everyday life where one could identify with or project onto a not-self from a position of relative safety behind the proscenium, renewing the frayed bonds of a common culture (see Turner). The cinema is also an empathy machine, inviting our identification with characters living lives quite separate from our own. In the cinema, like the novel and the theater before it, the fiction effect depends on a sense of safety or distance in time and space from the fictional characters and events on screen (Metz, *The Imaginary Signifier*).

Television offers an *impression of reality* constructed on an entirely different basis than the fiction of film—for television offers simulations of discourse and fictions of presence that attempt to virtually engage the viewer-auditor with the set in various ways. When Christian Metz applied the distinction *histoire/discours*, based on the linguistic theories of Émile Benveniste, to film narrative, he concluded that the fiction feature film is *histoire*, "narrated without the narrator, rather like in dreams or phantasy" (*The Imaginary Signifier* 92).[6] Film narrative is ideally transparent, as if stories were complete worlds without us, unfolding without reference to subjects, time, or space of the act of their narration. Metz describes different kinds of psychic regimes as well, noting that film is exhibitionist, but not in the reciprocal, alternating fashion between subjects of discourse. Rather, film knows, but doesn't want to know, that it is being watched; so, it pretends to be caught unawares, constituting its audience as voyeurs, who regress to "the seeing of an outlaw, of an *Id* unrelated to any *Ego*" (97). By not acknowledging the spectator or pretending not to know it is seen, a series of disavowals are set in play that structure the classic film as a full and separate world of the imaginary: "it is the 'story' which exhibits itself, the story which reigns supreme" (97).

However, by these same criteria, American television discourse adopts just the opposite approach, apparently baring its own act of enunciation to view, supplying narrators with regularity, speaking here and now in a context shared with the viewer. A talking head with a direct gaze regularly hails a virtual viewer it *pretends* to see. This might be a fairly innocuous shift in the function of "suture" from tying fragments of the fictional world together into a whole toward virtually tying the world and fiction together into a unified presence. There is, however, another important distinction between fictions of the past and present: virtualities are not contained and separate—we are not safe from fictions of presence. Our waning dominant cultural form, television, has no proscenium and no footlights; it is an instantaneous presentation of a realm that is virtually shared—anticipating the immersive and interactive commercial information society now in formation.

Because "live" media are temporally *engaged* or simultaneously transmitted and received, they seem, however speciously, to be more closely allied with everyday life and conversational flow than the authority of print or the detached realm of film fiction allows. The latter media *represent* a world that is past and elsewhere; television and the computer *present* virtually shared worlds, unfolding temporally in some virtual relation to our own, if not always actually simultaneously.

Even before the computer, instantaneously transmitted electronic messages were also capable of generating feedback loops, be they slack or taut. While closed-circuit video is designed to serve the interaction between physical and image space, news images on screen can induce and even change the events on which they report.[7] Speed-up of information-driven economies can be accelerated cybernetically, as for instance, when stock market blips up and down in interaction with global news are magnified still further by computerized stock management programs. As the time and space between the act of enunciating and receiving images closes in, it becomes more proper to speak of an image-world with which we will interact more or less continuously unless we make the effort to disengage ourselves from it.

Virtuality is a little-understood *fiction of presence* that operates on a different plane and most of all, has a different relation to *action* and to *cause and effect* than the fiction we know from the novel and film. As explained previously, fictions of presence play a fundamental role in everyday conversation in physical space. The advent of instantaneous transmission and feedback have simply made them more available to the mechanized transmission of culture. As a result, we are increasingly immersed inside a world of images—acoustic, iconic, and kinesthetic— capable of interacting with us and even directing our lives in the here- and-now, or rather, since the advent of instant decompression and processing via computer, in virtual space and "real time." *Images have been transformed* from static representations of the world *into spaces in which events happen that involve and engage people to various degrees in physical space.*

The conventions of fiction as representation (as in books or films) are more sophisticated and better understood than the fictions of presence, that vary in mood from persuasive performance to subjunctive presen- tation to outright lies and deception; *such utterances or performances include images meant to shape or invent a world, not represent it.* Virtualities become problematic when they are misunderstood as fictions of the past in which actions have no direct consequences for the material world. When the result is actual mass destruction, experiencing war conducted by means of manipulating symbols on a display on a com- puter as a kind of fiction or game can be a dangerous thing. However, even if the stakes are symbols and there is no intervention in the ma- terial world or physical body, virtual events can have actual conse- quences, as demonstrated by an example of telematic art (that is, art composed through operating on another spatial realm remotely or from afar) discussed later in this chapter.

Intersubjective/Interactive/Telematic

Once the simultaneity of *liveness* becomes instant *feedback* between images and the world, an inversion takes place in what was once called representation: neither image nor the world is "first," and each is likely to shape the other. *Interactivity* is usually conceived as a means of allowing the consumer/viewer to select or change the image with the help of an input device—telephone, keyboard, remote control, joystick, mouse, touch-screen, brain wave reader, et cetera. Interactivity like this has been mistaken for a kind of emancipatory self-expression that will change the very nature of communication. Two-way television, for instance, is touted as escaping the one-way and inert couch position for consuming television. However, if interactivity is an extension of the notion of immediate feedback of input on a display, that is, if it is operational and instrumental, does an input device of any kind make what is on the television or on a computer monitor any more inter-subjective or liberating?

This is not to discount the importance and necessity of interactivity between humans and humans, humans and machines, and even machines and machines—as long as the often unprofitable and inefficient forums of *intersubjectivity*, the *mutual* recognition, communication, and reflection of subjects that are the foundation of sociality and civility can also take place. The price of intersubjectivity is not only all sorts of infelicities and contingencies, but a process that can shift the framework that began the exchange between the parties involved in the first place.

Note that interactivity and intersubjectivity are not mutually exclusive, especially considering the murky status of the subjectivity we as a society regularly delegate to machines. Nor is instrumentality regarded pejoratively here, especially when it is further engaged with discourse on the values and priorities of cyberculture. Once subsumed into discourse, even the most instrumental relations can serve art and culture as metaphors that enrich our currently rather impoverished social imagination. (At present, very simple models of social relations prevail that pose individualism against fascism or communism, offering little means for comprehending complex patterns of cooperation that prevail even among machines.)

Consider the current fascination with "artificial life," for instance, as it "evolves" in the computer.[8] Self-generating patterns of interaction or what is known as "emergent behavior" over many computer generations may not be "life" (see Hayles, "Narratives of Artificial Life"), but it may be a way to figure complex dynamic interrelationships that help us to recognize similarly complex but far slower social and environmental patterns all over the world.

Once the interactive display evolves into an autonomous realm of images in which we are immersed, the image is more accurately an image-world that is enunciated around us constantly in *real time*. Computers allow duration to be simulated in a way that disguises the large amount of processing of information going on inside the black box; for instance, ADO or DVE computers can condense, expand, and move images on videotape at the same time that news or sports programming is being assembled live on air. Speech, writing, or drawing can be called up from store as if it were spontaneously produced on the spot; the data composing images can be decompressed and manipulated instantly to look as it were instantaneous in the same way as a world captured on video. So, *real time* depends for its very existence on the creation of unreal time that can mimic the clock. Of course, there are vast areas of the world in which time unfolds in the slow pace of duration. Even in a culture that prizes speed and instantaneity, some discourse such as hearings and trials must revert to duration for the event to occur at all.

Furthermore, if the image is linked up to apparatuses that control aspects of the physical world from a distance, the electronic image is no longer just a medium or a place, but an aspect of *agency*. Interactive control of the image and consequently remote control of the world is called *telepresence*, or, as it is known less oxymoronically in many European contexts, *telematics*. Any act of enunciation or symbolic kind of doing, once linked up to machines which execute instructions instantly, can take on an actual and deadly telematic power. The Persian Gulf War is the most obvious case in point for discussing the lethal dimensions of reconforming the world to fit the image. According to Paul Virilio in *War and Cinema*, war and "machines of vision" have a long and mutual history, though his comparison of the derealizing effect of modern warfare to a "life-size cinema" may no longer be apt (88). It also reminds us that to consider imaging systems in isolation from each other doesn't make sense. What is television without the counterpoint of camcorders in Eastern Europe in 1989? What is the Gulf War without global surveillance and military imaging systems or Pentagon-supplied graphics from the warhead's point of view?

These interactive and telematic capacities have taken us far from the normative ideas about the functions of images in relation to the world that prevailed until quite recently. What concerns cyberculture is not the fact of telematic imagery per se but the telepresent danger of engagement with the image world at the cost—ethical and psychic—of disengagement or remoteness from the actual effects of one's actions. I will offer two examples of "telepresent danger" that caution us that telematic agency is far from becoming framed and controlled like the regression of cinematic fiction—and it has far more potent and immediate consequences than televisual distraction. The responsiveness of images to our commands and the ability to act at a distance in the world by simply saying or pointing or gesturing also create a feeling of omnipotence that involves psychic regression of belief or complicity in word magic that can also be terrifying or delightful, depending on the context and the cultural frames constructed for virtual realms.

VIRTUALITIES AS FICTIONS OF PRESENCE

We are used to the symbolic presentation of force and terror via video and computer adventure and war games. We are not (yet) used to the symbolic presentation of horror that is actually occurring.

—Siegfried Zielinksi

FRAMING CYBERCULTURE: VIRTUAL WAR AND "TELEMATIC DREAMING"

The crisis in the Gulf that led to making Iraq a proving ground for electronic warfare suggests wider areas of crisis in the process of enculturation. Composing virtual worlds (that is, what are nonspaces that exist in effect, but not actually), and inducting the ordinary, nonexpert human, at least virtually, into the field of digits and machine vision (Virilio) require "interfaces" and display systems that translate "silicon-based intelligence" into our own "carbon-based" perceptual systems and ways of seeing (for more on this distinction, see Hardison). But once virtual contexts are produced and inhabited, other problems arise: "virtuality" is a dematerialized, and for that reason, ontologically uncertain mode of presence. Habitable cyberspace undermines long-term cultural notions of reality as well as systems of belief and identification. For the virtual does not yet necessarily (a) represent "reality" in ways we have come to expect; nor (b) distinguish between imaginary and real consequences of manipulating symbols; nor (c) is it always framed off from everyday life, like, for instance, theatrical or novelistic fiction. Consequently, (d) the reality statuses of virtuality have not yet been culturally mastered or regulated, nor are the subjunctive modes of virtuality well marked.

For instance, war conducted via interactive video display can have very real effects on another physical space instantly or with delay—or it can be just a game. The war in the Gulf on television resembled little about the physical world on a human scale. Television viewers of the Gulf War saw largely graphics, albeit transmitted live, and they heard the voices of reporters who could identify little of what was going on from their vantage point, beyond the explosions themselves, much like reporters who report live from the crowd at a media event are there to describe how little they can see (see White, esp. 128). Instead, the electronic imagery of television graphics provided the "first full-fledged video logo war."[9] Press censorship meant that the Pentagon supplied most of the rest of the visuals and the commentary; yet martial videos lacked "realism" in the iconic sense of "looking like," since they were based on the display of the machine vision associated with weapons like the F-117A Stealth fighter, the Hellfire missile and GBU-15 glide bombs (Denton 58). Deciding, or, better, feeling the difference may be problematic where similar-looking graphics lacking the resolution and indexicality of photographs may be guiding a weapon to target in the air war against Iraq or referring to an imaginary realm in which Saturday morning Nintendo takes "place." (One could imagine a paranoia-inducing situation similar to the children's rhyme, "step on a crack, break your grandmother's back.") A simulation can become rehearsal can become remote action and be virtually identical as to the look and response of symbols on a display.

The movies, Nintendo games, and virtual reality as the impression of immersion inside an artificial world have become abiding terms of comparison for the experience of the Gulf War that the media offered. (Richard Bernstein noted that "[The Gulf War] was so carefully scripted for television that it was in a way already a movie," and cites Ken Burns to the effect, "There's no reality to this war, but only a kind of virtual reality"; and General Norman Schwarzkopf made his famous statement, "This is not a Nintendo game.") Such apparatuses of fiction and artifice emphasize the intentional or controlled nature of instant Gulf War coverage on television, and the derealizing sense of artificiality in the war as graphic display, along with remoteness from the events and consequences of the war. This sense of remoteness extended from the conduct of the air war by bombing crews who had "no sensation of the havoc erupting on the ground," to the enthusiastic patriotism and moral remoteness of Americans toward a war "whose chief price has been paid with the lives," and we might add, the environment and economic well-being "of others" (Rosen). Such remoteness is fostered by the apparatuses of vision engaged in the conduct of the war—the electronic war machine and its public display system, the real-time television Gulf War.

Where virtual reality (in the narrow sense of real-time computer-generated, three-dimensional worlds) involves mapping of some of the sensory and kinesthetic properties of the body onto the image-surround—Renaissance space turned inside out—its purity is a consequence of interfaces that block out or blind the user to the physical world, giving the virtual image-world "absolute authority" over the physical.[10] For instance, the "eyephones" or head-mounted display could merely superimpose the virtual over the physical—however, display modes marketed today show a preference for occluding the physical field from view. This closure also creates a system over which the master-creator can exercise absolute control, and the user immersed in the system enjoys this sense of omnipotence secondhand. So, war as strong engagement and a sense of immediacy and nearness to the interface can coincide with a feeling of moral disengagement from a remote referent world of the enemy, for example, Iraq.

Where the virtual replaces the physical in everyday life, differing access to information or symbolic processing results in the actual, physical segregation of society and its institutions into techno-haves and have-nots. Only the person with an electronic scanning and display device can explore (and perhaps worship) "The Golden Calf" (1994), Jeffrey Shaw's ironically titled interactive sculpture. Anyone else in the room sees an empty pedestal. The cultural effects of such segregation are equally disquieting, for virtual interactions do not necessarily promote bonds of identification or sympathy, most especially with those inhabiting a physical reality beyond its virtual reach. Graphic modes of presentation in high-tech war, real-time television and virtual reality, the nature of image capture and display, and the spectacle of war itself have changed and along with it, the means for moderating war's psychic effects. Remoteness as the term of comparison slips between psychic metaphor, interface device, and physical description in the process, suggesting the fluid ontology of symbolic visualization of information in which mortal bodies may be made virtually invisible.

War conducted telematically forgoes a sense of physical contact with the enemy. Sunlight is banished in favor of the pale luminescence of the monitor; graphics generated on the computer display data from light waves beyond the spectrum that is visible to the human eye. Winograd and Flores argue that computers have an inherent "blindness" (a term borrowed from Heidegger) that is certainly demonstrated by machines for the virtual conduct of war. Seeing with night vision goggles, for instance, limits peripheral vision of a pilot as if he were "looking through a straw"—emblematic of an inability to see beyond the virtual interface and its zone of control. However, what displays for the conduct of war lose in realism, they gain in actual power—contingent on mechanical or computational failures and human error—to virtually affect physical reality and reshape the world according to directive. Instantaneous images, especially telematic ones that are linked to agency in the world, do not need to "look" realistic to be a powerful constitutive force of reality. Nor need a computer interface that occludes the visual field account for material bodies on the scene of battle.

Virtualities: A Conceptual Framework

Jeffrey Shaw's virtual sculpture "The Golden Calf" (1994) can be viewed from above, below, and on all sides by moving an LCD color monitor around the physically empty space atop the white pedestal. Interactive computer graphics installation. Software: Gideon May. Produced at the Institute for Visual Media, Zentrum für Kunst und Medientechnologie Karlsruhe (ZKM). By courtesy of Jeffrey Shaw.

VIRTUALITIES AS FICTIONS OF PRESENCE

The closure of such machine vision leads to particular sorts of blindness that might explain the curious absence of enemy or civilian Iraqis in our crosshairs as well as in our news. What broke through, occasionally, were brief moments of civilian outrage and grief at the al-Amariya installation/shelter/bunker or the gaze of a Kurdi woman into a camera, asking why? But what we did not confront for more than a brief moment is another subject with another point of view. Our Cold War systems of representation, identity, and belief were virtually if not actually maintained in a realm beyond sympathy or understanding, that is, beyond a second electronic skin.

Machine vision obviates the work of dehumanizing the enemy and producing ideological justification that precedes and makes martial conflict acceptable. For instance, "surgical bombing" is not only a metaphor for accuracy but also for an instrumental relation to a body, an objective mindset and high precision in distinguishing the bad object from the good object. In this martial machine of vision, the virtual world is global and panoptic as captured via remote sensing satellites in top secret high-altitude overheads. It is as if defense satellites could produce the imaginary map Borges described in one of his stories as the equivalent in every way, including size, to the land it covers: however, because this map exists virtually, images of any portion thereof can be processed (decompressed, enlarged, enhanced, and displayed) at will in real time. Furthermore, weather and night are not limiting factors when it comes to machine vision; access to the highest resolution data of remote sensing and imaging technology is restricted from the public as intelligence information. Such control of access to vision allows a concentration of information as power, when applied to convince, coordinate, or contain allies, attack enemies or contain the press.[11] The martial, virtual, panoptic map matches the body of a weapon and a trajectory on the virtual terrain contour map constantly against radar altimeter measures on board, point by point. The goal of this matching is, as Virilio describes, to rewrite the map, to impose a new terrain upon the physical world. Matching the crosshairs of the virtual to the physical world is what creates the line of sight—and to see is to kill. The only problem with the map is its aerial point and angle of view. It is the one least likely to reveal human beings—much less people as subjects, capable of calling us to account.

Even the cruise missile, credited by a story in CNN with the ability to follow street signs in Baghdad, actually requires virtual industrial scenes at a far lower altitude and angle of view against which to match its radar. The military has lamented its lack of tactical intelligence (with its nearer, lower point of view) in the Gulf War. One could even say the cruise missile requires a more human vantage point, except that the target images it needs can be synthesized from single high-altitude overhead photographs. (Could humans within the industrial scenes also be synthesized?)[12]

Although the Coalition goal was to "blind" Saddam Hussein, that is, to put out his infrastructure, each type of machine vision is already equipped with its own built-in sort of blindness. Similarly, dependence on image processing means that the "bad" computer in a Patriot's radar "never saw" the incoming Scud missile that destroyed an American barracks in Riyadh (Schmitt A9). The desire to create a closed system within which the map can obliterate the real adds a kind of willful blindness to what is inherent in technology—producing a realm where fantasies have few reality checks and physicality offers little resistance. Here is the fantasy of omnipotent thought and of interaction with a non-other, virtually but not really there, that unlinks the document from the world and transforms a medium into a kind of surrealestate all its own. That place could be coequal with the globe itself—the military version—or a place in nonspace where the world projection meets my living room—the television version—or a virtual world of the imagination or remote reality just the right size to wrap around you or me—the utopian nonspace of virtual reality.

Of course, in virtual reality taken on its own terms, any sort of interaction is morally acceptable because there is no one actually in its hallucinatory space. (Here the issue is virtual reality as a closed, "toy" world, not the vast field of cyberspace virtually distributed over many aspects of reality.) This machine is mapped over various sensory modalities of the body and its kinetic and propriocentric (the awareness of the body of itself) orientations by means of interfaces like the glove, the helmet, or eye phone with sensors that respond to head position. The result is the virtual immersion of the body and its capability of interacting with the display—not apparently a place of dialogue or confrontation with other subjects. In fact, because there are no natives, no prior inhabitants, and difference is as accessible as a costume, it is almost an alibi, a voiding of responsibility for what goes on within nonspace—no colonial metaphor need apply. Note that "interactivity" applies to the interface; it is not yet intersubjectivity. One can now have discourse with others, but only those with the same access to the inside of the same virtual world and then only with their virtual avatars.

We saw the degraded, infrared machine vision of warriors in the video footage supplied by the military to television in which bombs almost always hit their targets—and missed humans. In one of General Schwarzkopf's press briefings from Riyadh, for example, we are shown the "luckiest man" in Kuwait, a dark dot passing through the crosshairs and out of range of the extremely grainy, schematic image of a missile guidance system. Then, we saw a bomb fall and, again, there was no one there. The duality of us versus them becomes personalized only in the TV images of George Bush and a Saddam Hussein sometimes shown superimposed over the desert meant to represent Iraq itself. For the rest, "we" met the enemy and "he" was not just dehumanized, he was a nonentity, for there was no one there.[13]

But it is that no one is *actually* as opposed to *virtually* there I want to set in question. Actually, there are not merely two worlds—virtual and physical; there are at least four connected with virtual reality—all of them are populated. The felt or propriocentric body is the motor and source of agency for the virtual body. The virtual body can inhabit several degrees of person within a virtual world, from a ghost observer or "lurker," to a first-person participant, to being represented by an avatar or "me," to identification with third-person characters. Beyond the virtual is the largely male-dominated world where virtual reality is invented, produced, and programmed and the largely female world where it is assembled and maintained. To imagine the virtual without those who produce and service it is magical thinking on a par with the hidden servants of *Nosferatu*, *Beauty and the Beast*, or *Repulsion*. Then, there is the physical body seen making blind, infantilized motions that generate the feeling of "flying" or performing surgery or composing molecules within the virtual world.[14] This infant body is vulnerable, requiring not just an interface or second skin, but a fortress within which it can move with majesty and without fear. Finally, what is the virtual realm itself but externalized imagination, the product of a shared symbolic system and the unconscious? These symbols, furthermore, can be telematically linked to machine agents and very physical bodies. Then what happens in the virtual realm is a *symbolic event*, which is not without psychic or actual consequences. After all, the physical and felt bodies are linked to this symbolic world, and, so to some degree or other is the psyche, all the more so since, unlike the identification in fiction with third-person characters elsewhere, the felt body is linguistically and actantially engaged to some degree or other with the persons of "I" and "you" and is not just a voyeur. How could one have imag-

Virtualities: A Conceptual Framework

While sitting on a bed used as an image projection surface, Susan Kozel gazes at the
monitor that displays a virtual bed that is a mixture of her bed interpolated with another
distant one in Paul Sermon's "Telematic Dreaming" (1993). (See Frontispiece.)
Photo: Paul Sermon. By courtesy of Paul Sermon.

ined that the virtual realm, even when blank and empty, would be
devoid of other (un)consciousnesses or be a world without contingency
or history?

"Telematic Dreaming"

In writing on her experiences as a participant for several hours a day
over several weeks in Paul Sermon's first ISDN-based art installation,
Telematic Dreaming (1993), Susan Kozel describes her relation to her own
virtual body. The piece draws people in two separate rooms together—
in this case, on "a" bed—by combining their images via computer and
projecting it or screening it on monitors. For Kozel, the "experience was
one of extending my body, not losing or substituting it. My intuitive
conviction that the virtual body is entwined with the flesh was rein-
forced by my experiences of intimacy and violence" (12–13). While her
physical body was the ultimate ground for the image, "my electronic
body could do things that the latter could not, such as map itself onto
another or disappear, yet it could not exist independently" (31). She
could also disappear and reappear, fragment her body and reunite it.

VIRTUALITIES AS FICTIONS OF PRESENCE

Kozel describes interrelationships with others based on vision and motion as capable of a profound intimacy, and even responded with "little electric shocks" at a virtual touch. More often the behavior of visitors was predictable, constrained by an automatic code of behavior for sexual and social interaction called forth by the "bed." The only time she divorced herself from her virtual body was in reaction to "cyber-sexual violence" of two men who attacked the head and pelvis of her virtual image on the bed. Kozel began to see the "bed" as a "social and cultural space as well as virtual one," externalizing a symbolic field of behaviors, including gender roles, that "challenged visitors (and my-self) to identify their cultural formation and overcome it" (46–47). Events that occur solely in virtual image space—*symbolic events*—can have material consequences. The premise of virtual realms taken on their own terms—that any sort of interaction is sanctioned because there is no one actually in its hallucinatory space—is contested here. Symbolic acts in image space can be as potent and dangerous as physical force. So, even in a disconnected, autonomous world, in which no one is "really" there, how could one really elude responsibility for one's fantasies and actions?

When frames and conventions are lacking that set the everyday world in which we are responsible for most everything we do apart from a liminal realm where anything can happen, the task of discourse, including critical writing, is to invent ways of coming to terms with the situation. In a world undergoing a process of derealization, art can also serve this work of acculturation by refining our sensibility for the shadowy mixtures of delegated and deferred humanity invested in machines. "Framing" as a task does not entail a referential "mapping" of what is already there—the two-dimensional forms of the "map" and even the "frame" are no longer appropriate metaphors for what is an enunciative process, namely, the construction of cultural models. The task of constructing conventions and markers of the various fictions of person and of here-and-now would ideally be undertaken in a public sphere, mutually and intersubjectively, in a way that no longer relies on the referential "truth" but rather on the expression of many points of view.

Not too surprisingly, mass culture relies on the fallacies of referentiality and enunciation and uses engaged forms of imagery to enchant the world, not to come to terms with it. The critique of presence that began in speculative philosophy continues in cultural criticism. Art forms that disrupt and disengage the body from virtual relationships to images also perform this service in a way which involves learning with the body itself. The cultural task is to assess the very symbolic tools with which we think and express ourselves about experience—an assignment that this book approaches case by case.

VIRTUALITES: **AN OVERVIEW**

Virtualities is divided into three parts: the first part, "Virtualities as Fictions of Presence" includes this chapter defining the conceptual framework and theoretical tools of the book, while chapter 2, "The News as Performance: The Image as Event," takes a more historical approach to explore how power is inscribed in news discourse. After introducing a model of the subject, format, and levels of address in television news and talk shows in relation to the public sphere, the chapter looks to televisual events that happened during the Romanian Revolution to address how the news image and physical space interact.

Part two, "Immersion in Image Worlds: Virtuality and Everyday Life," begins with chapter 3, "Television Graphics and the Virtual Body: Words on the Move." After discussing the historical styles of television graphics, various figures and tropes associated with the "glitz" of network logo and ID sequences in the 1980s, particularly the vortex and the "fly-through," are proposed as anticipations of the immersive and interactive imagery of "virtual reality" and virtual environments in the 1990s. Chapter 4, "An Ontology of Everyday Distraction: The Freeway, the Mall, and Television," takes account of image-surrounds that are analogs of television: freeways and malls. Images in print and on television have surrounded Americans in everyday life incrementally since the takeoff of mass culture in the 1960s. While a television, magazine, or billboard advertisement is not strictly speaking a virtual image, its relation to the consumer can be. This chapter also refines the idea of a fiction of presence by describing its effects or the metapsychology of distraction associated with engaged cultural forms. The next chapter, "What Do Cyborgs Eat? Oral Logic in an Information Society," might be considered an extension of the movement into the image described first in "Television Graphics." The chapter grew out of an originally quite different paper I had delivered in the late 1980s on "Culinary Postmodernism." When I returned to the subject again in the early 1990s, I found that culinary culture had been transformed along with the advance of information society. Contemporary culinary fantasies involving the desire to be incorporated into the electronic machine are set in relation to the pervasive oral logic in cyberculture of immersion and wrapping or enclosure.

While sampling cultural forms of over a decade or more is not a very long-term study of cultural change, *Virtualities* assesses many fundamental assumptions about reality and electronic images that have shifted even within this time frame. In any case, the chapters in this book are concerned largely with aspects of culture that are part of the background or architecture of daily life, the features of which we have tangential awareness, but on which we seldom settle our conscious awareness or powers of reflection. Art, or more accurately, particular art forms and artists bring this tacit dimension to light. A trend in art began in the 1960s, if not earlier, and was concerned with the exploration of fictions of presence. Many movements from minimalism, pop art, and happenings to media art and virtual environments are part of this larger aesthetic field which investigates the dimensions and properties of a social and experiential reality in flux.

Part three, "Media Art and Virtual Environments," is arranged in order of the degree of virtuality of the media art discussed: chapter 6, "The Body, the Image, and the Space-in-Between: Video Installation Art," proposes a generic model and a metapsychology of an art form which composes electronic images within a three-dimensional material space. I regard the experience of a successful installation as a deep cognitive process that is a kind of learning with the body itself, in a mode of experimentation that is, unlike that of science, vastly underappreciated. Chapter 7, "Cyberscapes, Control, and Transcendence: The Aesthetics of the Virtual," uses specific examples of electronic art to discuss the construction of subjectivity in electronic culture and to propose ways of thinking about the reality status of the virtual. It begins with a description of the exhilaration of navigating in a virtual world and offers several propositions about art forms in which the image space is an immersive and interactive virtual environment. Then it explores the metaphor of travel or the journey through a virtual landscape, especially as it illuminates the relation between virtuality and a paradoxical status between life and death.

While the issues this book addresses are cultural rather than technological, new image and information technologies are imbricated with a global socioeconomic reorganization that is increasing disparities of wealth and well-being. The roots of social injustice are cultural as well as socioeconomic. Many commentators have noted the lack of sympathy (or feeling with) that characterizes many aspects of contemporary political and social policy, unwinding a web of sociality built over this century. Our image of sociality has become impoverished and the apparatuses which forge the bonds of affinity and link disparate groups into a well-functioning society are loosening. For instance, for those people without access to the worlds on-line where everything from business to scientific publication to communal life and intimate conversation is conducted, social differences become absolute. To be excluded from information society is to become invisible to those enveloped by virtual worlds and engrossed in interaction with machines.

As the century draws to a close, we face the challenge of producing a cyberculture out of or in spite of the instrumental economic imperatives of an information society. Commitment to social justice and the desire for varied and rich communal life cannot be approached through technology or political activism alone without a better understanding of how power is tacitly distributed by such mundane things as television formats or how a little recognized kind of fiction permeates contemporary life from freeway driving habits to the conduct of war.

TWO

The News As Performance:
The Image As Event

The drama of duration: the untelling of a dictatorship. [The Filipinos] watched the whole 50 minutes, the little family tyrant, repeating, obsessing ... holding on for ... the moments the Americans would cover.... they were watching a dead man, and every second was savored. TV had been reversed and now power flowed upstream. A dictator under surveillance, television stripping the emperor bare. A whole nation watched a machine hand out its own justice, as spectacle toppled before the wrath of the real.

—Steve Fagin, *The Machine that Killed Bad People* (1990)

The young news presenters in the Video Workshop of the Roŝka Refugee Camp in Slovenia in 1993 found that, "People had a particular model in their heads of what television was. It was in the minds of these people. So we had to make the news *look* like the news—what people were used to seeing. It was then that it became credible." The news in question consisted of reports of social unrest and armed conflict from around the globe (not just Bosnia), bootlegged off satellite from Radio Sarajevo, CNN, and Sky television and used as raw material to be integrated into a new narrative, edited by Bosnian refugees for Bosnian refugees. In the process of learning how to simulate the news, the refugees or "stowaways" found that it "was all one big manipulation." One of the two presenters sitting at the news desk in Chris Marker's documentary *Prime Time in the Camps* can't help breaking up as an ordinary person, or rather, a refugee, a "zero," performing an exalted role on the other side of the television screen.

However much the camp video succeeded in mimicking the format of the news, the refugees' project was different in instructive ways from American-style news productions, with their sharp role divisions and hierarchical structure. In the Video Workshop of Roŝka everyone was involved in capturing, sorting, editing, and performing the news: "We are all in the same situation and on an even footing. On both sides—those who film and those who talk." When the camp news producers/presenters found different interpretations of events in their sources, they simply juxtaposed them for the viewer to compare and evaluate her- or himself.

In another room in Camp Roŝka, refugees were invited to speak to the camera at length. Their willingness to participate and to pour out their hearts was not because these people were deprived of images of themselves: "Video has become part of daily life. In the room, the family explained that . . . even their departure [as refugees from Bosnia] has been filmed and they promise to bring the cassette." Their hunger was rather to be able to tell their own stories of what was now lost to someone who would listen and then to hold onto those stories in the flow of time. "These room stories show a huge need to communicate and, at the same time, an understanding that they are recording their memory." On the other hand, the ordinary person invited to tell his or her story to an American reporter will find that it is raw material for processing into a sound bite, a "cartoon bubble" of prepackaged thought that, according to Daniel Hallin's analysis, was an average of 4.2 seconds long in 1988, as compared to the 8.9 seconds granted to the elite of experts (94, 137). Admittedly, the camp "room" stories were not designed to become news per se, but to satisfy other needs for the *intersubjectivity* that is the foundation of the sociality and civility most sorely missed by refugees. However, those needs—to be recognized, to communicate, and to remember—belong to people everywhere. It is appropriate to ask how they are or are not being satisfied every day in American society as well as during upheavals and crises in distant places.

Of course, a format is freely displaceable—anyone, even a "zero," can pose as a "television news anchor" and use the "look" if not the production values of the waning form of American news on television to tell quite different stories. Yet this normative format is a product of history that exacts its own price on the democratic values so closely associated with the news.

FORMATTING POWER: NEWS THAT LOOKS LIKE THE NEWS

In research over the last fifteen years on the news, as well as other discursive formats and genres of American television employing the format of direct address by television personas to viewers—talk shows, commercials, sports, how-to's, logos, title and introductory sequences—I have concluded that disparities in power are marked into the format of the news, in stark contradiction to what has been called "television democracy." The American network news format is a very restrictive rather than inclusive discursive type with a monologic structure that both legitimates and severely limits the subjects produced by the news. While still drawing on the values and ethos of objectivity that evolved in print journalism (i.e., the referential fallacy), television news depends on a personality system employing virtual direct address to the viewer (that is, on the enunciative fallacy) in a "here" and "now" that is composed of what are actually highly processed and symbolic images. This format of news delivery cloaks what is, after all, an impersonal transmission with the impression of discourse across a desk with the quasisubjects or personalities in the machine. Far from confronting us with social reality, instrumental and impersonal relations are given their most disguised and utopian expression by simulating the paramount reality of speaking subjects exchanging conversation in a shared space and time. This is not at all to impugn the motives, integrity, or the journalistic methods of any particular news personnel, but rather to seek to identify large historical trends and to interpret their meaning. The resort to such charismatic and primary forms in the news suggests also that it is part of a larger cultural shift of dominance away from the disengaged forms of realism, literacy, and objectivity which have been dominant in Western culture since the age of industrialization.[1]

Full subjectivity in American television is reserved for representatives of television (i.e., talk show hosts, news anchors), the spokespersons of corporate sponsors and advertisers, and, under special circumstances, the president and a few other representatives of government and the armed forces. In a position of frontality in what simulates a first-order space shared with us, beyond the glass, the anchor speaks to us virtually as if fully engaged with us as viewers. The anchor is also the reference point for the division of the virtual realm inside the news image into planes that are arranged hierarchically nearer to or farther from the anchor. These planes sink in and out of visibility and audibility depending on transitional graphics and sounds and the anchor's words and gestures such as the gaze shift, the head "toss," and the chair swivel. Thus, the news anchor also acts as shifter between stories and levels within the news, as well as between television and the viewer.

The effect of American news conventions is to extremely constrain, if not actually deny members of the public the opportunity to speak as subjects, to shift the agenda under discussion, or to govern the length or context of a statement. The one-way structure and hierarchial conventions of television are ill-equipped to satisfy the desire of ordinary persons to "be someone," and to be recognized or to speak as subjects about the things that give meaning and structure to life in common.

In constrast, dialogue demands that we take the other seriously, that we take responsibility for our statements and their consequences in the world, and most of all, that we are prepared to change our beliefs or at least our demands in response to the other. However, the viewer's influence on television discourse consists largely of the power to switch channels or turn the power off. (Interactivity that does not serve intersubjectivity does not remedy this fundamental powerlessness.)

Yet why should anyone expect television to satisfy the need for intersubjectivity or substantive discourse? Though television de facto is a quasipublic realm, it is not a fundamentally democratic institution. Despite the catch phrase of "television democracy," the power of consumers to collectively influence television ratings must be strongly distinguished from voting (Meehan), just as popular entertainment meets other needs than does public discourse. Rather television is corporate and commercial and its programming dominated by entertainment designed to attract advertising through high ratings. There are admirable exceptions to this generalization, for instance, on public broadcasting, public access channels or the cable channel CSPAN; however, these forums are not really public in the sense that they can afford to display oppositional values or to air social conflict for very long. Even political candidates are forced to address the public largely in the form of commercial advertising.

The Great Divide

Perversely enough, the very barrier of the screen that anchors and hosts are empowered to overlook or disavow in order to virtually address the viewer is, according to Dan Hallin, actually a great divide between television and the public, at least on American television:

> [Television journalism] presents the interpretation of political events as belonging to a sphere that includes the journalists themselves and other political élites, but does not include the audience. This message is implicit in the treatment of the television screen as an impenetrable barrier. In Italy, political thinking is assumed to take place on both sides of the screen, which represents only a line between those who have current information and those who don't yet have it. In the United States politics takes place only behind the screen, and members of the public can become a part of it only to the extent that they are represented there by journalists. (Hallin 129)

Hallin concludes that "journalists need to move from conceiving their role in terms of mediating between political authorities and the mass public, to thinking of it also as a task of opening up political discussion in civil society, to use the term popular in the new democracies in Eastern Europe" (176).

Beyond the screen between television and the public, there is another divide or "wall within" the news which segregates members of the public from news personalities. "Sound bites" emanate purely from that other space about which the news is reporting and consist of very brief snatches of, for instance, comments made in interview, or a bit of ambient sound and speech from victims at a disaster site. Since the news is about putting the world as an object into words and images, sound bites provide that essential bit of authenticity that becomes all the more necessary in television news that is saturated with its own personalities. Sound bites are also at the bottom of the discursive hierarchy of the news, at two, three, or four degrees' remove from the anchor. Like the inhabitants of story space in the novel or film or behind the fourth wall in a dramatic presentation, the on-screen public in the news must pretend to be unaware of the camera and to address their responses to the second-degree narrator, the reporter. In other words, the counterpart of the fiction that the anchor in the image *can* address the television audience directly is the fiction that members of the public in the image *cannot*. Instead, members of the public are mediated by television itself as the only full subject.

The brevity of audiovisual material generated at the scene of an event and by people speaking for themselves rewrites history in a number of ways. First and foremost, all discourse in the world becomes raw material for the news institution's own performance. One egregious example of this occurred on CNN on December 27, 1989, in an aftermath-of-revolution story on the advent of free speech in Romania:

> "Now everyone wants to talk," said the reporter in a stand up. "Hold on a minute. Here's someone who wants to talk to you." The video

image cuts to a man looking directly at the camera, saying it was his first time on Western television and he had some words for Americans. Cut to a woman in 3/4 view saying, "I can die with a smile on my lips." Cut to a man saying, "I could before speak only to friends and family between four walls. I am asking the American people for information, foreign press accounts (fading out as the voice over of the reporter begins), educational materials."

Note the significance of the Romanians' shift from virtual address to American viewers into the conventional eyes-averted interview: we see a public being taught its place according to the conventions of power and position in news discourse. We see *that* members of the Romanian public speak, but hear next to nothing of what they say. The contradiction between conventional television practice and free speech is opened up in this typical and quite professional news story.

Between first-order (virtual) television discourse and the bottom level inhabited by the public, there are inflected and part-subjectivities. In my "Talk, Talk, Talk" (*Screen* 26, no. 2), I identified these intermediate levels as the speech of anchors and other news presenters among themselves, the second-degree narration of reporters and interviewers in the field, as well as the partial subjectivity of experts in three-quarter face. Persons on a monitor in the news set are held at a one-degree ontological remove from the anchor's physical space. Multiple interviewees can even appear in different monitors anywhere on the set and conduct a second-order virtual conversation among themselves.

Perhaps the most appropriate metaphor for the news stack of discursive levels that results is the *zoom* or shifting focus of a lens, that in moving from the macro through telescopic lens reveals utterly different worlds of reference that have in common their link to the anchor. Another contemporary metaphor is the computer desktop with a stack of hypercards that can be shuffled by strings of associations. (See chapter 3.) In any case, this multilayered space is hierarchically arranged around the anchor, who relates the news "personally," albeit virtually, to the viewer.

The "NBC Nightly News" has recently made the first "radical alteration" in a format that had been stable for the past fourteen years, garnering a surge in ratings in the process (Carman). This "borderline tabloid," or in the words of NBC, "populist" version of the news begins with Tom Brokaw standing in front of a kinetic video wall, in essence combining the "wallpaper" behind the anchor and the "window" or hanging box insert keyed in over the anchor's shoulder with the "stand-up" of a reporter in the field in front of a symbolic visual scene. Interestingly, objects impressionistically presented on the background video wall, for instance, windshield wipers in action or family photographs, are of such large scale that to me they give the impression of something life-size in my own viewing environment. This new format offers fewer news stories and one-third less foreign news, meaning fewer reporters and news correspondents. Thus, the new NBC format has collapsed many of the intermediate levels of subjectivity into the person of the anchor. One could say that as a result, the anchor enjoys even more prominence, at the same time that network news and the prestige of anchoring are actually in decline. John Carman cites a collective decrease of 30 percent in ratings by the three network evening newscasts over the past decade.

The public, though, plays a greater than usual role in the format via a regular NBC news feature titled "In Their Own Words," speaking without journalistic interpretation. However, my sampling shows what could be a miniature forum for address to and by members of the public consists so far of persons describing their feelings during a newsworthy experience with the same averted gazes as in the old format. The "more personal, psychological perspective" of such "subjective reactions" are borrowed from the arena of the talk show (Ellis 1996, 54).

Anchor Appeal

What is the appeal the anchor exercises in the old (and new) format? The credibility assigned to the news format (as I discuss at length in "The Television News Personality and Credibility") is a function of its engaged and subjective mode of presentation, exemplified by "the display of news personnel" and "the visual coverage of events" (Comstock cited in Morse, "News Personality," 55). Note that the anchor is a special kind of star supported by subdued sartorial and acting codes that convey "sincerity." Sincerity is the unification of social role and personal belief, as well as the unification of the speaking subject and the subject in the sentence that our own twentieth-century cultural experience tells us is *imaginary*. The news as institution, however, does not admit this disparity (which, to use Lionel Trilling's terms, would mean being "authentic" rather than "sincere"). It posits instead a subject who embodies "a shared viewer fantasy, a collective need" (Powers 2) for what has come to be, according to former CBS President Richard Wald, "the traditional sense of what an anchorman is: in effect, the all-wise, all-seeing mouth, that person who knows everything and will tell it to you. That person never really existed" (quoted in Barrett 22). However, that person may be constructed, even in the face of healthy skepticism, in order to maintain cohesive cultural fictions. Cronkite said recently he wanted to respond to people who tell him, "I believe every word you say" with "You're not supposed to" (James). In the language of disavowal or the "I know it's just TV news," the "but nevertheless" was at its strongest when television was newer, more centralized, and yet to be challenged by cable, satellites, and the Internet. As Caryn James writes, "As Cronkite talked to middle America, he came to stand for middle America, but such authority is not possible or even desirable today."

While the local news anchor team of mixed race and gender allude to a diverse community, since the early 1980s the network anchors have been three almost interchangeable "tall, white, Anglo-Saxon Protestants with dark hair coiffed very carefully, thin faces with an intelligent look."[2] Of course, network television news is actually performed by an entourage of news professionals, as well as by the TV producer and crew, and the on-screen network anchor or team (or in television terms, the "talent") is merely the most visible representative of this speaking collective subject. Interestingly, the part of the news consisting of "tell stories" was called "the magic" by Walter Cronkite, anchor of the "CBS Evening News" from 1962 to 1981. Indeed, it is the speaking subject or anchor as "talking head" that is the link between the message or utterance and the enunciation of the news, performing the "magic" of binding so many elements and cultural institutions together to form a coherent "reality."

For the anchor represents not merely the news per se, or a particular network or corporate conglomerate that owns the network, or television as institution, or the public interest; rather, he represents the complex nexus of all of them. In this way, the network anchor position is a "symbolic representation of the institutional order as an integrated totality" (Berger and Luckmann 76), an institutional role on a par with that of the president or of a Supreme Court justice, although the role originates in corporate practices rather than political or judicial processes. Then there are those who are forever offscreen, unless like AIDS activist group ACT UP, they are willing to take an unauthorized sprint in front of the camera at the "CBS Evening News" and the "MacNeil/Lehrer News Hour."[3]

Even the president's preeminence as television subject over any news anchor or advertising spokesperson is not self-evident; rather, it must be won. Then presidential candidate Vice President Bush established his priority in the control of discourse in the infamous on-air shouting match with Dan Rather on the "CBS Evening News" on January 25, 1988. Reports of that story featured striking recursive monitors with anchors and news windows—almost a *mise-en-abyme* (an image repeated within an image ad infinitum).

An unscheduled presidential address interrupting regular programming (and, of course, without ads) conventionally signals the power of the office and an extraordinary situation. The then President Bush's address and quasideclaration of war ("The Liberation of Kuwait has Begun," January 16, 1991) suspended commercial imperatives on television, in favor of the martial imperatives. Subsequent analysis of polling data shows that a significant gap in public opinion against and in support of war remained that was simply suspended for a time, in a bandwagon effect of patriotic fervor (Mueller 138–39). The flurry of discussion that began in the crisis mode quickly abated; dissent was discredited and downplayed. The computer graphics had long been prepared to roll; the experts from Brookings and the retired generals were on the network and cable payrolls. But the militarization of television went deeper. Instead of sound bites from "real" people, that is, troops or civilians, weapons such as the Stealth were personalized as hometown heroes and military spokespersons became television hosts with the power to make the press into secretaries for oral dictation. Reporters in the field were sent into the desert without an uplink. Even the president had to defend his supreme anchor position against the wild popularity General Schwarzkopf had garnered as the chief anchor of war reporting.

President Bush's televisual address to the nation concerning the riots/rebellion in Los Angeles was a reprise of the Gulf War call to national unity, flanked by flag and family photos.[4] Promising a return to order, and nationalizing the guard under the central control of General Powell, Bush offered a martial solution to pressing needs for social change. Again, quite explicitly, our (old) identity or self-image as a nation was at stake. "Slow war" against the urban centers where minority populations live had fashioned "a crucible of violence" (Terry 1), or else the outcome of the trial of police officers in the beating of Rodney King could not have sparked social rebellion, looting, and vandalism in Los Angeles and other cities. The president's television "anchor" position is one of legitimating force, but one that is limited by the very superficiality of its persuasive and even coercive potential.

Since there are few other organs for inclusive and substantial discourse on social and cultural values in American life, the responsibility for interpreting the world and posing a political course of action and a social agenda falls on a very limited number of public personas, including such news personalities and the presidency.[5] (Relatively more personas in entertainment enact our dreams and nightmares and are rewarded to varying degrees with money and unrelenting public fascination.) The rest of us are the voice on the phone on the shopping channel, an inhabitant on the floor of a talk show, or are trapped in a sound bite that, as Dan Hallin's research shows, grows shorter by the year. Our restrictive discursive system not only drastically reduces the number and kind of subjects who can speak for themselves to a wider public, it also might explain why, despite hundreds of hours of news and talk per week on American television, television as a cultural form seems to have said little about "what's really happening in this country."

Tabloids

The hierarchical model of the news has been challenged by even more engaged and somewhat less hierarchical formats in daytime talk shows that feature an on-screen audience of "real people." The audiences acts as a kind of jury that evaluates onstage discourse and often pronounces judgment on the guests, other ordinary or "real" people who represent some aspect of socially controversial behavior. Daytime talk show guests are usually singled out by means of a low dais or stage, signifying their slightly different plane of performance and their availability as objects for scrutiny by the crowd. The home viewer may be positioned variously as a voyeur, a member of the audience, or may share collusive glances with the host. The talk show host acts as mediator between realms of the dais or stage, studio audience, and television viewer.[6]

The subject matter of daytime talk shows is controversial but with few exceptions, trivial. Elaine Scarry, writing in the critical context of the deliberations that preceded the Gulf War's announcement (not declaration), pronounced talk shows on the crisis with Iraq a spectacle of communication that lacks substance. Rather than functioning as public discourse or as a genuine populism, the burgeoning numbers of talk shows "perform a kind of *mimesis of deliberation*," that infantilizes and marginalizes the American population (Scarry 1993, 59). Thus the issues we see debated on television talk shows are not the grave matters for which we are responsible, but private affairs which are not a public concern. We are asked to authorize only what entails little to no risk or sacrifice on our part.

Contemporary daytime talk show discourse on television is not organized around the slow payoff of working through an issue or controversy inclusively and over the long term. Instead a kind of discursive virginity is preferred, in which something is disclosed or done or someone is confronted, preferably for the first time, live. Far from allowing truth to surface, such a performance elicited by the camera is designed to create a spectacle that might otherwise never have happened or might never have been such an exaggerated, or on occasion, deceitful way to provoke the emotional reaction of the parties involved. Then the participants are left on their own to sort out the aftermath of this intervention in their lives. In extreme instances, the ambush and shock tactics of talk shows have resulted in actual mayhem, injury on the show or, subsequently, murder.[7]

Considering how potentially humiliating the situations on the dais in daytime talk and evening dating shows can be, why are "real people" so willing and eager to participate in them? Presuming they have some rights and must give permission, why do even malefactors on police "reality programming" allow themselves—without pixellated faces— to be frisked spread-eagled by police? Perhaps even a minor role of being bad on television is good, a kind of confirmation that, yes, one has lived and even mattered in the social drama; the largely thwarted desire to speak and be recognized and to know and be known is such a powerful motivating force in ordinary social life that any context serves better than oblivion.

Tabloid news magazines use exaggerated techniques of virtual address to the viewer, but they are less concerned with "real people" than with featuring celebrity interviews and gossip. Hallin regards the tabloids as a "deeply problematic development for culture," threatening to divide the news even further into knowledge for an elite and reports for the poor and less educated that appeal to irrationality, fear, and personal threats. However, it could be argued that the tabloids, with their relentless, even persecutory attention to the personal lives of celebrities, may be a perverse manifestation of the hunger for a discourse on changing social values. Is the obsession of American media with quirky areas of celebrities' personal lives and fates so consuming because prurient interest in this pantheon of stars is so extraordinary or because it is a displaced discourse on larger social values, albeit stripped of political significance and personal responsibility? Television tabloids and talk shows are pleasurable and titillating forums that do challenge social conventions and probably do appeal to the profound mysteries of human desire—without, however, plumbing them.

The weakness of a public sphere in the United States has long been recognized and criticized in different ways by social critics, philosophers, and scholars; and, it could be said to be endemic to a system where democratic access is almost universally subordinated to the commercial exchange-value of discourse. Television discourse is with few exceptions a function of the market value of time sold to advertisers and sponsors, a crippling limitation on public and civic life, now largely conducted in the media and on the Internet rather than the piazza or public square. Fewer yet are the forms (such as the archaic and rarefied town meeting) in which members of the public are invited to air their differences with each other. The discourses that could bind disparate social groups together, build empathy, and convey a sense of responsibility for society as a whole are feeble on television, and in vast areas of society they do not figure at all. Rather than addressing the obstacles to achieving a fair and free society, representations of the good life in advertising and entertainment have become the "cultural glue" of the American dream, with little attention to the hope or dignity needed to achieve it. The mood of dissatisfaction and disillusionment with politics, government, and social engagement of all kinds in large sectors of the population suggests that this "glue" is losing its grip.

The lack of public discourse also makes any exposure of tales and images of victimization on television into a dilemma. If television viewers sense that watching images of horror from all over the globe entails a kind of moral responsibility, no wonder they are said to fear the "CNN syndrome" (that is, emotional anguish at the sight of the images of victims of atrocity or disaster on television, leading to short-term international attention to those victims whose plight was most recently aired) and to suffer from moral, sympathy, or donor fatigue in what seems an amorphous and overwhelming task of living up to our image as "the world's only remaining superpower." While we caught glimpses on television of the victims of what Daniel Schorr called a "living room holocaust" in Bosnia (in his PBS radio commentaries), there was very little public discussion on what meaning the ethnic conflicts in the former Yugoslavia might have for Americans, what values were at stake, and what moral as well as mortal risks were involved in the ultimate intervention of the United States and NATO in them. The domestic American response was long in a state of near paralysis, lacking the direction and conviction, if not consensus, that such a public (not merely a grudging congressional) airing could have given it. The problem has often been identified as one of leadership, though it appears to be more fundamentally institutional. Bosnia is only the most recent of the great ruptures in the post–Cold War world in which Americans appear to drift. Not quite knowing who we as a people are, or, more accurately, how we perform ourselves, either in our own domestic eyes or abroad, we don't know what is worth our sacrifice.

"THE TURNING"

While discourse as conversation and even public speech is usually characterized by the reversibility of "I" and "you," discourse simulated on television is presented as if it were direct and permeable, when it is actually one-way and irreversible. Or rather, it just seems that way. Depending on the extremity of the circumstances, the tables will turn—subject becomes object—and the valence of power and fame can shift from plus to minus in a matter of seconds. The electronic spectacle that makes or breaks celebrity is equally capable of sanctioning or undermining the dictatorial power of a Marcos or Ceauşescu in a matter of hours. Extreme situations also highlight the potential for twists and reversals in what can never be a simple or straightforward speech-act.

In 1989, the historical shift the Germans call "die Wende" or *the turning* took place, "a staggering news story . . . the crumbling of communism as the sole official truth in the nations of Eastern Europe and now even in the Soviet Union. There will not be many bigger stories this century, if ever" (Du Brow). Unlike the "velvet revolution" that seemed to fold into Western socioeconomic expectations without resistance, the Romanian revolution and atrocities in Bosnia signaled that despite "winning the Cold War," "the turning" wouldn't go smoothly—even for Americans.

The favorite U.S. television icon of the end of the Soviet or Evil Empire is the Berlin Wall chipped at by thousands, eventually falling bloodlessly like the walls of Jericho. Yet, in a way, the Wall might as well have been a photographic negative or a left/right mirror inversion of America, for it reflected the projections of not-self against which a sense of Americanness was constituted. Communism had been our major stabilizing and unifying force, the justification for a belief system that has framed and hierarchized American values, deciding the allocation of resources and damping down the acceptable degree of public dissent since the end of World War II (see Hallin, "Where?"). Now that dark mirror was broken after more than four and a half decades of military potlatch—that is, the destruction of economic resources for deterrent display or, as President Reagan put it, "spending them [that is, the Soviets] into the ground." The end of it all seemed suddenly as dreaded as it was desired. "Winning" the Cold War paradoxically shook

American confidence and its sense of mission.[8] Even its sense of time would have to change from that of a constant state of emergency. (The alternative is not a nostalgic view of an intact America uncontaminated by government and illegal immigration.)

Is anything more uncanny than to lose a prime foundation of one's identity—the orientation "East" and "West"? In such a situation, an air of unreality or tentativeness hovers over recent events. The narrative of reform or revolution in Eastern Europe did more than any other news story, including stories about domestic issues of a staggering deficit or social and environmental ills, to allow awareness of the inadequacies of the American media–political superstructure to surface, however briefly. Though Gorbachev cried "uncle" first, the long-term toll of the Cold War on our own economy and social fabric had become very conspicuous by 1989. A growing sense of the failure of "television democracy" was expressed (largely in the print media),[9] at the same time that television and other high technology were considered at least partly responsible for freeing Eastern Europe, namely the heroic "revolution in a box," extolled by Ted Koppel. These two strands of media self-criticism—a self-questioning mode and a celebratory mode—also influenced the tone of American press and television coverage of Eastern Europe.

American televisual coverage of the Romanian Revolution reveals as much about Americans and our public sphere as about the events in Romania in 1989. It is instructive to compare American coverage to the "televisual events" on Romanian television. In a "televisual event" the image on screen and acts in physical space interact with and change one another. On such occasions, televisual hierarchies can fall apart. The televisual events in Romania were presented "live" and in duration, not in the "real time" that simulates duration of American television. Processed and compressed, computer-generated, and packaged images and stories control the flow of time and are "live" only by virtue of their simultaneity of transmission and reception. The heterogeneous temporalities channeled into simultaneous strands of "flow" on television may simulate the *duration* of time unfolding, but do not open into the unknown, nor do they accumulate or invite knowledge or favor reflection. The news is rather an effort repeated daily from zero and delivered in packages moving at an ever-faster pace. Banishing duration from the American form of the news—with the exception of disasters, wars, crises, trials, hearings, and the like—has economic rationality and strategic advantages in the deployment of power as spectacle.

VIRTUALITIES AS FICTIONS OF PRESENCE

When a *media event*—a ceremony in real space staged for televisual transmission (Katz and Dayan)[10]—is disrupted or gets out of control, it can become one or more *televisual events*, often marked in the flow of images on-screen by such things as wobbling and mobile framing, freeze-frames, masking, and "snow." The revolution, the uprising, and, in the light of subsequently compiled evidence, the coup d'état[11] in Romania commenced during a media event on December 21, 1989, televised from the square in Bucharest in front of party headquarters. Much like Ferdinand Marcos, speaking directly, albeit virtually, to his nation-state as the all-powerful Father, Ceauşescu suddenly shifted from subject to pathetic object of terror under the electronic gaze of the camera. Some people in the crowd, a compulsory assembly frozen below the dais under a claque of Securitate, were enraged by rumors of a massacre in Timişoara. Apparently willing to risk imprisonment or death, they had begun to shout down Ceauşescu's address to television. The state television camera began to shake as it caught the shift of terror from the space under the gaze of absolute power to the frozen body and impotent voice of an old man, who didn't at all resemble the "Genius of the Carpathians" on huge banners below. As one of those later inside a car honking in celebration exclaimed, "To think that it was just an idiot we were afraid of. People had to die to get rid of him!" Suddenly, "snow" interrupted the image transmission for three minutes, but left the sounds of catcalls and a patriotic song on the screen. Stock footage of crowds waving giant banners was quickly substituted for the emptying square. Then television transmission ceased for a while. In untransmitted footage of the moments following Ceauşescu's humiliation, Ceauşescu can be heard continually shouting "Hallo! Hallo!" as if this lapse of image were a simple interruption in television transmission that could be restored if only the power came on again. Ceauşescu's visible loss of power—marked by loss of television signal—created the vacuum in which subsequent events could occur. Many of those events were captured via camcorder, while still others remained unrecorded conspiratorial moments, the content of which can only be surmised.

In this case, "the turning" was expressed in the perceptible shift of power from the screen to the physical space in the public square beyond the frame. According to Geert Lovink, "What was special about the Romanian tele-revolution is that the cameras faithfully rendered the dynamics and rhythm of the events, and that for a few days they were not following any orders from above" (Lovink 59). Thus, shifts of power were all the more clearly marked in manipulations of the image stream, including instances when cameras (televisual and camcorder) actually turned around and sought out events out of curiosity and without agenda or supervision. The following sections will compare "the turning" or reversal of power as it occurred in Romania with the Romanian Revolution on American network news, CNN, and "Nightline" coverage, plus a camcorder record compiled by Harun Farocki and Andrei Ujica's documentary *Videogramme einer Revolution*.

Romanian Televisual Events

The relation between television images and the world is easier to grasp as dis/simulation when news is alloyed with plenty of lies, deception, and betrayal, and is designed to inculcate terror backed up by the show or exercise of force. The televisual event that ignited the revolution/uprising/coup depended on the peculiar power that is invested in being an image *on screen*—an especially restricted position in Romania, considering that spectacle was as severely rationed as everything else, in a general strategy of dehumanization by means of privation. Air time and even the vocabulary of the Romanian language, as well as food and light were rationed; birth control and access to public life were banned; homes and villages systematically destroyed. Certainly Ceaușescu made use of the extravagant display of processions and pageants in grandiose architectural settings to constitute and reveal power, a technique prominent since the days of Louis XIV.[12] However, Ceaușescu's power was not based on display alone, and his hyperinflated image as patriarch (and for the foreign press and diplomats, Soviet rebel), unlike the Western cult of personality, was controlled by coercion, not mechanisms of desire. Privation also paid Romania's international debt accrued for state spectacle and Ceaușescu's opulent private lifestyle, which was exposed, like Imelda Marcos's shoes and what was supposedly Noriega's red underwear, to the gaze of television and the populace after the Revolution threw open the doors of the Ceaușescus' palaces.

Such a subsistence strategy supports the generation of terror by allowing people no control over their lives. There is just enough spectacle, and just enough evidence of surveillance and brutality to suggest an otherwise invisible and vast machine of control. (Fake and real can be equally intimidating in suggesting the rest to the imagination.) Thus, terror is best sustained by partial visibility, and media events characterized by masking are among its hallmarks. Like a blinking and swiveling surveillance camera, a mask is meant to be seen and to announce the presence of something that can see but that is out of sight—whether or not there is actually anything there. The orchestration of terror via spectacle, the enforced performance of the populace, and the focalization of subjectivity into one talking head would seem to have been Ceauşescu's strongest as well as weakest point. For Ceauşescu, the apparatus of television shifted from serving as the foundation of power and a tool of statecraft into a means of his own humiliation as an object before the crowd, and far more terrible for him, exposed his naked vulnerability before the virtual viewers of television far beyond Romania.[13]

Deceit as well as lies, shams, errors, and subterfuge are events in the world despite their truth value, and they can be televisual events as well. Take, for instance, the December 23 broadcast of a grisly laying out of bodies dug out of mass graves in Timisoara into a line for the press. The numbers of the dead of December 17 had been reported (erroneously) in the thousands. The uncanny vision of these relatively few bodies unearthed just before Christmas served to confirm that atrocities had taken place. But this televisual event was exposed as the false evidence of paupers' graves.[14] Indeed, suffering long invisible under Ceauşescu was given visible, albeit borrowed flesh by means of this subterfuge—an event is written as a productive deception.

In the meantime, the crowd was discovering itself on television. It is seldom that what is on the monitor is confirmed by what can be seen around the ordinary viewer in physical space. When there is an unexpected mutual confirmation of the screen and the world that is a doubling effect or even a coincidence of physical and screen spaces, it comes as a *shock* that exerts a powerful fascination and sense of confirmation.[15] This shock was a powerful motivating force in Bucharest during the Romanian Revolution, when the crowd in the street was egged on to more resistance by the vision on television of its delegates in the studio, and, once a remote camera was set up outside the station, of itself as crowd in the street. However, remembering the enunciative fallacy, and the experiments of closed-circuit video art in the 1970s (see chapter 7), a perfect spatial and temporal match between a view of "real" space and a view of screen space is an unlikelihood and, ultimately, an impossibility, considering the radical difference between two- and three-dimensionality and the very rarely identical positions of the camera and the monitor. Nonetheless, during these heady days, the crowd became obsessed with its own image on television, the confirmation of an experience of spontaneous community acting in concert against op-pression. Yet there was a spatial and temporal discrepancy even here: people on the streets could not at the same time be glued to the televi-sion at home. Some televisions in windows turned to face the street; other protesters reportedly solved the problem of being both a part of the crowd on the street and seeing the crowd on television by oscillating between the two spaces.

The televisual event that made viewers into on-screen protagonists of the revolution occurred on December 22, the morning after Ceau-şescu's debacle and after Ceauşescu had escaped from Bucharest by helicopter from the Central Committee Building under siege. Part of the crowd heading toward the state television station in Bucharest met the poet Mircea Dinescu, newly liberated from house arrest, and put him on their lead tank. The crowd entered the studio and formed a memorable image of collective subjectivity at and behind a table in the tiny and somewhat antiquated television studio. "What one sees here is a nation packaged into a compact-image, where ethnic groups are being put together in a brotherly way. Everybody gets his pick here: young and old; man and woman; and not only for the Romanians, but for the whole world" (Lovink 60). Dinescu, after being passionately introduced, proceeded to speak a blessing from amidst a tableau of people on the screen: "God has turned his face toward Romania again"—in effect televisually declaring the end of Ceauşescu's govern-ment (Cullen 104). (Later, behind the scenes in the Farocki-Ujica docu-mentary, he says, "I hope things will turn out all right.") After he spoke, others in the tableau of people around him on-screen took turns speak-ing. This example of power grasped from the bottom up was an op-portunity seized for autonomous and creative public discourse, though speech from the tableau of a crowd on-screen to the television audience remained one-way. Furthermore, the position seized was an unstable inversion of Ceauşescu's speaking subjecthood and the speeches ut-tered there were as likely to be based on lies and deceit as on shattering emotional release and vulnerability.

The National Salvation Front used the tableau in the television stu-dio to establish its legitimacy operationally, essentially allowing it to govern by issuing directives that called the army to the aid of the populace, declared solidarity with the people, warned against poi-soned water, and gave orders deploying troops and provisions. It is hard to imagine a more direct convergence of the television as a stage and social reality into one virtual whole—not to ignore the staging that was going on behind the scenes.

After the December uprising appeared to have been hijacked, crowds began again to gather in front of the television station in Bucharest, demanding that their protests against continued communist control (and for an independent Romanian television) be shown on Romanian television. In response, a monitor was set up outside showing the crowd on television to the crowd, in another doubling effect. Perhaps the drive for agents in "real" space to see their own images, to see and be themselves, or better yet, to see their desire confirmed, is underestimated wherever television is understood as "representation." There was a glimpse of success in fulfilling the crowd's demand for self-confirmation; a utopian vision of self-determination was realized, if only on the screen and without immediate consequences for social change. Later, many Romanians reportedly played cassettes of the Romanian television of those days in December over and over, again and again until utter disillusionment set in.

There was another fateful switch point in the flow of subjectivity and power, inside and outside Romania during the revolution: a freeze-frame, the close-up on the face of the corpse of the executed Nicolae Ceauşescu: behold the man. This was a grisly sight in the screen on which one usually finds talking heads. (Oddly enough, the face of the nearby Elena was not as controversial.[16] Could it be that she was positioned in the frame so as to preclude a gaze that could possibly be directed at the viewer?) Michel Foucault, describing the torture and execution of "Damiens, the regicide" in March 1757, in *Discipline and Punish*, told how the public spectacle of ripping Damien's body limb from limb as an edifying example for derision and horror suddenly became the vehicle of Damien's transformation into a subject of heroic suffering, deserving of the sympathy and admiration of the assembled crowd (3–31). While to display Ceauşescu's open but vacant eyes had strategic justifications in Romania at the time (see Longworth), nothing could have better served to make the dictator into a victim to the viewer outside of Romania.

This still image of Ceauşescu was itself the culmination in a series of extremely controversial freeze-frames and obvious temporal gaps edited into the record of the trial and execution of Nicolae and Elena Ceauşescu by unknown parties—since there were no reverse shots. These marks of absent footage were an obvious attempt to conceal part of the record of the trial and possibly to rewrite the time and mode of execution. Edited and restored-or-faked versions of the video became the object of a detective story and the focus of obsessive speculation in Romania and a number of conferences throughout Europe.[17] Of course, routine editing by cutting would not have preserved an uninterrupted sound track of the exchanges between the Ceauşescus and their judges either. The entire controversy is dependent on duration and the notion of recorded liveness, or unedited footage. (Chris Marker edited his own version of the Ceauşescu trial by filling in the missing trial footage with advertising, in his own wry comment on the growing adoption of American commercial editing practices.) A freeze-frame is like a mask in that it shows *that* it hides—but only if it appears in a context of temporal duration. The instability and the "turn" of subjectivity in spectacle become apparent only at the everyday rate at which both experience and discourse unfold.

Ironically, later in June 1990 the very same performative use of television that constituted the revolution served newly elected President Iliescu to brutalize protest into submission and to rewrite the significance of this act, in a procedure reminiscent of Chinese publicity after the massacre at Tiananmen Square. Such rewriting is another kind of performative act and a televisual event.

The American Romanian Revolution

The Romanian revolution in the country in which it occurred was not the event as it was reported in national news and CNN in the United States. In Romania and much of Eastern Europe, the events in the state television studio and on the streets unfolded on screens almost without interruption—except for significant lapses in transmission or "snow." American viewers saw the surreal spectacle just before Christmas of a crowd of half a million people in the streets, tank warfare and house-to-house fighting, bodies wounded and dead, and cries of grief, that appeared on various national and satellite-cable networks. However, reviewing many hours of archival recordings of American television confirms that Romanian television was almost never discussed in American programs about Romania, nor was it retransmitted at length. Nor did the "universal hallmark of the revolution," the tableau of the crowd in the television studio, have the significance in the United States that it held elsewhere in Eastern or Western Europe.

The network news, even Ted Koppel's half-hour of analysis on ABC, "Nightline," is the antithesis of duration, a model of brevity and immediacy, focused on telling stories, and hearing from experts in the immediate present, and hence not a tool for analysis of long-term trends or in-depth investigation of issues.[18] Although there are different registers and a wide disparity in the degree of news condensation and "processing" in network news, CNN, PBS's "MacNeil-Lehrer NewsHour" (now "The NewsHour with Jim Lehrer"), and Ted Koppel's "Nightline," in each case, discourse in the world of events is compressed rather than allowed to unfold. (The only exception might be CSPAN.)[19] However, it is important to remember that truth does not reside in any particular pace or editing strategy.

Reports of a crackdown in Romania began on network news on December 18, followed on the 19th by interviews with dissident Romanians, conducted in a "terrorized" mode—disguising voices and using black silhouettes on screen.[20] Though coverage in the U.S. was typical of each news institution's presentational style, and the news stories, even on the networks, were slightly longer than usual, footage from Romania was offered typically in brief sound bites. It was, however, as part of "the reform movement in Eastern Europe," the most heavily covered news story of 1989 in the United States (Center for Media and Public Affairs).

Many were ready to congratulate Western media for "the turning," though Tom Wolfe exclaimed on Ted Koppel's June 1990 PBS special, "World Without Walls," "Ted, CNN did not cause the Romanian Revolution." Yet the Romanian revolution was also debated in the West as if it were only a simulation on a vast scale, resented by those who had (or had not) been so easily taken in. Certainly there are many instances of duplicity, deceit, shady dealings, and simulation discussed above, and most of all, the use of brute force to support this conclusion. The bad press of the Romanian revolution in the United States was framed by a profound sense of disbelief in the reality of the events themselves and a mistrust of the motives behind them.[21] Perhaps Western guilt for Cold-War collusion with Ceauşescu and his regime—the good guys in our morality play—fed a diagnosis of Romanian national and immanent wickedness or corruption as an explanation for the violence and brutality that was so startling on screens so used to portraying violence as make-believe.[22]

The framing of the Romanian revolution on American television was influenced by the simultaneous occurrence of the American invasion in Panama.[23] Indeed, Panama and Romania were often compared: both were labeled "Just Cause"; both share motifs such as hunting down the dictator, emptying the palace, and a trial—but these probably owe their similarity more to the syntax of a metanarrative of revolution than to mutual resemblance.[24] Perhaps such a moralizing stance to justify American intervention in our hemisphere fed the expectation that justice and purity of purpose should be at the heart of events in Romania.

An additional factor in the news space given to the Romanian story was the relative spatial and psychological distance of the Romanian news to Americans. The nearness of Panama and the involvement of American troops would seem to have demanded a crisis mode of coverage, whereas Romania would seem remote and out of the sphere of interest of most Americans. In a larger sense, however, the distant and yet disquieting Romanian revolution was as much a part of a larger post–Cold War crisis as was the later domestic Los Angeles rebellion/riot in identifying what it means to be American. Work on the imaginary of Americanness would need to overcome self-righteousness and our own sense of disbelief as well as the awareness of our own shortcomings. ("I just had to cross my fingers and think, 'Gee, I hope it turns out better for you guys [the Czechs] than it has for us.' Clearly, they believe in us more than we do in ourselves these days" [Mike McCurry of the Democratic National Committee, quoted in Baum].)

In covering breaking stories, CNN, as a twenty-four-hour satellite-cable service, has the advantage of an "open newsroom," when it chooses to use it, where the viewer can follow the progress of news story consolidation. As a result, CNN rewards the analyst by wearing the contradictions of American news practices most openly. The initial coverage of the events from December 21, 1989, on CNN showed a news story out of control. The anchor read text off a computer while video that no one could identify from Romanian television via Yugoslavia, in a language that no one at CNN could interpret, appeared in a frame. Meanwhile, the anchor conducted a telephone conversation with a Hungarian who had been in the Timisoara area about another Transylvanian city. There was no coherence and no center of knowledge. All information came from sources regarded until recently as of dubious credibility. Yet, despite the situation of news out of control, Romanian television itself was not presented at any length. Then, on came a series of commercials.

Another example of loss of control occurred on December 23, when CNN showed extensive video of night fighting. There was almost nothing to be seen, except for occasional bursts of light. Then, there was a series of commercials, indicating the commodity-nature of the very image of terror, albeit distant, and of not knowing that one would think the antithesis of the American news style of centrality and mastery. So it seems that the prime contradiction revealed in the CNN broadcast in the Romanian situation and the almost simultaneous Panamanian invasion is a format that appeals to the taste for the real by regularizing and commodifying crisis and catastrophe mode of television coverage.[25] But televisual events in Romania were barely glimpsed on CNN; the real event was the gradual constitution of authority over the news itself by television, that is, the unfolding presentational event, or what has become known as "the process."[26]

"Nightline" and "Television Democracy"

In his earlier 1989 ABC special, "Revolution in a Box," "Nightline" host Ted Koppel had expressed faith in television democracy, referring to popular access to technological means of capturing, storing, and distributing images—the camcorder, the VCR, the portable satellite dish, and the computer, technologies that he appears to regard as social change in and of themselves:

> Television used to be the exclusive province of government and enormously wealthy corporations. They decided what you would see and when. Not any more. Television is falling into the hands of the people. The technology is becoming more affordable and accessible. They haven't mastered it yet, but they will. A form of television democracy is sweeping the world, and like other forms of democracy that preceded it, its consequences are likely to be beyond our imagination.
> I am Ted Koppel. Good Night.

Koppel was not anticipating anything as low-tech as the takeover of the Romanian state television station in Bucharest. Indeed, his "Nightline" report on Romania in April 1990 ignored the series of televisual events with very real political consequences discussed above in favor of focusing almost entirely on power at the top: the fall of the Ceauşescus—their opulent lifestyle, their escape, capture, trial, and execution, all set to ominous underscoring. (Koppel's program on Tiananmen Square has been criticized on similar grounds.) "Nightline"'s research team gathered amazing footage of the fate of the Ceauşescus supplied by camcorders operating seemingly everywhere, supplementing "Nightline"'s own footage of the regime's secret listening posts in underground tunnels and behind double walls. Of course, the documentary report featured Koppel as narrator and editorial commentator throughout and submitted all its documentation to extensive editing and electronic manipulation. For instance, in response to Romanian joy at the sight of Ceauşescu's body, Koppel's "Nightline" offers an implicit critique of Romanian (not Ceauşescuan) barbarism and corruption, by augmenting the close-up of the dictator's dead body with an underscore on the sound track of maniacally repetitive or perhaps electronically extended laughter of Sylviu Brucan, a respected long-term critic of Ceauşescu and now of the current regime. (Romanians on the street also responded to American reporters with smiles about Ceauşescu's death—*Videogramme* shows a room of Romanians watching television and applauding as his corpse was displayed.) Brucan went on, in the interview that was the source of the laugh, to express happiness at Ceauşescu's death with an oddly serious face.

While, by his own reckoning, approximately sixty percent of Koppel's Romania program in April consisted of roving camcorder footage, it was framed by Koppel's very strong presence and his project of debunking both the revolution and Ceauşescu's apparatus of terror as a sham. And despite Koppel's belief in the camcorder as "television democracy," he himself has framed the issue of video footage made by "real people" on the news largely in terms of its tenuous reality-status. "The same technology that can be used to reveal truth can be used to conceal it, to confuse reality. . . . Manipulation or altering reality is now within the budget of almost any political group in the world."

Why is such amateur footage of disasters, uprisings, riots, and hostage situations used as the sign of the real so often discussed as potential fraud? Why is what on one hand seems so real—the finality of death or the spontaneously "live"—greeted with such uneasiness and disbelief? Perhaps the most superficial explanation is that the expansion of nonprofessional access to television is a threat to any notion of reality or truth in a single and authoritative sense. The sense of mastering and being actually above world events conveyed by the American news media is set at risk. The program demonstrated techniques for manipulating video, such as compositing images together with electronic mattes; but it implied that once ordinary people, presumably in spontaneous (or planned) situations with camcorders, become sources allowed access to the air, technical finesse is not needed to perpetrate hoax and fakery. Fake Chernobyl footage that proved to be of a cement factory in Italy and the Shiite tape of a hanging body claimed to be the hostage Colonel Higgins were particularly problematic instances that underline what the loss of control over every step of image capture, processing, and display by professional news organizations can mean.

Camcorders in the hands of the general public enlarge the capacity for real-time recording, as well as the possibility of continuous surveillance of a society from below without pause, always. The advantage of surveillance from below is not in its greater reality or truth, but in its multiplicity—provided it is disseminated in a way that allows discourse to unfold. Media "democracy" as a private camcorder culture of oppositional video not only in Poland and Czechoslovakia but in the American gay subculture, in Chile, or the West Bank can be a force that eludes not only state but corporate control and transcends national boundaries as well as professional protocols. Consider, however, that camcorder footage is almost never allowed anything more than a sound bite presence in conventional formats on American television.

One wonders how much of the spectacular camcorder footage shown in Koppel's documentary had been disseminated in Romania and how much was sold exclusively to various international news media. The camcorder record of the deliberations to take over the television station, for instance, was sold in an exclusive to Japan. What this suggests is that the function of surveillance from underneath may be compromised when it is also a precious commodity. On the other hand, the record of the killing of protesters by Soviet police in Georgia shown there and in the West played a role of enormous significance in setting limits on the use of force in subsequent nationalist struggles, just as camcorders recording the evacuation of the square and the vigilante attacks of miners set limits on the ability of the Iliescu government to rewrite history—presuming that footage is aired or disseminated in a way that preserves it as voices and positions. In fact, in considering the value of camcorder footage as a view and a voice below, the enunciative context is everything—how is this image being made and disseminated, by whom and to what end?

Camcorder Events à Farocki and Ujica

Harun Farocki and Andrei Ujica's documentary on the Romanian Revolution, *Videogramme einer Revolution*, is a concordance of camcorder footage, reconstructing the same events from multiple vantage points in counterpoint to what was happening on official Romanian television. The footage in question was available in archives because it was no longer a fresh and thus valuable commodity. Perhaps because many of the camcordists in question were television and governmental workers, we also have astonishing access to what is going on behind the scenes.[27] The documentary's approach honors its sources with lengthy shots in chronological sequence and few voice-overs. Shots are allowed to implicitly comment on each other. Long, one-shot sequences with an utter lack of photogenia are embraced.

The opening segment of the documentary offers a prime example of camera-induced performance. A wounded young woman is seen on a gurney moaning in pain in Timisoara, Romania on the same day as Ceauşescu's failed media event—December 21, 1989. Told (citing the translation in subtitles) "Speak to the camera, you'll be on TV," a mask appears and a podium-style speech is elicited as she speaks lucidly and directly to the camcorder without pause for over three minutes, concluding, "in the name of the Co-op, I wish to join the great revolution, the youth of Timisoara and Bucharest. We want a better life, freedom for young people, bread to eat and happiness." Her speech is so eloquent throughout, it has the flavor of something preprepared or canned, yet it is spoken by someone wounded and in pain—hardly a media event. Seeing her performance in its entirety from the gurney is the only way to fully appreciate the effort involved. Instead, the performance points to the other side of the image, the camera in an *offscreen* space of enunciation that teaches us to ask, who elicited this performance and where were they situated? That is, we consider the station point of the photographer also as a metaphor of social position and vested interest.

Camcorder images from early in the uprising still show the work of censorship. The nearly three-and-a-half-minute shot that is the second one in the documentary—violating an American sensibility with the inexorable pace of unedited liveness—shows demonstrations in Timisoara that were the catalyst for the disrupted media event in Bucharest as almost unreadable motion in the upper-right corner of the screen. Later camcordists turn the lens around toward the crowd with impunity and nose in almost, but not entirely everywhere: a camcordist is barred from a secret session at the TV session. The documentary supplies voice-over commentary on key sequences missing from the camcorder record. Yet, amazingly, we can see the "ex-head" of the Securitate, General Vlad, behind the scenes, terribly busy on the telephone orchestrating the coup.

Videogramme documents duplicity in events behind the scenes and on television with strategic contrasts. At one point in the Bucharest TV station, something is held up as a symbol of the revolution that proves to be a lipstick; later, in a tearful Christmas celebration, another symbol of the revolution, a little red heart, is held up by one of the people in the tableau on screen. There is also a fairly humorous discussion about whose helicopters have been shot down in confusion—supposedly by Libyan terrorists, though we hear men behind the scenes exclaiming, "What terrorists?! The helicopters could only be yours [the army's] or mine [the Securitate's]!"

We also see a struggle over whom television will transmit once the motley crowd in the TV station was replaced by the provisional government of Ian Iliescu. Would it be an ex-diplomat and dissident in a public sphere of the most old-fashioned kind, addressing the crowd and calling for democratic reforms? Or would it be the National Salvation Front (with a name that "sounds like a coup d'état" according to one in Iliescu's contingent) in the studio? Iliescu's eventual control of television and the old infrastructure of power in the countryside did much to guarantee his landslide election on May 20, 1990.

Meanwhile, shooting seemingly at random continued in the streets for days after the outcome of it all was quite decided. Somehow the snipers fighting the revolution were never active on the scene when the camcorders or news cameras arrived. Again, *Videogramme* teaches us to ask about vectors reaching beyond the field of view on screen: who is shooting at whom and why? There is a particularly funny sequence of outtakes of an American reporter on the scene of what purports to be a gun battle. Every time he begins his "crouch-down" report, the soldiers around him start to shoot, clearly performing for the camera, but drowning him out in the process. In commentary about the shooting, a voice-over informs us that "later there was talk of combat units from the military intelligence service which in simulated skirmishes had to feign an armed opponent in order to assist the army to victory on the side of the revolution."

However, the documentary also offers moving performances of testimony: the last shot is an address to a crowd and the camera that suggests that despite the futility and sorrow of the uprising, the speaker had learned something about privation and its effects:

> I just wanted to add, the dictator, the criminal we saw today on TV is dead. He lied to us so much that we hated someone if he earned 300 more lei. His children had millions in the bank. He forced us to do without . . . "our land needs every dollar" . . . and all the time the money was shared among the party. We had no fun. The lights went out at 6 pm. We grew up hating minorities. And the Hungarians and the Germans are our friends; we've lived together for ages. And now our children have died . . . and many of us have died.

Tiny Power Grabs

American news anchors are not immune to "televisual events," particularly in situations of protest and upheaval. In commentary on an archival sample of one news day—August 6, 1968—on all three networks, I noted two particular stories connected with the civil rights struggles against segregation (Morse, "The Television News Personality," 67–68). CBS's Ed Rabel reported on an incident in the small Southern town of Luverne, Alabama, where an elderly white man, once a member of the Ku Klux Klan, was being boycotted and ostracized for hiring a black man who sent his child to county schools. This white man naively broke the rules of television news as well, by talking and weeping directly into the camera in an emotionally moving and discomfiting way. On the other hand, there was a glaring example of the "wall within" on ABC news, with Ted Koppel reporting from the home of a poor African-American family in Miami. The striking thing about this report was that the black family was never asked to speak at all, and, needless to say, was never allowed to look at the camera that roamed intrusively around the apartment looking at them. This convention was not regarded as unusual at the time and prevails today, but probably not so nakedly. Twenty-three years later, during coverage of the Los Angeles rebellion/riot, one of those brief periods on television associated with the confusion of a disaster and upheaval occurred when gang members, welfare recipients, unemployed men, even looters and other unusual spokespersons on television could be solicited to speak. In Ted Koppel's "Nightline Special" with the African-American community in South Central Los Angeles on May 1, 1992, the format of the show itself and the authority of the anchor were challenged by the people sitting in the audience as well as by those onstage near Koppel. First, the news tactic of pitting members of the community against each other (in this case, gangs versus church members, possibly in an attempt to achieve "balance") was roundly condemned.[28] The practice of speaking through the anchor (and not for oneself and directly to the audience in the church or to people at home via television) and the practice of cutting off a statement for a commercial were all commented on and criticized: all these once self-evident practices were suddenly no longer so transparent, but were seen as obvious tools of power. Koppel was asked whether, if he was not merely grandstanding, he would come back again. On Monday, to his credit he did and received more instruction from the black community on its way of formatting the show. Here was the admirable beginning of a larger public discourse that ended abruptly.

This salutory example occurred in a larger context of catastrophe-style reporting, a prime example of "the process" in which spectacular footage of fires, looting, and mayhem from surveillance and traffic helicopters made with high-powered lenses and mikes was repeated again and again, until just a few images solidified into symbols for events as a whole. The world below seemed as remote as the desert of Iraq. In the meantime, the George Holliday camcorder footage of the beating of Rodney King alternated like a mantra with all the other coverage. Such repetition functions to assuage trauma, wearing away the flow of information into a few well-polished narrative images—a way, ultimately, of forgetting.

CYBERCULTURE IN CONTEXT:
THE PROCESS AND "WORKING THROUGH"

Remembering how "the process" functions on CNN, John Ellis has hypothesized that television as a whole works in a similar way that he calls "working through" ("Television as Working Through" 48). Drawing on Pierre Sorlin's suggestion that in the face of the often inadequate and totally contingent image material of the news, documentaries, soap operas, and television fiction are all involved in a metaphorical "steadying of the image" (Sorlin, cited in Ellis 1996), Ellis proposes television to be a vast "forum for interpretations" (71).[29] Events that are "radically incomplete," yet that "demand explanation" or "incite curiosity, revulsion and the usually frustrated or passing desire for action," are submitted to a "process of repression that psychoanalysis describes: a process that does not eradicate but places them elsewhere" [in what might be called the Symbolic order], "a process necessary for civilized life to remain possible" (53). Beginning with the news as "wild footage from a wild world" and passing through various genres—chat or talk shows, soap opera, documentary, sport, and narrative forms, in a progression of increasing narrative closure—television "comes to terms" with the flood of information that would otherwise overwhelm us. Ellis stresses the openness of this process, in which no material is ever entirely explained or resolved, just "continually worried over until it is exhausted" (48). Then, what chapter 2 is about, in Ellis's terms, would be the rules of engagement of television as a forum and their inadequacy, in a process that, apparently, gets its impetus and material from television news.

While Ellis cautions that the process is not like sausage making, his notion of working through does rest upon a nature/culture contrast in which the news is raw material for civilization, as if news were the first footfall into jungle or desert. It also implicitly considers the news in terms of representation, not presentation. However, Ellis would probably agree that the raw material of the news is already "culture," that is, already full of many voices telling stories which news conventions effectively silence. "The news" is not a found object, but a cultural product and its reality is the social reality that we perform and call forth together.

While I question assumptions in the progression from news to narrative, Sorlind and Ellis's fundamental point about the repetition on television of similar material in genre after genre can be illustrated with numerous examples. Take, for instance, the justice system as it passes through transmission of the actual "live" trial and the recorded trial with commentary, to the reenactment of an actual trial by actors to "People's Court" (a television surrogate court that "actually" decides cases) and "The Judge" (offering dramatic reenactment of legal cases), to docudramas and fictional court cases on "Perry Mason," "L.A. Law," and "Murder One." The enforcement of the law takes shape in camcorder footage, "live" and recorded transmissions, reenactments and simulations in, for instance, "Cops" (direct documentary), "Top Cops" (reenactments), and "America's Most Wanted" (reenactment and audience interaction as a surrogate justice system allied with actual police departments). The proposed airing of state executions is the limit condition of what appears to be an incipient parallel system of justice with its own televisual codes that operates in a virtual space between police squad cars and helicopters, the courts/television studios, and our living rooms. This mix of simulated and actual justice is not only ontologically confused with real consequences, it could gradually change the law itself in ways that are more televisual and directly "interactive." As part of a surrogate justice system, viewers have gradually been asked to become both judge and jury (in the court of public opinion) by watching television. "Working through" then takes ontologically diverse forms that reach beyond the television set and, as I show in chapter 4, into the built environment. If "the process" functions as a means of enculturation (chapter 1) and to "steady" (and far more rarely, to "unsteady") the symbolic order (chapter 2), the passage through and circulation of images are also linked to the exchange of other symbols and objects, money and bodies (chapter 4).

Post-Television and Convergence

Over the next two decades, it is predicted that the apparatuses of the computer, the telephone, radio, satellite and cable television, electronic games, and the cinema will have been integrated into global, if not universally accessible electronic networks. A global subculture has evolved around electronic networks that offer two-way and communal exchange. The amateur and public uses of the Internet strongly distinguish themselves from contemporary television, which despite its proliferation of channels and "interactive" call-in programs, is still a corporate-owned and commercially oriented mass-produced culture in one-way distribution.[30] Point-to-point communication in electronic mail, posting on news groups bulletin boards, the collective construction of on-line communal spaces, and self-publishing on the World Wide Web have the potential to sustain an individuated and democratic discursive realm, with this limitation—any *one* message is unlikely to reach the millions that Hollywood cinema or the broadcast network and satellite transmissions of television can attract.

Soon television will no longer be the mass medium that dominated the second half of the twentieth century, but one of the many that have been subsumed into a computerized information society. However, we are not witnessing the end of television per se, especially in emerging or declining modern societies. For one thing, while the cinema and television are relatively cheap and available to all but the very poor, the public sphere in cyberculture is limited by the problem of access: one estimate is that at best, twenty percent of the world will possess the requisite infrastructure to participate in this symbolic realm guarded by digital gates and computer terminals (Crary).

Media activists concerned about the future of public access to the data sphere might compare our contemporary situation to the period after World War I, when the freewheeling sending and receiving of amateur radio signals before the war gave way to legislation which regulated the airwaves. Corporate leaseholds on the electronic spectrum were granted and the structure of radio and later of television was resolved in favor of one-way commercially supported broadcasting owned by a cartel of corporate conglomerates. In the shift to commercial networks, the Internet or electronic network of networks may diminish or no longer support exchanges tantalizingly like Brecht's call for a medium in which every receiver is also a sender and in which fantasy and experimentation are given reign, often with no relation to their economic cost. The exemption of electronic networks from economic imperatives is already ending and when it ultimately does, this transitional period will also.

Another historical point of comparison with our own transitional situation is the late-nineteenth-century and early-twentieth-century period before one cinematic apparatus took hold and the conventions of the realist fictional narrative came to dominate over the variety of nonnarrative experimentation that preceded it. This precinematic period included devices such as Marey's photographic recording gun, Muybridge's motion studies, the zoetrope, Edison's wax cylinder sound recorder and his kinetoscope.[31]

The apparatus and conventions of convergence are still being invented. However, in the meantime, the presence of television as a structuring metaphor on the Internet is growing. The television metaphor is "the most logical route to increasing [the Internet's] audiences," according to Jon Swartz, who points to language on the Internet borrowed liberally from television: desktop "channels," "channel surfing," "producers," "Netguide" and "programming," plus visual metaphors such as the virtual TV set of Microsoft's on-line service. Currently, in its attempt to become an advertising medium, the World Wide Web is said to be more and more like television or the world's largest, and some say, most boring shopping mall.

While the computer and other imaging and display technologies are innovative, they are not in and of themselves revolutionary. Furthermore, the institutions around these technologies are as likely to resist as they are to promote social change. This transitional period is one of struggle for control by megacorporations with global interests over the rules of ownership and the conventions and practices of the data sphere—a global and virtual surround of electronic networks for exchanging information. How power will be marked into formats and networks of cyberculture differently than television remains to be seen.

PART TWO

IMMERSION IN IMAGE WORLDS: VIRTUALITY AND EVERYDAY LIFE

THREE

Television Graphics and the Virtual Body:
Words on the Move

It is true in general that words are treated in dreams as though they were concrete things.

—Sigmund Freud

"I felt freed from *the powers of gravity*, and, through memory, succeeded in recapturing the extraordinary *voluptuousness* that pervades *high places. . . .*" When the dreamer really experiences the word immense, he sees himself liberated from his cares and thoughts, even from his dreams. He is no longer shut up in his weight, the prisoner of his own being.

—Gaston Bachelard

COSMIC LETTERS

A development began in television graphics at the end of the 1960s, when a vortex seemed to pull the viewer virtually "inside" the set and into a miniature cosmos occupied by an animated logo.[1] High-end television graphics subsequently evolved into elaborate three-dimensional forms choreographed in complex patterns of motion. Despite their brevity, television graphics in openers for movies, sports, news, and entertainment specials of up to thirty seconds, images for network or station identifications of about ten seconds, and even bumpers or identifications between ads of three seconds have become ubiquitous expressions of a cultural fantasy of induction into another world on the other side of the screen. Especially in the 1980s, a visual and aural repertoire of images functioned as entry points or "star gates" into a fantasy with roots in childhood experience as well as links to a cultural construction of the future.[2] These letters, numbers, and/or pictorial symbols that swooped or tumbled across the void in intricately shifting trajectories and speeds not only identified and advertised television networks and cable channels, they constituted incipient virtual worlds. Like the slipping and sliding of signifiers in dreams, a television spectator's traveling point of view and a graphic symbol in motion could virtually zip and zoom past one another along the z- or depth axis of television space, anticipating the development of computer-supported immersive and interactive media. The z-axis extends from the illusory depths of the set to the material space beyond the frame of the television screen; so, a glowing logotype could mysteriously appear on the screen from a vector behind the viewer and might even seem to pass through the viewer's body on its way into the visual field. The viewer (or perhaps reader) seems to be freed from gravity in a virtual experience of giddy speed through a symbolic universe of abc's. Assumptions about the word shaped by centuries of paper, ink, and printing machines were altered in the process.[3]

A sense of the word schooled in an iconoclastic biblical tradition and Enlightenment logic considered the written page to contain disembodied expression, the essentially static, two-dimensional trace of an absent subject, distanced and reflective. Machine-mediated print is yet more distanced and anonymous. Yet, it is interesting how much of the nomenclature of both writing and typographics—*hand, face, character*—are metonymies of the absent human body and of the subjectivity which we presume is responsible for them. No wonder a logo composed of a particular style of letters and/or pictorial symbols can act as the image, proper name, and bearer of the personality of a specific corporate being. After all, a corporation is a person in legal fiction only, and it is distributed unevenly over a mixture of the physical and the intangible. Only symbolic means can create or express its corporate unity and give it a body, a face, and a character. Television networks, stations, and channels also transmit logos identifying the owner of a broadcast frequency or cable channel on which airtime is sold. The on-air logo has a circumscribed, hierarchical field of operation: as a clocklike mechanism, the logo signals a temporal, linear shift between programs and program types in television flow; as the design of its motion underlines, the logo represents an exchange along the depth or z-axis between the viewer and the screen.

The most famous broadcast logo, and "one of the most successful trademarks of the twentieth century," was the CBS pictographic eye designed by William Golden that first appeared as an on-air logo on November 16, 1951. According to Phillip Meggs, a historian of graphic design, the eye "was superimposed over a cloud-filled sky and projected an almost surreal sense of an eye in the sky. . . . Translucent and hovering . . . it symbolizes the awesome power of images projected through air into every home."[4] I myself have heard several people tell stories about their uncanny feeling in childhood that the CBS eye was looking back. Evidently, this logo could convey the uncomfortable sense of being under surveillance by a consciousness on the other side of the screen.

Even when graphic space is quite flat, it serves the exercise of the power to identify or change the subject. Add depth and motion, especially as highly controlled patterns of acceleration and deceleration that suggest the operation of volition, and a logo symbol is imparted with what is intuitively a sign of an anima or soul. The logo that seems to move of its own accord and to engage us in a shared virtual realm functions much as any other indicator of a person in television discourse, namely as a *shifter* or switch between discursive levels and narrative worlds. A "live" audiovisual medium such as television expands the linguistic concept of shifters (such as "I" and "you," "here" and "now") to include the gestural—tosses and swivels and eyelines—of anchors, hosts, and now, logos. In a sense, the flying television logo might be thought of not only as the proper name of a network or a station, but as a very special kind of television host or narrator, leading the viewer deep into and through the layers of television space.

After a brief sketch of the history of television graphics in the second section of this chapter, the third section will explore various motifs, figures, and tropes of television graphics. In particular I will examine how a logo sequence or opener conveys in a matter of seconds the fantasy of the viewer's virtual *induction* at great speed or gives the impression of *immersion* in a world beyond the screen to be explored in *weightless flight*. I will also consider how the experience of hyperrealistic depth and extreme nearness lends a sense of monumental scale to logo objects.

Spatial motif refers to the virtual location of a logo, for instance, "outer space" or "America." Shapes and boundaries within screen space form *spatial figures*; movement, rendered in a style which is not to be taken literally, but figuratively, is a *trope of motion*—for example, the star gate or the squeeze frame. Rendering most of the figures pictorially would be difficult, although not impossible, without a computer. (Of course, spatial figures have a history that began long before television or the computer and even before the primitive era of moving pictures.) Beyond distinguishing themselves from competitors, networks and cable channels were at least partly motivated to employ a new and expensive computer technology for on-air IDs in order to partake in the aura of futurity associated with the computer itself. It is the look of digital technology in a particular stage of development and the ubiquity of such figures that produced the unmistakable style of television graphics in the 1980s.

The fourth section of this chapter considers graphics as shifters and transitional devices in the exchange function of television in culture. I conclude by questioning whether tropes of motion will have the significance they now possess once motion ceases to signify subjectivity and once spatial transit becomes moot as a metaphor for transformation. "Morphing," telepresence, and augmented or enhanced reality don't require travel to change bodies or places, and the object-world itself is personified with speech and agency.

In the beginning was *Logos*.

—John 1:1

A BRIEF SKETCH OF THE HISTORY OF TELEVISION GRAPHICS

The earliest television graphics were cards in front of a camera; if informational content were all that mattered, that could still suffice. Not that such simple means precluded showmanship: as Roy Laughton describes the process, "Glitter [real, not electronic] flowed like water. The epitome of success was a roller caption filled with every conceivable style of typeface, laboriously hand-lettered and decorated with stars, spots and spangles from top to bottom" (14).[5] Aside from their actual televisual transmission and the use of the kinescope or the caption scanner to transfer film and slides to live television, graphics for television were most commonly produced by traditional methods such as drawing, hot press, and various methods of film animation—until the advent of the computer. The character generator was the first electronic graphic tool in a profession, which at least one commentary on television graphics has divided into two periods: from the beginning until 1975 B.C., or "before computer," and from 1975 on, that is, A.D. or "aided design" (Merritt 46).[6]

In the late forties and early fifties, CBS was in the forefront of corporate identity design, thanks to its President Frank Stanton, and William Golden, who is consistently remembered for the sense of quality conveyed by his designs for television and for commissioning artists such as Ben Shahn to produce art work for corporate promotions.[7] Today what might strike a viewer of the most admired graphic designs of the period, such as Golden's logo or Saul Bass's film titles, is that they are modern, clean, hard-edged, and flat.

Golden's successor, Louis Dorfsman, Creative Director of the CBS Television Network from 1960 and Director of Design of CBS Inc. from 1964, effected a high-modern corporate design strategy by carving out a unified identity for CBS in seventeenth-century Didot typeface with delicate serifs (supplemented by a sans serif, CBS Sans). CBS Didot signified quality and quiet refinement, and it appeared on everything from the television screen to letterhead, mail chutes, fire-alarm boxes, and the corporate lunchroom at CBS corporate headquarters. In retrospect, this total corporate environment seems to anticipate the desire for immersion in a symbolic world, albeit one that is richly material. Letters, eye, globe, and star symbols in Dorfsman's animated film promotions and logos in the 1960s and 1970s glowed tastefully, spun around or expanded and receded, demonstrating that even after television took off as a marketing medium in the 1960s, the desire to signify quality and prestige could still support a design strategy that eschewed razzle-dazzle.[8]

However, as the competitive pressures on networks and cable channels increased, the need to differentiate corporate identities from each other with elaborate signatures and fanfares increased as well; new design strategies and modes of production were adopted. Analog animation techniques form a bridge between film animations like Dorfsman's and the digital computer animation of today. This technology was based on the Animac, the invention of Lee Harrison, whose "animated cute, springy character transformed itself into a means for moving logos and high contrast graphics about the screen."[9] The graphic bodies of corporate symbols were produced by "bone generators" and "skin scanners" but the motion design was still a far cry from the glitzy graphics performing fancy z-axis moves that characterize the postmodern trend in television graphics.

Though sophisticated choreography had already begun in the late 1960s without the aid of computers, the years from 1975 to 1981 were the formative ones for the development of computers and computer graphics.[10] The subsequent decade from about 1983 on (when, for instance, the "Fantastico" title for Brazil's TV Globo was produced) might be characterized as the high baroque to mannerist period of computerized graphic design for television. Of course, the often artist-commissioned, constantly changing logos of MTV, established in 1981, are a special case. Here the cable channel's identity is signified not by consistency in visual appearance over a year or more, but by the concept of rapid change itself, conveyed by quick editing and the continuous variation of visual motifs, amidst which nonetheless the pattern "MTV" is always recognizable.

If we look at three NBC IDs for the years 1984–87 (in the "graphics packages" produced at Pacific Data Images with Harry Marks of Marks Communications), we find a record of changing fashions in computer graphic design as the logos shift in composition from the simulation of chrome, to neon, to transparency. Each ID involves elaborate motion design based on flight simulation. In 1985, our vantage point is in flight toward a gleaming logo object, an abstract "N" adorned with the peacock-color spectrum, floating in space. We are banked to the right over horizon lines, gradually coming upright as we fly under the logo, revealing the object behind it, the slogan "BE THERE" in block letters, and reflected below as in a mirror (that is, THERE is reversed; BE mysteriously isn't). Meanwhile, a squadron of glowing balls deposits the pink flashing banner "Let's all!" The letters of the slogan become monumental as we fly down toward them, ultimately flying through an enormous passageway formed by an "E." Elapsed time: three seconds. The 1985 logo object, a neon marquee seen from the back, turns slowly around toward the left, as the viewer seems to fly backward, so as to ultimately reveal the logo in a frontal view of the N-peacock, as "Let's all" flashes and lights advance across "BE THERE" (three seconds). The 1987 ID is an extravaganza of transparent layers with surface modeling that advance left to right across the surface of the set, as our viewing position seems to travel backward, revealing transparent letters on their sides and seen from below. The letters gradually right themselves into full frontality, revealing that they are indeed a multilayered, transparent, and monumental NBC peacock logo. Thereupon the logo adopts a more ordinary flat and more opaque appearance (five seconds, leading into individual station IDs).

In 1987 the exuberance of television logotypes drew the attention of the architectural critic of the *New York Times*, who posited them to be the ultimate indicator for trends in stage, film, and architectural de-

Television Graphics and the Virtual Body

**Computer graphic network IDs, logos, and openers.
By courtesy of Pacific Data Images.**

An animated logo object for Globo Fantastico (1983), produced for TV Globo by
Pacific Data Images. Creative Director: Hans Donner, Globo TV.

sign. At the time, what struck this critic was the "movement, change
and sparkle" or what he variously called "visual excess," "razzle daz-
zle" or "overdesign" of the prior five years in visual design (Goldberger
1, 34).[11] Television graphics were at that time the most technologically
innovative and highly produced visual design commonly available in
our culture at a cost per second comparable to the same average cost
per minute of video. A single logotype or opener could take weeks of
computer time to render. Of course, these most radiant expressions of
corporate identity also marked a period of economic vulnerability for
broadcasters.[12] At the same time, they anticipated a major social and
cultural transition—even if the audience was out in the kitchen getting
a beer.

Now broadcast television networks are dimming stars in the media
universe and television itself is being subsumed into cyberculture.
Faster computers and the availability of graphics technology and programs to television stations and producers and even independents have
taken three-dimensional computer graphics for television largely out

Two frames from the animated NBC ID for 1985. Produced by Pacific Data Images for Marks Communications. Creative Director: Harry Marks, Marks Communications, 1984.

Television Graphics and the Virtual Body

Two frames from CBS Tuesday Movie Opener (1987). Produced by Pacific Data Images for CBS Entertainment. CBS Producer: Lewis Hall. PDI Producer: Roger Gould.

A z-axis move down a celestial landing/film strip.

Two scales of lettering serve legibility and monumentality.

of the hands of a few specialized computer graphics firms, who have turned their businesses toward advertising and special effects for the movies, theme parks, and now even feature-length films.[13] Common visual effects have been standardized for instant or "real time" use on television by means of, for instance, ADO, DVE, and weather graphics systems. The sensibility that informs visual design has changed as well: the once-glowing neon look of the NBC peacock can assume a flat, hand-drawn, childlike innocence or historicize itself with a rapidly edited review of peacock logos. Other contemporary logos present a fairly shallow theatrical space or a composition with historical referents such as the searchlight and marquee. However, the fantasy of induction and virtual flight, far from being played out, is finding far roomier fields of expression in the production of commercial virtual environments for arcades, theme park motion-platform ridefilms and now even the communal space on-line on the World Wide Web with its "VRML" or virtual reality mark-up language. Ultimately, the trope of induction into a world of corporate imagination comes to fruition in the impression of being immersed in a seemingly infinite virtual realm, filled with nothing but projections of our own symbolic system posing as celestial objects.

Thus the minuscule, a narrow gate, opens up an entire world. . . . Macrocosm and microcosm are correlated.

—Gaston Bachelard

INDUCTION INTO LOGOLAND: FIGURES OF SPACE AND TIME IN GRAPHIC SEQUENCES

Figures of induction are literal representations of an act of the imagination that permits the reader or viewer or visitor to a virtual environment to enter and explore worlds that are otherwise inaccessible by virtue of their two-dimensionality, scale, solidity, immateriality, or imaginariness. How does a viewer experience virtual entry into television as if it were an imaginary realm of outer space populated by letters the size of asteroids or planets? Visual figures promote this feeling of "being sucked in," though the fantasy of induction itself is archaic, part of the liminal function of culture, and is not dependent on technology. It is rather an invocation that shifts attention from immediate circumstances in order to enhance our capacity to suspend disbelief in a symbolic world. There are many precedents in folktales, fantasies, and reveries: the French literary theorist Gaston Bachelard, for example, cites Tom Thumb, a one-inch-tall boy who drives the constellation of the Great Bear or Big Dipper, as his prime instance of this cosmic fantasy. In fact, any act of reading that involves being "carried away" has this very scenario of entry into the miniature letters of the text and finding another world inside them.[14] While in reading or in daydreaming such an act occurs in the imagination, on television it can be represented literally, often by an actual motion along the z- or depth axis.

The realism of motion in fiction film is ascribable only to lateral motion along the x- and y-axes. By contrast, motion on the z-axis is inherently unreal, for the means by which we interpret nearness and farness (that is, changes in scale) can also act as disconcerting, even magical changes in the size of objects (see Weinbren 328–35).[15] The turn-of-the-century pioneer of trick films, Georges Méliès, used the magical effect of scale in a seventeen-second space flight in *A Trip to the Moon* (1902)—though only the first twelve seconds are presented as a z-axis subjective point-of-view shot.[16] Narratively, the moon grows larger on screen because the camera/rocket is getting nearer, but technically the background with the moon's (literally personified) face is moving forward. This trick is at the heart of absolute inertia in all virtual travel: "the bedridden man," in Paul Virilio's words,[17] does not move; the background and/or the ground itself does.

Of course, the trip to the moon is not just the ticket to another world but to another ontological status and state of mind: movement along the depth axis is consistently associated with a transformation, be it a change of worlds or condition. Méliès's moonscape tableau is no terra incognita, but rather a magical scene watched over by alluring female bodies who broadcast stardust from the heavens onto stuffy academic moon visitors, whereupon male demons, brandishing pitchforks at them, issue from below.

The depth axis can also act like a microscope or telescope in motion through worlds in different scales, that is, like an incredibly powerful virtual zoom that is not merely motion *through* homogeneous space but also *between* heterogeneous worlds.[18] Of course, even the sense of movement itself is virtual in a zoom: a variable focal length lens creates the impression of movement and of getting closer or farther from an object without requiring the camera to move from its station point at all.

Z-axis moves or zooms from a subjective point of view possess the advantage of allowing the viewer to identify all the more with visually induced kinetic experiences. However, z-axis moves in the cinema, as opposed to television, are special effects that would threaten to burst the viewer through the line between representation and reality if they were not almost always recaptured for the fiction by what is essentially a reverse shot of the eye or body of the hero. At this point, they are interpreted as safe lateral moves along the line of action that divides the viewer from the fiction.

Yet there are some moves in the cinema that remain subjective, uncaptured by a reverse field, because they are associated with a supernatural being or, more commonly, a narrator. Consider, for example, the trope of a film title sequence or opener that begins with a wide-angle view that gradually dollies/zooms in to witness a single story or fate. The reverse move signals the end of the narrative. Unassigned subjective z-axis moves within the body of a film may also be associated with a narration or serve as a hermeneutic device in which the camera is a weaponlike organ for exploring a space, discovering its dangers, and taking away its treasures.[19] Note that in film such apertures inside a story-world are usually sinuous and lateralized and rarely the perpendicular zooms which mark the breakthrough into Logoland—at least until 1968. That was the year Stanley Kubrick's *2001, A Space Odyssey* established the archetypal z-axis move in outer space, signifying evolution induced by extraterrestrial intelligence. It was also the year Charles and Ray Eames composed the finest modernist expression of the zoom as a hermeneutic tool of discovery in their eight-minute film *A rough sketch for a proposed film dealing with the powers of ten and the relative size of things in the universe.*

With the earliest "depth" logos in television graphics (according to designer Harry Marks, then working for ABC in Los Angeles and, in fact, responsible for its "Swiss" look)[20] the viewer virtually enters screen space along the z- or depth axis through a "star gate" or vortex borrowed from the sequence realized by Douglas Trumbull in *2001*. In this particular instance, the mysterious matte monolith was replaced with the shining letters "abc" and the viewer took the place of "Dave." The television screen became like a viewport of a spaceship moving into outer space—the inner space of the television—at such a rate of speed that space itself seemed to fold in upon itself along a vertical or horizontal axis just ahead of the viewer. This is the trope of an *extreme or forced perspective*, and it can produce a visceral feeling of excitement or unease.[21] As Trumbull explains what he calls the Slitscan process, "The camera was mounted on a track moving in one direction, while the artwork was moving behind the slit in another. There's the sense of plunging into a space that has infinite depth."[22] Note that the trajectory of motion at this stage is resolutely linear—the swoops and fly-throughs were a later development.

The streaking colors in the late 1960s acid palette were similar in effect to the motion-blur of the stars around a spaceship at warp speed exponential to the speed of light in the *Star Trek* films. These effects became more pronounced in the subsequent *Star Trek* series *The Next Generation*, *Deep Space Nine*, and *Voyager*. The impression of speed also offers a sense of *time compression*: what might ordinarily take light-years to experience is available here in seconds. We are meant to feel that we are engaged in a subjective experience of time in which we break through "bodily" into a story-world in which clocks run at a different rate (a popular rather than scientific rendition of Einstein's theory of relativity). The prime temporal reference for the people who make television graphics may be the time of enunciation or production, be it a matter of weeks or instantly, in "real time." However, from the point of view of the receiver, the logo is an utterance of a few seconds in duration. Ultimately, the experience of subjective time is of a fourth dimension in a fictional world of the future, characterized by a capacity for speed beyond our ken.

In contrast to high-speed streaking and blurring as a transition be-tween worlds, Charles and Ray Eames offer a cosmic exploration of exponentially expanding and receding scale in high-modern style. In *A rough sketch* we are virtually zoomed "up" to and "back" from the outer reaches of the universe and "down" to the atom and back through a rapid chain of coherent image-worlds arranged perpendicularly to the surface of the earth and in alternation (like spacers) with what the Eames voice-over tells us are near voids or blank spots in our solar system. While Michael Snow's seemingly inexorable zoom across a New York loft in *Wavelength* lasted for forty-five minutes, the speed of the Eames zoom[23] was evidently a function of the intended psycho-logical effect of conveying immensity rather than duration: the jacket copy of the current laser disc version of this film, "shot long before George Lucas," suggests that Charles and Ray Eames were eager to be as mind-boggling and transformative as *2001*, albeit in a more rational vein: "It employs the technique of telling and showing viewers more than they can absorb in the time allowed. Images are a fraction too short to imprint on the mind's eye, but not so short as to be subliminal: the mind races."

What is "inside" the television, once a perpendicular subjective high-speed zoom virtually smashes through into the other side of the screen and allows one to bodily enter the symbolic world inside the television set? Unlike the coherent, referential world that opens up when a text becomes transparent, here it is as if there were a gate into the literal space of letters such as "abc" as opaque objects in a void. Clearly the influence of *2001* has contributed to the predominance of outer space as a motif; however, the dark void in which the logo figure floats is also a perfect three-dimensional counterpart to the ground or negative space of the page in print. Outer space also does not need to look particularly "real" to maintain a credible, albeit surreal atmosphere on the television screen. Colors on television are additive, that is, painted in light, and the earthy or gritty look of subtractive colors that we think of as realistic was long difficult to achieve. Yet the simple geometric shapes of celestial objects could be rendered in a way that simulates complex textures and the reflective properties of multiple light sources on a surface. No wonder the computer-generated universe of Logoland in the viewport of our spaceship was characterized by garishly colored geometric primitives in a usually black void. (Even the satellite images of "real" planets in our solar system were enhanced with color in that period.)

In addition to its practicality, the motif of outer space is part of a general cultural shift of imagery away from the historical reference points that oriented Americans for the greater part of the twentieth century and toward a rather limited range of images and motifs that signify the future. For the next quarter century, outer space replaced the Old West as the frontier of imagination: even Levis blasted off into the stratosphere, along with the alphabet. Today, the frontier has migrated to the virtual realms supported by the computer itself.

The symbolic world that is revealed inside logos and openers is largely self-referential. For instance, the HBO movie logo has long been organized around the theme of entering not only a city and a theater but film space itself, sprocket holes and all. A common motif for a football opener is the field itself, altering from the size of a chessboard to a size big enough for automated giants. Other motifs of location are not specific places but rather symbolize imaginary social unities, serving the ambition of broadcasting to speak for and represent the public. For instance, the 1984 Olympics and presidential campaign reporting relied on logos of flying over gigantic maps of the globe and the United States respectively. In the same period, the NBC news logo of the Statue of Liberty allowed us to fly around the symbol of America as mother giantess (a decade later, we could discover Michael Jackson on the Statue of Liberty in the music video "Black or White").

Another series of NBC openers in the mid-1980s were based on "Las Vegas"–style marquees, full of neon lights the size of planets in planes revolving in counter directions. This marquee had indeed "learned from Las Vegas" (Robert Venturi's classic guide to architectural post-modernism), for it borrowed the properties of the "pleasure zone" that Venturi's team identified on the exterior and interior architecture of the urban strip: outside, an eclectic assemblage of symbols was designed to be approached and viewed in motion, while inside an autonomous space of light surrounded by darkness became a limbo world without edges. The complex spatial planes of the logotype or symbols in an opener are also similar to the "decorated shed" construction Venturi identified: two-dimensional graphic forms were extruded, sliced, and texture-mapped by computer. And it appears that Las Vegas has learned from computer graphic design in turn, as those casino oases in limbo have been supplemented by full-fledged virtual worlds in theme parks designed, for one, by the same Douglas Trumbull of *2001*.[24]

It was the adoption of flight simulator conventions for film and then for televison graphics by, among others, the graphic designer Harry Marks in work with Colin Cantwell, that allowed the flight path of the viewer to veer from a straight line into infinity, and to swoop and change direction, in motions coordinated with other objects moving in entirely different ways and trajectories.[25] Its supreme expression is the evasive flight of a spaceship through the "Death Star" in George Lucas's *Star Wars* (1977). The twisting narrow valleys and tunnels inside the Death Star function like a vortex or space of passage; however, they are not only a more interesting background on which to demonstrate the visual effect of speed, but allow the hazards and obstacles of the space itself to act as a dramatic antagonist. Indeed, the winding "tunnel" trope has become a stock figure in computer-generated special effects for film, opening and / or title sequences in film and television, as well as in amusement ride films, which may also be synchronized with a motion platform under the audience's seats.

The twenty-six-second "CBS TUESDAY MOVIE" opener for 1987 (Pacific Data Images and Creative Director John Le Prevost, Associate Creative Director Lewis Hall) manages to allude to the tunnel trope while swooping through a celestial logo organized as a constellation of spatial planes. The music swoops as we seem to fly backward, revealing a blue layer with sprocket holes above us; then, a layer of glowing balls and another of transparent stripes come into view as it advances and we recede. At three seconds, letters become discernible which pull upright revealing "CBS." At five seconds, a gigantic "C" moves left to right across our field of view, becoming legible as another CBS at seven seconds; likewise, a small "TUESDAY" and a monumental "TUES-DAY" pass by, and at thirteen seconds, a small and a big "MOVIE" have been revealed frontally, as we gradually descend between the spatial planes. As the fanfare crescendos, we fly into the z-axis toward a celestial layer very much like a landing strip, in a move that bears the unmistakeable imprint of the flight simulator. However, we don't land, but come out of the constellation through an enormous "E," as another logo constellation comes into view. At twenty-two seconds, the new star group moving away from the viewer becomes legible as "CBS TUESDAY MOVIE," becoming monumental and frontal letters seen from a low angle. The various planes of sprockets, balls, and stripes evoke film, stars, marquee lights, and the flag, while moving the viewer away from as well as into the interior of logo space. What at first seems to be a gratuitous doubling of words and logo objects for the purpose of sparkle and glitz also serves the same function as the motion design—combining legibility with a sense of monumentality.

Many other television openers offer sinuous trajectories, including, for example, the opening animation sequence of the children's and cult program "Pee-wee's Playhouse" with its subjective point-of-view swerving to avoid trees and animal life in an enchanted forest.[26] Once we meet the host (Paul Reubens as Pee-wee next to his dollhouse-sized playhouse), he acts as a transitional object into deep story space by "shrinking" until he is toy-size, able to enter the playhouse door, where the show begins. This spatial transformation is also a discursive change from a level of the presentation of a toy world narrated by the host to a story enacted in a "real"-sized space virtually shared with the viewer.

It was variable motion design that moved television graphics beyond the breakthrough theme and into the creation of a virtual world in which the viewer could fly and explore. Once inside Logoland, the viewer's virtual motion can be quite daredevil: it might include a sudden switch from a point of view facing ahead toward the object to flying backward, looking at the object behind one. It is at this point that the hidden and readable side of the celestial object is revealed. One could say that this transformation is *hermeneutic* and that the choreography of viewer and logo is designed to provide an adventure of discovery in which a fantasy world suddenly becomes a graphic world or vice versa. On the other hand, flying around, through, and between the discursive planes of discursive space in logos sometimes reveals an illogically organized series. The NBC opener for 1986–87, for example, might be considered cubist in spatial organization, showing the same elements from various angles and entry points—but its topology of over and under or behind and in front of makes no sense in the two or three dimensions to which we are accustomed. In any case, complex motion design serves the *repeatability* of such logos and openers over one or more seasons of a network or cable channel's programming.

Another interesting facet of the viewer's subjective motion deep within Logoland is the capacity to circle around objects and see the sides which are ordinarily hidden from view. This ability to virtually move behind an object and see its *back side* is precisely what is forbidden in monocular perspective and, one might add, representation in the photograph and the classic fiction film. In the world governed by an iron 180° rule, what one would see if one crossed the line would be the back of the canvas or the trusses and props of the backstage factory.[27] Until recently representation was like a Potemkin village of two-sided facades, one side supporting the impression of reality aided by the psychic mechanism of disavowal, and the other side accrediting the fiction to the efforts of human subjects in discourse. However, the televisual fantasy of going behind the objects within a story does not reveal a world of makeup and plaster, but instead a total fictional world that could enclose the viewer entirely (if television only possessed the full-fledged immersive capacities of virtual reality or another type of virtual environment). The proclivity of television in general for disclosing a backstage to view could be cited here, but the "backstage" here (and maybe there) is ultimately revealed to be a kind of pocket within the space of the fiction itself.[28] This anticipates the techniques of virtual reality that give the viewer the impression of enclosure in an image envelope that functions as a full-fledged environment.

Interestingly, the perpendicular zoom technique is still favored as a metaphor for organizing and shifting between databases. For instance, the screen-based interactive globe named *T-Vision*, produced by the Berlin design firm ART+COM in 1995, allows the visitor to turn the simulation of a globe wrapped with satellite imagery on screen in any direction with an input device. The visitor can also "fly" over the earth or descend to inspect a city or a street and even a building more closely (but only in those areas where the data in question has been filled in).

Much like Eames's technique (which was itself borrowed from a Dutch textbook [see Boeke, and Morrison and Morrison]), different features of the earth/universe are revealed at different scales, but unlike the Eames zoom, the flight path is determined by the user and need no longer be perpendicular—you can fly at the same altitude (and in the same database). The goal of the ART+COM program is to produce utterly seamless transitions between databases, producing the sense of one homogeneous virtual world.[29] In contrast, in the Eames zoom, different scales remain distinct and well defined, as if each were edited by the universe itself, without too much messy streaking or too many distorted in-betweens.

There is an ideological assumption embodied in *T-Vision* and other hermeneutic zooms that to get nearer to the screen in an electronic display is to get a more detailed view—that is, to achieve a better understanding—of the visual field. The photographic correlate of this assumption is the enlargement or blow-up. Jeffrey Shaw's interactive videodisc installation "Royal Road" (1993) is an experiential demonstration that electronic images are not like the analog information in photographs: getting closer to an electronic pixel can reveal nothing that is not already on display or contained in the electronic database that generates it—though the computer can "enhance" the image, that is, simulate a guesstimate of details. As Shaw describes the piece, it also embodies the electronic metaphor of "the viewer as traveller who enters and explores a virtual space of stored audiovisual information" by offering the viewer a path lined with sensors in physical space that is a chain of six virtual monitors in virtual space. Walking past a series of sensors triggers an antihermeneutic process. As the visitor nears a virtual monitor, the "pixels" get larger on the monitor at the end of the path, making the image coarser and less legible. Then, at the beginning of the next virtual monitor, the image returns to normal size and the process of enlargement can begin again, without having resolved anything about the prior image. In this way, "Royal Road" thematizes a way of dealing with problematic or unresolved images much as television would—by simply bringing in a fresh layer of imagery (see *Multimediale 3* 54).[30]

Having objects on the other side of the video screen get nearer to the picture plane is no more enlightening than getting nearer the image. In fact, nearness is one of the tricks of scale that contributes to a sense of the overwhelming size of logo objects, along with placement in frame and the inverted horizon. Scale is a mental construct we surmise from the

Digital Transmutation

In Jeffrey Shaw's "Royal Road" (1993), walking down a path marked with blue lights interactively triggers changes in the imagery on the large video monitor at the end. A sonar sensor measures the person's position and walking direction. The images are a sequence of digital metamorphoses that are seen on six virtual monitors arranged architectonically along the path. Interactive videodisk installation version of "Going to the Center of the Garden of Delights" (1986). 3–D animation: Tamás Waliczky. Produced at the Institute for Visual Media, Zentrum für Kunst und Medientechnologie Karlsruhe (ZKM). By courtesy of Jeffrey Shaw.

Midpoint in the metamorphosis from automobile into Exxon Tiger (1991). Produced for McCann-Erikson (Houston). Animation/Special Effects: Pacific Data Images. Live Action: Griner/Cuesta & Schrom. By courtesy of Pacific Data Images.

size of an object as we know it in real space, not from the absolute size of the image. Relative size in relation to other objects, placement of the object in relation to the edge of the frame, and whether the object is fragmented or seen whole and centered are all of importance in distinguishing the miniature from the monumental. For example, a fly-through that "slices" the viewer through objects in television space might virtually place the viewer right next to an object on the other side of the television screen.[31] When only a tiny part of the object can be seen and the rest is cut by the frame, it will appear to be massive. It is not until we pull away (or it pulls away and rights itself vertically) that the object is frontally revealed as a cosmic letter of vast proportions. In actual dimensions, of course, the letters ABC, CBS, NBC, the eye, the peacock, HBO, and MTV are just inches tall on the screen.

Even though we might be feet away from the television screen, the aspect of view is far closer than we ever come in normal life to see an object, just millimeters away from, say, a celestial object, a car, or a cubic zirconia tennis bracelet. In effect, the "eyes" of the camera are substituting for our sense of touch. It takes time to explore the planet/car/bracelet in such extreme close-up and even then we can know it only microscopically, but not necessarily in toto. This trope of *extreme nearness* is very common in logos and contemporary advertising and dominates the presentation of objects on home shopping channels. In logos such a use of scale conveys immensity and power—like the pyramids or fascist architecture or the door handles in *Metropolis* which the man-child had to reach on tiptoe. Even the mysterious monolith in *2001* was more accessible than monumental logo objects at just three times human size.

Many logos or openers begin in medias res, that is, already inside the outer space created inside the television. Because they appear to be floating in outer space that we know intellectually as infinite, logo objects may also seem enormous. This sense of floating is created not only by making negative space a void, but also by putting massive objects above what would be the horizon line, leaving the ground below empty. The *inverted horizon* is typical of *Star Trek* and *Star Wars*, where starships always seem to station themselves below a relatively huge planet, empty space below them. Thus, a point of view weighted by the world and stabilized through the x- and y-axes at the horizon line and anchored at the plumb line of gravity is unhitched and made independent of weight, mass, and all coordinates. Clearly, such a detachment from earth would be a significant change in the ground of representation and our basic assumptions about orientation in the world.

This figure of the inverted horizon was the prime trope of the movie *Top Gun* (1986), where it is an index of the skill and sovereignty of the intuitive flyer released from the common social and rational anchors of representation. The Cold-War hero makes a minus Mach 4 inverted contact with an MIG, using this means of alien contact to make an obscene gesture at the Russkis. Interestingly, this trope was then appropriated for the Pepsi commercial that preceded the video release of *Top Gun*, where the inversion is used to pour a liquid commodity into a cup—a return to gravity. A look at other fictional renderings of outer space shows how partial the trope of inversion remains in recreating the weightlessness. In contrast to footage of astronauts inside their capsules showing them sleeping at every angle of the compass, the interior of Cloud City in *Return of the Jedi* is somehow subject to gravity. Luke Skywalker even suspends himself from the exterior of a space station upright, earthlike clouds around him. When space objects are revealed as letters in logos they also regain the upright, vertical axis.

Though it seems that virtual worlds are psychically preparing us for the weightlessness of outer and now "inner" or virtual space, our bodies act nonetheless in real space and in irreversible time on earth. Nevertheless, the *fantasy of weightless flight* is supported for all of a few seconds in Logoland, recalling some of the most euphoric experiences of childhood that, according to Freud, recur later in dreams. "Children are delighted by [games involving movement]," he states, "and never tire of asking to have them repeated especially if there is something about them that causes a little fright or giddiness. In after years they repeat these experiences in dreams; but in dreams they leave out the hands which held them up, so that they float or fall unsupported" (*Interpretation* 428). In Logoland, the displaced hand movements allow letters and the body of the dreamer/viewer to move at breathtaking speeds without volition. Our living-room starship has no Captain Kirk, but like Lohengrin's swan, the capsule goes where and as fast as it desires. Though our virtual flight might be rapid or abrupt, it accelerates and decelerates smoothly and it only threatens to become dysphoric and to let us fall in order to entertain. Whereas the worlds in miniature discussed by Bachelard are "dominated worlds" (161), the speed and the roller-coaster trajectory of movements out of our control underline our powerlessness in the immensity of (corporate) outer space: we are made small. Television graphics have been called a "real time flight simulator," but we are not pilots, only passengers without influence on the flight path, supported in thrills of motion by invisible hands.

**Mecka Lecka Hi,
Mecka Heini Ho!**

—Genie's incantation in
"Pee-wee's Playhouse"

WORD MAGIC

The flight path of a graphic symbol through televisual space is, oddly enough, at least as significant for its role in the exchange of cultural values among objects, bodies, and other symbols as any information it may communicate. How the word is choreographed through television's illusory depths, what it can be exchanged for or transformed into, or what it can cause to happen is more important from this perspective than how the graphic symbol was made, what it means, or to what it refers. The word or *Logos* takes pride of place in general among other great signs of exchange, for it is the symbol—be it written or drawn, a verbal utterance, referent object, or associated mental image—that allows values and meanings to pass through different systems of exchange, reality statuses, and material states. Television is still the great engine that enacts the virtual exchange of all these symbols. The logotype is the symbol (both trivial and fetishistically overvalued) of a network's place and position in that exchange function per se. The logotype has taken on what Karl Marx called a "fantastic form" (*Capital 1.1*) of corporate *jouissance* that reenacts its "operations of specula(riza)tion," that is, the transformation of ordinary objects and everyday language into commodities. No wonder that the logo glitters and glows with *plus-value*, the aura of saints and celebrities, holy objects and beer bottles.[32]

However, even quite ordinary words within program space can be fetishized. We shall see how graphic phrases in a game show serve the transit of prizes and money from distant to near program space and how a subtitle can toss a speaking role, shared with hosts and characters on screen, to the child watching. Just as the logo sequence can bring the word to life, other graphics can kill three-dimensional worlds, flattening them into images like a stack of cards and blowing them away. The following examples from a game show, a children's series, and the news illustrate the role of graphics in the mediation of value and subjectivity.

A graphic display of letters composing a commonplace phrase is the focal point of the syndicated game show "Wheel of Fortune." The letters are hidden on the back side of blocks on a glittering wall deep in stage space, seemingly parallel to the plane of prizes/commodities. The letters are the locus of exchange between verbal utterances, dollar amounts, and distant prizes, facilitated by the letter-turning hostess and representative of "Fortuna," who also implicitly, albeit chastely, introduces the female body and sexuality into the equation.[33] The male host facilitates each contestant's spin of a wheel that establishes the exchange-value of a contestant's correct guess of letters in the hidden phrase; he is also the agent largely responsible for the shift of address between contestants in near space and the studio audience and the television viewer in the virtual space in front of the screen. What "Wheel of Fortune" circulates and the television viewer ultimately observes is the transfer of symbolic and economic values through graphic letters and phrases, verbal utterances, dollar amounts, and objects, in a choreography of male and female bodies and graphic objects in near and far space. The advent of game shows that interact with the home viewer is simply the next interactive level and spatial layer in this exchange.

Even the word "the" could be fetishized in "Pee-wee's Playhouse," which provides a tongue-in-cheek case study of the process of singling out and overvaluing the trivial. Once inducted inside Pee-wee's playhouse, the viewer is not only engaged by glances and direct address from the host, and introduced to the playhouse characters, he or she is also offered a word much like the secret word in Groucho Marx's game show, "You Bet Your Life." In that early 1950s show, the secret word was written on a card held in the mouth of a toy duck that was dropped into the frame from on high as the word was simultaneously whispered by the announcer. The word in "Pee-wee's Playhouse" is far from secret, since whenever "the" word is spoken—irrespective of its insignificant context or innocuous meaning—it flashes in subtitling three times and causes an outbreak of screams of all the animated characters and actors on screen, and, by express invitation of the show, of the children and willing adults in viewing space. The word itself is singled out by a toy robot, avatar of technology, and printed on something akin to supermarket register tape that descends from a robot's mouth (much as the divine word flows from the mouths of prophets and saints in medieval paintings). So the mundane becomes a precious kind of karaoke script or minus-one text of which anyone can become the subject or enunciator, producing a magical contagion that allows viewers to participate in an event on the other side of the television screen.

"Pee-wee's Playhouse" also consistently used puns literally and declaratively, embodying them in program space. Chanting "let down your hair!" transforms a lyric into a mop of hair that enters the frame from above. The wish altar or closet inhabited by a disembodied genie is another point of transformation: genie leads Pee-wee in uttering the incantation, "Mecka Lecka Hi, Mecka Heini Ho!" while mentally forming a wish and it comes true, at least in this playhouse (see Doty, esp. 94–95). So the power of words to circulate through graphic and verbal utterances, mental images, and physical objects transports the child viewer into a world of symbols in free play, where everything, including the floor, is animate.

Even the most pedestrian use of graphics over the image has consequences for representational logic and style, shifting modes from the diegetic and referential (story-world) in favor of the discursive (story being told). Television graphics can function in a seemingly transparent way as a means of anchoring images with captions, of presenting credits of a show, or of identifiying speakers and reiterating or commenting on verbal information in the news. Such traditional graphics serve similar purposes as graphics in films, for example, the credit sequence that scrolls over images at the end of the movie and intertitles or subtitles, although in sound film they are used sparingly as narrational devices in the body of the story: as discourse, such graphics violate the diegetic value or "realism" of the image. On the discursive medium of television news, however, burned-in graphics are common, even though they flatten out photographic depth, giving news images the reality status and depth of photos in a magazine. Other graphic devices (such as borders or a diagonal band or "violator" over the image) and figures of transition contribute to a flattening effect that Herbert Zettl calls "graphication" ("Graphication").[34] Since these devices and transitions insistently remind the viewer of the discursive agency in question and the television station or network that supports it, realistic imagery is clearly not the sine qua non of discursive genres on television.

The best known graphic frame and transitional device is the news window or hanging box inserted over the shoulder of a news anchor. The hanging box is not a window that bites into space; rather it forms a distinct spatial plane with its own independent capacity to display two and three dimensions and to advance over the plane of the news studio, acting discursively as a kind of supernarrator and product of symbolic activity over the representation of the "real" trace of an external world. This "window's" true counterpart is not an architectural form but the balloon in comic strips. When a window expands algorithmically from one point to fill the whole screen or contracts until it disappears out of sight (progressively replaced by another image), it is a *squeeze frame*, a common narrational transition in between anchor, reporter, and story space or market, between one story and another, or in sports, between one replay and another. Variations on this spatial figure include tumbling blocks, flipping pages and the like; in every case, multiple planes occupy televisual space together. One spatial plane may give the impression of moving toward or away from the viewer and of getting larger or smaller, but it does not function as a star gate or virtual entry into the image world but as a means for bringing up and disposing of images.

The squeeze frame is but one expression of the overriding spatial figure of television—not the segment, and not even the virtual realm deep within televisual space, but rather a series of discontinuous planes, arranged in depth along the z-axis that can advance and recede (as in news narration), or even, in the case of music video, alternate at random. The space and time to which a spatial plane refers and the means with which it is represented become heterogeneous; each image plane is capable of using different graphics and images of different scales and types (drawings, photographs, moving images, writing, or typing) than the other image planes in a stack, sustaining a different discourse or level of discourse in the process. A plane may even cross over segment boundaries, as in a news promo over the credits at the end of the previous show. The underlying metaphor that governs this construction of space is indeed the "magazine."[35]

Considerable effort is expended on techniques for editing such digital effects and digitized images *seamlessly* (smoothing the edges of objects within the image, for example, through anti-aliasing, using fractal, nonadditive mixes, minus-value black, and various segues to move smoothly from one image to another). However, a wide variety of other digital effects are applied to realistic video images with the goal of making them more like graphics (that is to say, less "real"), among them "posterization," "mosaics," or "solarization" effects and various transitional figures.[36] This suggests that the goal of "seamlessness" is a technique to create a psychic and aesthetic flow, not a way of lulling the viewer into thinking that what she or he witnesses is raw and unprocessed reality itself. In fact, the "excess" of manipulated imagery and the heterogeneity of elements within the frame amount to an open declaration of discursive and symbolic intent.

BEYOND THE BOX

Graphic tropes of motion are ultimately not about covering ground but about transition and psychic or cultural transformation. We have seen how the virtual traveler can sit utterly still and visit one world after another as the background moves, and how graphic symbols can expand into three-dimensional worlds and move, "leaving out the hands which held them up," or be collapsed and discarded by an external enunciative force. *Movement* is what suggests the animating force of an enunciating subject, whether from within or without. In thrill-oriented virtual rides in arcades and theme parks, the cultural imagery of induction—vortex, tunnel, fly-through—seems to have become an end in itself. Virtual motion means going nowhere at great speed. Meanwhile, immersive virtual worlds remain imaginatively underdeveloped. It is as if as a culture, we have prolonged the effort of getting somewhere because we don't quite know where we'll be or what to do once we get "inside."

On the other hand, graphic tropes of motion—words on the move—may be on the wane, supplanted by digital tropes that challenge the very notion of *movement* as a means of passage, in favor of an even more dreamlike world of metamorphic inconstancy, telepresence, and network cyberspace. While the hermeneutic shift from celestial object to logo letters, numbers, and symbols required virtual motion, metamorphosis—or "morphing"—is a transformation from one thing into another *in place*. Perfected as a two-dimensional digital technique in Lucas Films' *Willow* and familiar from the longest sequence to date for Michael Jackson's rock video "Black or White," morphing has become a prime trope of television advertising in general in the mid-1990s.[37] The digital effect allows a smooth sequence of images that transforms one image into another, for example, car into Exxon tiger or Michael Jackson into black panther. In "Black or White," racial, gender, and geographical differences melt into each other and separate again. Ideologically, the *work* of achieving harmony among different people disappears along with the space in between them.

However, it is foolish to blame magical thinking on the availability of morphing techniques. Long before the digital morphing of the late 1980s, such transformations were achieved *mechanically* or *magically*, especially in children's programming. The spatial transformation of scale that served the induction of the host into "Pee-wee's Playhouse" is displaced by a *mechanical* transformation that manipulated machine into robot in commercial toys such as Gobots and Transformers. With the help of its on-screen character, the toy serves as a transitional object into the space of fantasy. *Magical metamorphosis* from one form to another (for example, from a "real" cartoon boy or girl in the frame story to the powerful He-Man or She-Ra, or from ordinary teenagers to "Mighty Morphin' Power Rangers" in the fictional world) is aided by ritual, plus

editing and costume changes. The toy product endowed with the magical power to induce such a dreamlike inconstancy of shape and size in
characters/objects also invites the possessor of that toy into fantasy.
Such toys also colonize physical space as precursors of a physical reality
that has been augmented or enhanced by the computer. Interactive
experiments of children's television include controlling the action of
toys in the "real" space of the viewer by means of signals generated in
the on-screen program, making viewing space "actually" and "telematically" as opposed to "virtually" part of the program. The toy, like
the graphics before, is then endowed with the appearance of autonomous motion that "leaves out the hands which held them up."

Telepresence or telematics means that objects—physical or virtual—
can be animated or acted upon from afar without the need for the
controller to move from position. Furthermore, many different subjects
can share a virtual space together, like the bed in Paul Sermon's pieces
"Telematic Dreaming" (1992), discussed in chapter 1, and the couch in
"Telematic Vision" (1993). A blue-screen links people in different places
onto one virtual item of furniture—allowing visitors to experience virtual touch and the overlap of bodies and gestures in an arena that is
already loaded with social meanings. As far as on-line nets and webs are
concerned, the only material spaces that matter are the ones in front of
computers all over the world. All the space-in-between collapses in
nanoseconds, while virtual realms fill in the breaks with virtual realms
that can literally be graphic worlds constructed "room" by "room" in
the text-based virtual environments of communal cyberspace or multi-
user dungeons.

While the figures and tropes of television graphics have considerably
enriched our audiovisual language, there have been consequences for
what we might classify as the ability to decipher "figuration" itself.
Since it has become feasible to edit invisibly within the frame, even
realistic presentations of everyday life have become contaminated with
a more graphical, that is to say, symbolic status and the indexical reality
that photography still enjoys has become ever more suspect. Categori-
cal distinctions—photography versus drawing, for example—and generic conventions which cue the reader/viewer on how to "frame" the
intention behind what he or she is seeing in terms of fiction or nonfiction
have become confused or blurred. Mastering the nuances of what
Howard Gardner described as the ability "to appropriately construct
that *membrane* which stands at the interface between the worlds of
television and world of daily life" will become more difficult once even

the physical frame of television, the box, disappears, in favor of flat monitors and image projections. Then, in effect, that membrane will be wrapped over the physical world.

The logic of the box as container is quite different from the logic of video- and computer-aided projection onto the world or immersion in a virtual environment. Projected or liquid crystalline images are surfaces of light, not bodies in space. Fine-grained phantoms in saturated colors lack a body or frame to contain them or a luminous path to betray their origin. Their scale can be superhuman in larger-than-life projection, while liquid crystals can be miniatures worn like jewelry. Such images need not coincide with a frame or support. Like shadows of stained glass without the need of window or sun, they are easily wrapped over any architectural frame or object. An architecture of giant or miniature skins of light can be condensed over walls or objects in real space. With the help of a computer, an image can be broken over a surface or object in the world in any shape, in any size, in whole or in fragments. Ultimately, we can invest these images and objects with speech and the ability to perform as agents: even now, video walls alive with motion speak with human voices in the mall.

Our box of symbols and words is emptying out, spilling husks of speech, wisps of letters, and gestures into the air. Without the shelter of the niche or box *from* as well as for words, inside has become outside and outside has become inside without a frame to call us home from dreaming. What once was television is becoming life itself, wrapped with metaphors in light and sound, a world without edges or end, a space without place, where planes overlap and intersect without boundaries or frames. Without the taming work of culture that marks and maps and frames, we would risk regression in a world of mundane magical transformations and commodity terror.

FOUR

An Ontology of Everyday Distraction: The Freeway, the Mall, and Television

Thus television turns out to be related to the motor car and the aeroplane as a means of transport for the mind.

—Rudolf Arnheim

This chapter articulates an intuition that has been expressed from time to time in critical literature—that television is similar or related to other, particular modes of transportation and exchange in everyday life. The investigation of the subjective and formal bases of this intuition is limited here to the built environments of freeways and malls.[1] Television and its analogs, the freeway and the mall, are conceptualized as a nexus of interdependent two- and three-dimensional cultural forms which don't so much *look* alike as observe similar principles of construction and operation. These shadows or inverse aspects of the work world are forms of communication that also function interdependently.

Freeways, malls, and television are the locus of virtualization or an attenuated *fiction effect*, that is, a partial loss of touch with the here-and-now, dubbed here as *distraction*. This semifiction effect is akin to but not identical with split-belief—knowing a representation is not real, but nevertheless momentarily closing off the here-and-now and sinking into another world—promoted within the apparatuses of the theater, the cinema, and the novel. Its difference lies primarily in that it involves two or more objects and levels of attention and the copresence of two or more different, even contradictory, metapsychological effects. Ultimately, distraction is related to the expression of two planes of language represented simultaneously or alternately, the plane of the subject in a here-and-now, or *discourse*, and the plane of an absent or nonperson in another time, elsewhere, or story.

However, beyond the invocation of an *elsewhere* and a "spacing out" or partial absence of mind described here, many aspects of "distraction" are left to the imagination or to later treatment: a review of the rich field of the iconography of automobiles, freeways, malls, and television,[2] an account for the shifting relations between mastery and bondage and the feelings of pleasure and boredom involved in their use, and the ambiguous value the analogs of television enjoy in our culture— each in its own way being considered a "vast wasteland" and a waste of time as well as a devotion allied with the American dream.

The preconditions of distraction are postulated in the phenomenon of "mobile privatization," and the general features that promote this divided state of mind are described as "the phantasmagoria of the interior." Furthermore, freeways, malls, and television are posed as interrelated and mutually reinforcing systems organized in a way which allows for "liquidity," the exchange of values between different ontological levels and otherwise incommensurable facets of life, for example, between two and three dimensions, among language, images, and the built environment, and among the economic, societal, and symbolic realms of our culture.

Television is a key element of these exchanges and transformations, not only because it invests images with exchange-value, but also because it models exchange itself, both as an apparatus which includes the viewer virtually in discourse and via representations of constant shifts through various ontological levels, subjective relations, and fields of reference. The dualism of *passage* and *segmentation* which is part of the freeway, mall, and televisual realms is discussed more theoretically in relation to *discourse* and *story*.

There is nothing discrete about television, for its very nature is to annex pretelevisual culture and leisure time to itself. This chapter seeks, in broad strokes, to situate television as a cultural form in a larger sociocultural context of everyday life. This speculative project draws explicitly and tacitly on previous works of synthesis to support its premises, for example Raymond Williams's relation of broadcasting to the changing social context of mobile privatization in which it developed; Walter Benjamin's *Passagen-Werk* or arcade project of research on the genealogy of commodity fetishism in the nineteenth century in glass- and steel-enclosed shopping arcades, dioramas, and such exhibition halls as the Crystal Palace; and Mikhail Bakhtin's notion of the *chronotope* or unit of space/time that oscillates between literary representation and the spatiotemporal experience of everyday life. The archetypal chronotope, the *road*, for instance, invites comparison with the *freeway*, as does Benjamin's conception of the *arcade* with the *mall*.

Michel de Certeau's *The Practice of Everyday Life* is an inspiration to the basic premise of interchangeability between signs and objects described here. Noting that "in modern Athens, the vehicles of mass transportation are called *metaphorai*" (115),[3] de Certeau articulates concepts of language and narrative with such forms of everyday life as architecture, transportation, and food. His vision of liberation from formal determination, surveillance, and control is based on the distinction between language and society as formal systems versus language as it is enunciated or as a social form enacted in practice at any one time. This distinction is expressed spatially, for example, as the difference between *place*, a proper, stable, and distinct location, and *space*, composed of intersections of mobile elements, taking into consideration vectors of direction, velocities, and time variables. He concludes that "space is a practiced place," a geometry of the street redefined and made habitable by walkers (117).

De Certeau's vision of liberation via enunciative practices bears the marks of its conception in another time and place, that is in a pre-mall, pre-freeway and largely print-literate, pretelevisual world. In the meantime, in the United States at least, the very nature of the street and pedestrian activity as well as the predominant modes and media for linguistic communication have changed. However, the notion of praxis as enunciation, be it linguistic, pedestrian, or other, which evades predetermined paths and escapes from literal reality into an *elsewhere* and to other levels of consciousness is, as we shall see, one fully congruent with the operation of malls, or for that matter, freeways and television. Indeed, *distraction* is based upon the representation of *space* within *place* (in which, as we shall see, space becomes displaced, a *nonspace*) and the inclusion of (for de Certeau, liberating) *elsewheres* and *elsewhens* in the here-and-now.

Thus, de Certeau's very means of escape are now designed into the geometries of everyday life, and his figurative practices of enunciation ("making do," "walking in the city," or "reading as poaching") are modeled in representation itself. Could de Certeau have imagined, as he wrote on walking as an evasive strategy of self-empowerment, that there would one day be videocassettes which demonstrate how to "power" walk? This investigation takes stock of this new cultural environment.

To contour this new terrain is less to map postmodernity than to explain why a map per se is virtually impossible to construct. For the level of iconicity shared by television and its analogs is one of common preconditions and principles of articulation rather than one of resemblance in shape or the boundedness of contiguous or even specifiable locations in space. Rather, these analogs share the *nonspace* and the simultaneous temporalities of *distraction*.

DEREALIZED SPACE

The late twentieth century has witnessed the growing dominance of a differently constituted kind of space, virtuality or a *nonspace* of both experience and representation, an *elsewhere* that inhabits the everyday. Nonspace is not mysterious or strange to us, but rather the very haunt for creatures of habit. Practices and skills which can be performed semiautomatically in a distracted state—like driving, shopping, or television-watching—are the barely acknowledged ground of everyday experience. This ground is without locus, a partially derealized realm from which a new quotidian fiction emanates.

Nonspace is a ground within which communication as a flow of values between and among two and three dimensions and between virtuality and actuality—indeed, an uncanny oscillation between life and death—can "take place." One finds the quintessential descriptions of nonspace in the postwar generation which was first to explore suburbia. Tony Smith's description of a car ride along a newly constructed section of the New Jersey Turnpike at night (quoted in Hobbs 14) expressed a formative experience of *elsewhere* out of which grew (in the 1960s) the conception of environmental art by artists like Robert Smithson. With earthworks such as *Spiral Jetty*, Smithson undermined the object-hood and the locus in space of his sculpture, lost somewhere between documentation in a gallery or museum and an inaccessible referent somewhere else. Robert Hobbs explains Smithson's nonsite and non-space sculptures as a profound assessment of mid-twentieth-century experience:

> In an era of rootlessness, massive reordering of the landscape, large-scale temporary buildings, and media implosion, he viewed people's essential apprehension of the world as a rejection of it. Vicariousness,

projection to some other place by rejecting where one actually is, has become a dominant mid-twentieth-century means of dealing with the world. Making the nonsite (which brings together nonseeing and nonspace under one rubric) a primary determinant of his aesthetic forms, Smithson emphasized ways people nonperceive. (15–16)

Later descriptions of nonspace (for example Baudrillard's notion of simulation) also emphasize it as a focus of derealization. Baudrillard conceives of simulation as a loss of referential anchorage to the world or the insecurity of denotation as it applies primarily to objects, whereas his own spatial allusions to *networks*, inert *masses*, and *black holes* lay claim to a kind of poetic scientificity. But this mixed metaphor in "The Ecstasy of Communication" is the vehicle which conveys the full complexity of his conceptualization of spatiality in postmodernity: "The vehicle now becomes a kind of capsule, its dashboard the brain, the surrounding landscape unfolding like a televised screen (instead of a live-in projectile as it was before)."[4] The interiors of the home television viewing space, the automobile, the space capsule, and the computer are ultimately associated with the interiority of the human mind. The image of the exterior world from these interiors is no longer a "Western window" onto reality, but for Baudrillard, the dubious vision of television.

In his popular and playful ontology of the shopping mall, *The Malling of America*, William Severini Kowinski goes even further, calling the mall a "TV you walk around in." Here the mode of locomotion is different, but the interiority (not just exterior vision) of the viewer is equated with television itself: "The mall is television, [in terms of] people's perceptions of space and reality, the elements that persuade people to suspend their disbelief" (71). These spatial comparisons depend on a common experience of some degree of fictitiousness within their (un)realities. The implication is that television epitomizes a new ontology of the everyday: vast realms of the somewhat-less-than-real to which significant amounts of free time (unpaid leisure, the shadow of work) are devoted on a routine, cyclical basis. The features of this derealized or *nonspace* are shared by freeway, mall, and television alike.

The first distinguishing feature of nonspace is its dreamlike *displacement* or separation from its surroundings. Freeways are displaced in that they do not lie earthbound and contiguous to their surroundings so much as they float above or below the horizon. The freeway disengaged from its immediate context is "a bridge over the barriers of both social and natural geography," offering as well "a continued shelter from engagement with ghetto areas" (Kevin Lynch, quoted in Brodsly 39–

40). In Kevin Lynch's famous study of cognitive maps of the city, from the point of view of the streets, the freeway is almost invisible, "not felt to be 'in' the rest of the city" (quoted in Brodsly 31). Similarly, from the subjective point of view of a driver or passenger experiencing motion blur, the city isn't visible either except at times as a distant miniature seen from a freeway which is usually also physically depressed or elevated from its surroundings or shielded by its own greenbelt. To paraphrase Charles Kuralt, the freeway is what makes it possible to drive coast to coast and never see anything. In fact, the freeway divides the world in two, into what David Brodsly calls "local" and "metropolitan" (24) orientations. These also denote two realities: the one, heterogeneous and static; the other, homogeneous and mobile. The passage between them can be accompanied by a shock, a moment of "severe disorientation" (Brodsly 24).

Furthermore, the process of displacement is a prelude to condensation. The freeway not only represents transportation from the city in the suburbs, but it is also a greenbelt and an escape "from the world of stucco into an urban preserve of open space and greenery" (Brodsly 49). Suburbia is itself an attempt via serial production to give everyman and everywife the advantages of a city at the edge of the natural world. Thus, the suburbs are "a living polemic against both the large industrial metropolis and the provincial small town," which nonetheless manage to "maintain the facade of a garden patch of urban villages, a metropolitan small town, without ever compromising the anonymity that is a hallmark of city life" (Brodsly 33, 45).[5] Freeways and the suburbs they serve are thus examples of the "garden in the machine," which provides mass society with a pastoral aesthetic and rhetoric.

Malls are similarly "completely separated from the rest of the world." Kowinski calls this separation "the first and most essential secret of the shopping mall":

> It was its own world, pulled out of time and space, but not only by windowless walls and a roof, or by the neutral zone of the parking lot between it and the highway, the asphalt moat around the magic castle. It was enclosed in an even more profound sense—and certainly more than other mere buildings—because all these elements, and others, psychologically separated it from the outside and created the special domain within its embrace. It's meant to be its own special world with its own rules and reality. (60)

The mall is a spatial condensation near a node where freeways intersect, serving a certain temporal radius; it is "a city, indeed a world in miniature."[6] Shops that are four-fifths of normal size[7] are linked together within a vast and usually enclosed, multileveled atrium or hall, devoted solely to the pedestrian consumer (albeit served by autos and trucks).[8] A regional center saturated by chain stores which turns its back on local shops,[9] the mall is the paradoxical promise of adventure on the road within an idyll of Main Street in a small town before the age of the automobile (see Graham and Hurst).[10]

The mall is not only enclosed, Kowinski adds, but it is protected from exposure to the natural and public world through unobtrusive but central control. This private surveillance escapes the kind of sharp vigilance in the light of democratic values to which it would be subject in the public world: we do not expect the consumer to possess the same kinds of rights or responsibilities as the citizen. Shopping malls are essentially governed by market planners (that is, by a fairly limited pool of mall entrepreneurs, builders, owners, and managers) and market forces. Each mall is carefully situated and designed in terms of its architecture; the "retail drama" of its syntax of shops and types of commodities, promotions, and advertising conveys a unified image that attracts some parts of the surrounding population and discourages others.

Consumers of all ages (but probably not all social conditions) come together to recreate the lost community of the street and the agora now under the private management of the arcade. The courts of foot traffic allow consumers and "mall rats" (nonconsuming loiterers) to intermingle in an attenuated and controlled version of a crowded street. Thus the mall retains elements of the milling crowd, but as a private space in which anonymous individuals, preferably ones with particular demographic characteristics, gather en masse. So the paroxysms of release from individuality via bodily contact described by Elias Canetti in *Crowds and Power* are unlikely; the street celebrated by Bakhtin as a place of festival which erases boundaries between self and other is scarcely imaginable.[11]

Rather than a site of "contamination," the mall is a place to shore up the boundaries of the self via commodities which beckon with the promise of perfection from beyond the glass or gleam of the threshold in brightly lit shops. These commodities with roles in retail drama have a somewhat dreamlike quality even in terms of their use-value, for they are less often connected with labor or the small necessities of life (for example, needles and thread, nails and hammers, seed and fertilizer, and so forth) than linked to leisure and a designer lifestyle (note the category shift of pots and pans, now that cooking is linked to luxury living). Rather, the preferred commodities of retail drama are "lost objects," the very things a subject desires to complete or perfect his or her self-image. And, rather than being unique, these objects are mass-produced, the very ones to be seen advertised on television, in print, and on display beyond the glass.

Television is likewise premised upon private reception in an environment isolated from events "out there," which determine the conditions of life outside the home. John Ellis has described this practice as the "double distance" of television's complicity with the viewer against an "outside world" represented as "hostile or bizarre," and the viewer's delegation of "his or her look to the TV itself."[12] Both means of distancing constitute "the opposition 'inside/outside', which insulates the viewer from events seen by TV" (169).[13]

But this division of the world is complicated by the reconstruction of an idealized version of the older forms of transport, social, and media communication within the very enclosures from which they are excluded. The past inscribed within the present is constructed *as past* through this very act of separation; a local and heterogeneous world beyond continues to exist but with fading resources, a phantom from an anterior world. This interior duality has symbolic dimensions as well: oppositions between country and city, nature and culture, sovereign individual and social subject are neutralized only to be reconstituted within nonspace in a multilayered compromise formation, a utopian realm of *both/and* in the midst of *neither/nor*.

This process of displacement from context is also one of dislocation. In a quite literal, physical sense, freeways, malls, or television are not truly "places." That is, they cannot be localized within the geometrical grids that orient the American city and countryside.

As Brodsly explains in his essay on the L.A. freeway, a freeway is not a place but a *vector* (25–26);[14] even its name or number is a direction rather than a location. Channels of motion dedicated solely to one-way, high-velocity travel, freeways are largely experienced as "in-betweens," other than as places where one enjoys the full reality of a point of departure or a destination. And magnitude on the freeway is popularly measured in minutes rather than miles. Yet, within that waste of time spent in-between, usually alone and isolated within an iron bubble, a miniature idyll with its own controlled climate and selected sound is created. In this intensely private space, lifted out of the social world, the driver is subject, more real and present to him- or herself than the miniatures or the patterns of lights beyond the glass, or farther yet, beyond the freeway.

Television is also dislocated, insofar as it consists of two-dimensional images dispersed onto screens in nearly every home in the United States, displaying messages transmitted everywhere and nowhere in particular. Television is also a vast relay and retrieval system for audiovisual material of uncertain origin and date which can be served up instantaneously by satellite and cable as well as broadcast transmission and videocassette. Other two-dimensional media including newspapers and periodicals (the prime example being the hybrid satellite/print production of *USA Today*, that appeared briefly as a television magazine program as well) are increasingly identified less with the specific location(s) from which they emanate (insofar as that can be ascertained) and more with a range or area of distribution they "cover"—indeed, mass-circulation media have constituted the "nation" as a symbolic system of common associations as well as a legal and political creation. The freeway and the mall provide the greatest evidence and manifestation of a homogeneous, material culture, just as television is the main source of shared images (visual and acoustic). There is also a "national" weather within these enclosed spaces of mall and home and auto—the even temperature of the comfort zone.[15]

Nonspace is not only a literal "nonplace," it is also *disengaged* from the paramount orientation to reality—the here-and-now of face-to-face contact. Such encounter with the other is prevented by walls of steel, concrete, and stucco in a life fragmented into enclosed, miniature worlds. As Brodsly explains: "Metropolitan life suggests the disintegration in space and time of individual's various dwelling places. Often living in 'communities without propinquity', the individual metropolitan must somehow confront the task of reintegrating his or her environment. . . . One does not dwell in the metropolis; one passes through it between dwelling places" (2). This task of reintegrating a social world of separated, dislocated realms is accomplished by means of an internal dualism, of *passage* amid the *segmentation* of glass, screens, and thresholds. Thus, each form of communication becomes a *mise-en-abyme*, a recursive structure in which a nested or embedded representation reproduces or duplicates important aspects of the primary world within which it is enclosed.[16]

The freeway, for instance, is divided into a realm of passage, both over the outside world and from inside an idyllic, intensely private, steel-enclosed world of relative safety. At the same time, the sociality with the outside world that has become physically impossible inside the automobile is recreated via radio, compact disc, and tape.

Television is similarly derealized as communication; that is, the primacy of discourse in television representation is not anchored as enunciation in a paramount reality of community, propinquity, and discursive exchange. While every act of enunciation disengages an utterance from the subject, space, and time of the act of enunciation (see Greimas and Courtes),[17] television—with its temporal and spatial separation of interlocutors into a one-way, largely recorded transmission—is *doubly disengaged*. Hence televisual utterances waver uncertainly in reality status. However, the primary levels of "interface" with the viewing audience of television are those televisual utterances which represent direct engagement or address oriented proxemically on face-to-face discourse, that is, the discursive level of presenters, hosts, and spokespersons. The discursive plane of television includes all sorts of unrelated, nonprogram material from ads, logos, IDs, and public service announcements, to promotions and lead-ins, as well as the discursive segments within programs themselves, from openers and titles to presentational segments. This primary plane of discourse seems to be an overarching presumption of television representation even when it isn't directly on-screen, and it builds the framework of television flow as a whole.[18]

Further acts of internal disengagement install second- and third-level segments as units of narrative (disengaged) or dialogue (engaged) within the primary discursive plane of the television utterance. However, the nesting order of disengagement does matter, for Greimas notes that the effect is different when dialogue is included in narration rather than when narrative is included in dialogue. In the former situation, predominant in the novel, for example, dialogue is referentialized, that is, given a spatiotemporal locus (however fictive) by the narration; in the latter situation, predominant in U.S. televisual representation, narration is dereferentialized, that is, lifted out of a spatiotemporal context (however real) into a symbolic or affective realm. That is to say, even in nonfiction genres such as the news, the dominant reference point of the utterance will be a simulacrum of an ultimately fictitious situation of enunciation rather than a world outside.

METAPSYCHOLOGICAL EFFECTS OF PRIVATIZATION

In "Paris: Capital of the Nineteenth Century," Walter Benjamin anticipated the everyday world to come and discovered the roots of nonspace in the phenomenon of *privacy* and enclosure. Indeed, the nineteenth-century arcades of Milan served as a direct model for the contemporary American mall.[19] While *privatization* has largely been conceived as an economic and political term,[20] it appears to have meta-psychological effects associated with its derealized surroundings—the postmodern development of what Benjamin called the "phantasmago-ria of the interior," a mixture of levels of consciousness and objects of attention. The process of distancing the worker from the workplace and the enclosure of domestic life in the home, separated from its social surroundings, allowed a compensatory realm of fantasy to flourish, a conglomeration of exotic remnants in which new and old are inter-mingled. This phantasmagoria of the interior broke with the immediate present in favor of a primal past and the dream of the epoch to come. However, the twentieth-century phantasmagoria idealizes not the pri-mal but the immediate past, and is an agent responsible for its decay. And the utopia or dystopia which these forms anticipate seems less a vision of a future earth transformed for good or ill than a hermetic way of life liberated from earth itself.

The temporal world is also lifted out of history in favor of cyclic repetitions less determined by than modeled secondarily on daily and seasonal cycles of the sun, the stages of life, and the passage of genera-tions. As labor is more and more liberated from solar and circadian rhythms, cycles of commuting, shopping, and viewing become shift-able as well. Television program schedules are "intricately woven into the fabric of our routine daily activities" (Moores 23), because they are organized by the same division of labor outside and inside the family which recruits the daily commuter and the recreational shopper. And it is the demands of labor itself that may produce a state of mind and body which is best compensated within the comfort zone.

Time is largely experienced as duration on the freeway, a "drive time" guided by graphics in Helvetica, connoting a clean, homoge-neous or unmarked publicness and a vague temporality from the 1960s on (Savan). Continuity with the past is represented largely in terms of automobile model and year. Similarly, within the mall (as in Disney-land, McDonald's and other realms of privately owned mass culture), decay or the fact of time itself has been banished from cycles of destruc-tion and regeneration via a scrupulous cleanliness and constant re-newal of worn parts.

On television, duration of viewing time is also the prime experience of temporality. The work of time itself as decay is seldom represented in images of the human body or everyday life. Nor is the past so much remembered via narrative as it is rerun or embedded as archival images within contemporary, discursive presentation. Even the image quality of the past—records of grainy black and white—is gradually undergoing electronic revision to meet today's expectations. The phantasmagoria of television and its analogs is thus less to be imagined as escape to flickering shadows in the cave than as a productive force that shapes spatiotemporal and psychic relations to the realities it constitutes. The state of mind promoted within the realms of nonspace can be described as *distraction*.

Distraction as a dual state of mind depends on an incomplete process of spatial and temporal separation and interiorization. The automobile, for instance, is connected to the world outside via the very glass and steel which enclose the driver. However, the dualism of outside/inside within these separate realms means that a connection with "outside" drifts between a "real" outside and an idealized representation.

A sheet of glass alone is enough to provide a degree of disengagement from the world beyond the pane. Add to this the play of light which appears to be part of the *mise-en-scène* of the mall, the freeway, and television—the world beyond the glass glows more brightly than the darker passages and seats we occupy. Beyond its glow, even the "real" world seen through a clear glass windshield, shop window, or screen has a way of being psychically colored and fetishized by the very glass which reveals it; the green glasses of the inhabitants of the Emerald City of Oz are a mythic expression of this vitreous transformation.[21]

However, green visions promote a state of mind that remains somewhere between Oz and Kansas, or between regression to the primal scene and a commercial transaction: because mental life on the freeway, in the marketplace, and at home is linked to very real consequences for life, limb, and pocketbook, it requires vigilance while it also allows for and even promotes automatisms and "spacing out." "Being carried away" to a full-blown world of fantasy is not in order—but the "vegging out" of the couch potato is a well-publicized phenomenon. Malls and freeways also can induce a state of distraction: for example, the very design and intentions of the mall taken to extreme can induce what the "cosmallogist" Kowinski diagnoses as the "zombie effect" (floating for hours, a loss of a sense of time and place) which he diagnoses as a copresence of contradictory states of excitement enhanced to the point of overstimulation mixed with relaxation descending into confusion and torpor (339). In discussing the habit of driving Brodsly calls "detached involvement" (47) an awareness of the outside environment mixed with that of an intensely private world within the interior of the automobile. Noting that the automobile is one of the few controlled environments for meditation in our culture, he describes how even the temporal link with the outside world may fade: "Perhaps no aspect of the freeway experience is more characteristic than the sudden realization that you have no memory of the past ten minutes of your trip" (41).[22]

In his mythological investigations of everyday life, Roland Barthes made the subjective experience of driving a metaphor for the operation of mythology itself. In "Myth Today," he turned from analysis of objects and scenes like the "cathedral-like" "New Citroën" to the practice of driving as an alternation between two objects of attention:

> If I am in a car and I look at the scenery through the window, I can at will focus on the scenery or on the windowpane. At one moment I grasp the presence of the glass and the distance of the landscape; at another, on the contrary, the transparency of the glass and the depth of the landscape; but the result of this alternation is constant: the glass is at once present and empty to me, and the landscape unreal and full. (123)

For Barthes, this constant alternation constitutes a spatial category of a continuous *elsewhere* which is his model for the alibi of myth. If we were to expand Barthes's metaphor of semiotics and driving with concepts of discourse, the alternation of which he wrote would also be one which shifts between planes of language and subjectivity. That is, the awareness of a subject would shift between a here-and-now in the interior of the automobile and awareness of a world elsewhere beyond the glass (in which the interior is also lightly reflected) through which the subject speeds. But because the interior of the auto is disconnected and set in the midst of a new kind of theater of derealized space, the experience of what is normally the paramount reality—the experience of self-awareness in a here-and-now—becomes one of unanchored mobility. This mobile subject in the midst of *elsewhere* is a cultural novum and the model for a new kind of fiction effect, a fiction of presence unbound and uncircumscribed by the fourth wall, without a 180° line to separate the world of the imaginary and the subjunctive from the commonplace.

The freeway provides the most obvious examples of *mobile subjectivity*:

> Each [freeway] exit ramp offers a different visual as well as kinesthetic sensation. The interchange is like a mobile in a situation where the

> observer is the moving object. It is the experience of an effortlessly
> choreographed dance, with each car both performing and observing
> the total movement and the freeway architecture providing the care-
> fully integrated setting. (Brodsly 50)

Yet from the observer/moving object's point of view, this mobility is
a paradoxical feeling of stasis and motion. In *nonspace*, the body in
motion is no longer a kinesthetic key to reality, for at the wheel of the
automobile or of remote control engaged in small motor movements
which have become highly skilled and automatic, it explores space as
an inert mass, technically or electronically empowered with virtual or
actual speed. Indeed, what we experience is not an erasure, circumvention, or fragmentation of the body, but its investment with a second and
more powerful skin within which a core remains secure, intact, and at
rest in a vortex of speed.

Of course, mobility is a multifaceted and paradoxical concept per se,
with many fields of reference: from displacement from one location to
another to the freedom of movement which is symbolically equated
with social mobility, to the feelings of pleasure in effortless flight which
has roots in infancy, to the fundamental psychic link of motion with
causality and subjecthood first described by Aristotle. But mobility also
suggests the opposite of subjecthood, the freely displaceable and substitutable part, machine or human, which enables mass production and
a consequent standardization brought to the social as well as economic
realm. *Nonspace* engages all of these possibilities.[23]

Motion is not only paradoxical, it is also relative. Safe within the halls
of consumption, the body may stroll with half a mind in leisurely
indirection. But the shops passed in review are themselves a kind of
high-speed transport, the displacement of goods produced in mass
quantities in unknown elsewheres into temporal simultaneity and spatial condensation. And on the freeway as well as the airplane, a new and
paradoxical experience of motion has evolved: on one hand, the relative
motion of an enclosed space beyond which the world passes in high-
speed review; or inversely, the dynamic sensation of movement itself
experienced by a relatively inert body traversing the world at high
speed.[24] At least before the advent of the simultaneous and multiple
perspectives of cubism, motion in Western representation was usually
confined to the world of the story beyond the glass, stationary or moving images presented for the eyes of a stationary (and one-eyed) subject.
A "bubble" of subjective here-and-now strolling or speeding about
in the midst of elsewhere is one of the features that constitute new,
semifictitious realms of the everyday.

Of course, any mobility experienced by the television viewer is virtual, a "range" or displaced realm constituted by vectors, a transportation of the mind in two dimensions. Our *idyll*, or self-sufficient and
bounded place, is the space in front of the TV set, what Baudrillard calls
"an archaic envelope" ("Ecstasy" 129). Yet Baudrillard thinks bodies
left on the couch are "simply superfluous, basically useless," "deserted
and condemned," like the immense countryside deserted by urbaniza-
tion. But these couch bodies are also travelers, responding in a checked,
kinetic way to the virtual experiences of motion we are offered as
subjects or view in objects passing our screens.[25] Television also offers
the road in the midst of the idyll, reconstituting a virtual world of face-
to-face relationships shared between viewer and television personalities displaced or teleported from elsewhere in the process, a fiction of
the paramount reality of discourse. Thus *discourse* or represented acts of
enunciation can be understood as a container for both the viewer and
the personalities of television which provides protection from a world
thereby constituted as beyond and elsewhere.

Discursive segments also constitute a plane of passage between the
shows, items, and stories embedded within the plane. Sometimes *passages* are even marked as such via the motion of subjects who can speak
as if directly to us, the viewers within the televisual representation. For
instance, the syndicated yet local program, *Evening Magazine*, often
showed its local hosts in motion, walking as they introduced unrelated,
packaged stories (produced at many different stations) to the viewer.[26]
While this practice seems strange and gratuitous, it is quite simply a
visual realization of the virtual power of language as a means of transport. The use of movement as passage marker is echoed, for instance, in
the work of visual anthropologists Worth and Adair,[27] who, in trying to
understand the films they had incited members of the Navajo tribe to
make, concluded that "almost all the films made by the Navajos portray
what to members of our culture seems to be an inordinate amount of
walking" (144). Worth and Adair concluded that for the Navajo, walking itself was an event and "a kind of punctuation to separate activities"
(148). On television, such marking may also be represented in far more
minimal than spectacular ways, for example, spatially via shifts of an
on-screen subject in body orientation and eyeline or verbally via the use
of discursive shifters. Thus the overall discursive framework of televisual representation, including the use of hosts and presenters of all
kinds, provides a means of passing between object-worlds, be they
stories provided for entertainment or fantasies which surround commodities, in a way which virtually includes the viewer.

IMMERSION IN IMAGE WORLDS

In *Visible Fictions*, John Ellis determined that the *segment* is the basic unit of television (in opposition to or modification of Raymond Williams's notion of flow).[28] The basic dualism of televisual representation opts for neither concept alone but helps to explain why, despite its segmentation into unrelated items, television is not commonly perceived as fragmented, but rather experienced as unified and contained. Nor is that coherence achieved simply by virtue of "flow" or the juxtaposition of items on the same plane of discourse. The duality of *passage* and *segmentation* in physical as well as represented space is related in turn to the dual planes of language, the engaged discourse of a subject in passage, and the disengagement of stories from the here-and-now of the subject.

The separate segments that disengage from discursive passages are recursive or embedded "hypodiegetic worlds" (McHale 113) at one level removed from the frame of passage. Segments with widely disparate topics in contrasting expressive moods from the tragic or the comic to the trivial or traumatic can be united via discourse into flow. Other sub- or "hypo" levels of narration can appear within any one discursive or narrative segment—three, for instance, are typical of news reports (115) (see part 1). Thus television discourse typically consists of "stacks" of recursive levels which are usually quite different in look and "flavor." These stacks are also signified at different spatial and temporal removes from the viewer and have different kinds of contents. Thus a shift of discursive level is also a shift of ontological levels, that is, to a different status in relation to reality. Television formats then amount to particular ways of conceptualizing and organizing "stacks" of worlds as a hierarchy of realities and relationships to the viewer.

Formally, shifting from one televisual segment to another may be a shift in the hierarchy of discourse—but shifts and passages between levels can also occur within segments. For instance, there is a category of television segment, including advertisements, logos, and rock videos (see my "Rock Video"), the *raison d'être* of which is to engage the viewer with a sign, image, or commodity by means of a represented passage through a whole range of discursive and ontological levels. Such segments are *condensations* of what are ordinarily dispersed in syntactic alternations of discursive segments with embedded stories or fantasies.

Furthermore, televisual representations may include several layers in the same visual field *simultaneously*. An obvious example is the image of the narrating news anchor against "world" wallpaper and over-the-shoulder news windows. Like television, freeways and malls provide similar examples of multiple worlds condensed into one visual field: for example, the automobile windshield is not merely glass and image of the world into which one speeds, but also a mirror reflection of the driver and passengers; a rearview mirror provides a window of where one has been as well as side views of landscape unfolding and distorted by speed.

The representation of the copresence of multiple worlds in different modes[29] on the television screen is achieved via division of the visual field into areas or via the representation of stacked planes which can be tumbled or squeezed and which, in virtual terms, advance toward and retreat from the visual field of the viewer. Discursive planes are differentiated from embedded object-worlds via *axes*: changes of scale along the z-axis of spatial depth indicate a proxemic logic of the shared space of conversation with the viewer. In contrast, embedded stories are oriented around x- and y-axes, actually or virtually by means of the field/reverse field of filmic continuity editing. The primary logic of alternation in television segments is then not that of suture of the story-world, as in filmic fictions,[30] but rather of communication with a spectator in various degrees of "nearness." The constant reframings in and out along the z-axis of depth which David Antin saw as part of the television form apparently do have a function as links with a spectator rather than as inexplicable or gratuitous reframings of a spatially continuous, diegetic world. Even in fictional worlds beyond the plane of discourse, a relation to the z-axis of discursive relations with the viewer can be discerned. For example, in her discussion of soap operas on television, Sandy Flitterman notes the lack of continuity editing and the practice of alternating framing of characters in a two-shot as nearer to and farther from the viewer (200). This practice can be explained historically by the television studio situation of live editing by means of switching between two cameras. But it can also be explained as part of a proxemic logic of relations with the spectator which pervades even fictional worlds.

What is ultimately at stake in this insistent relation to the viewer is a site of exchange. For the representation of mixed and simultaneous worlds is deeply allied with the cultural function of television in symbolically linking incommensurabilities of all sorts—the system of goods or commodities and the economic relations it orders, the sexual-matrimonial system which orders sociality, and the symbolic order of language, including images, symbols, and the spoken and written word. If television itself is a great storehouse for tokens of all these cultural systems, exchange-values are created by their juxtaposition, but even more by means of passages through them, in which television programming offers many different itineraries from which to choose.

The viewer as mobile subject has remote control over trajectories and channels plus power to take the off-ramp and leave the zone of televisual space. However, the television viewer who enters a car to go shopping, or even to work, hasn't left *nonspace* behind—these realms are variations thereof. (For this reason "home shopping" channels represent less the interaction of television with the world than a "short circuit" of communication and growing withdrawal into enclosed systems.)

Thus the realm of *nonspace* is divided again via the play of motion and stillness organized by passages and thresholds to the worlds behind the glass, by a *mise-en-scène* of light and darkness, and by proxemic indicators of nearness and distance within an unanchored situation. This very mobility allows what could be a profoundly disorienting and fragmented experience of life to act as a powerful means of reunifying the flow of time and space into a virtual here-and-now of a communal world. Voices and images offer community to a disengaged and enclosed world of the home, the automobile, and the mall. A banished, paramount reality is recreated as a phantom within elsewhere. The result may be the "secular communion"[31] of the freeway, the shared passages of the mall, or parasociality in relation to television personalities. Thus the institutions of mobile privatization restore a vision of the world from which they are disengaged and which they have largely displaced.

A NEXUS OF EXCHANGE BETWEEN ECONOMIC, SOCIAL, AND SYMBOLIC SYSTEMS

Realms of everyday experience—the freeway, the shopping mall, and television—are part of a sociohistorical nexus of institutions which grew together into their present-day structure and national scope after World War II. Transportation, broadcasting, and retailing displaced the earlier sociocultural forms of modernity such as the railroad, the movies, and the shop windows along a brightly lit boulevard (Williams 26).[32] These earlier forms of modernity were in themselves means of surveillance and control. Like the cinema, the railroad is an odd experience of immobile motility, virtual and actual, in which spatiality retains a semipublic nature.

Institutions of communication after World War II intensified processes of privatization and massification which had begun far earlier. Private life in the postwar era presumed a significant amount of leisure or discretionary time and "an apparently self-sufficient family home" which "carried, as a consequence, an imperative need for new kinds of contact" (Williams 27). Raymond Williams pointed out the paradox which the notion of "mass" communications hides—the increasing functional isolation and spatial segmentation of individuals and families into private worlds which are then mediated into larger and larger entities by new forms of communication.

In the United States, the paradox of mass culture and social isolation is even more acute, for to a far greater extent, the public airwaves, rights-of-way, and places of assemblage have been given over to private ownership or use and to market forces. Perhaps because the principles of mobile privatization are congruent with widely and deeply held American values of the good life along with dreams of social mobility which hold that ideal attainable for all, the choice of the private automobile over public conveyances, for instance, "seems to reflect an overwhelmingly popular consensus rarely matched by social movements, and it flourishes because it continues to serve that general will" (Brodsly 36). The principles of mobile privatization guided the creation of systems of transport and social communication that promise liberty in the midst of sociality, privacy amongst community, and an autonomy of protected selfhood nourished by its environment.

What the institutions of mobile privatization then represent are a means of social integration and control which can dispense with the need for any "central" or panoptical position of surveillance, visible display of force, or school of discipline, because they are fully congruent with the values of individualism and hedonistic pleasure, as well as desires for social recognition and dreams of community. Furthermore, the practices of driving, shopping, and television viewing are dreams become habit.

Take, for instance, the perception of freedom and self-determination experienced by the driver of the automobile in comparison with that public mode of transport, the train. An automobile driver, Otto Julius Bierbaum, exclaimed in 1902:

> The railway just transports you—and that's the immediate contrary to traveling. Traveling means utmost free activity, the train however condemns you to passivity. Traveling is getting rid of the rules. But the railway squeezes you into a time-table, makes you a prison of all kinds of rules, and locks you into a cage that you are not supposed to

leave and not even to unlock whenever you want. . . . Who considers that traveling may as well call a march in review a stroll. (Quoted in Sachs 3–4)[33]

The automobile represents an apparent freedom from the lockstep of a public time-schedule as well as "the complete subversion of the traditional sanctuary of the public realm—the street," so that merely driving a private automobile can be understood as a ritual expression of national faith: "Every time we merge with traffic we join our community in a wordless creed: belief in individual freedom, in a technological liberation from place and circumstance, in a democracy of personal mobility. When we are stuck in rush-hour traffic the freeway's greatest frustration is that it belies its promise" (Brodsly 5). This faith in mobility sustains cultural homogeneity rather than diversity; and paradoxically, the feelings associated with vast improvements in the freedom of motion are in lockstep with submission to demands for greater conformity.

A common faith in freedom of movement and of choice among commodities, destinations, and channels sustains the institutions of mobile privatization. They are the realms of answered prayers, embodiments of dearly held beliefs and phantoms of desire become commonplace, a field of action constituted by the automatisms and chains of associations which make up vast networks in the symbolic system of our culture. Constraints built on these chains of associated ideas are owned, not imposed, and require very little surveillance. As an early theorist of representational punishment cited by Foucault in *Discipline and Punish* explained:

> This link [between ideas] is all the stronger in that we do not know of what it is made and we believe it to be our own work; despair and time eat away the bonds of iron and steel, but they are powerless against the habitual union of ideas, they can only tighten it still more; and on the soft fibres of the brain is founded the unshakable base of the soundest of Empires. (103)

The empire of the habitual is the matrix of mental and social life, made of mundane opportunities and choices and composed of practices conducted half-aware, which assemble one's very personhood. What is new in contemporary life are not these institutions of mobile privatization per se, but the interpenetration of layer upon layer of built environment and representation, the formative and derivative, the imaginary and mundane. Embodying values as neither here nor there, both present and absent, they are ideal expressions of the *zones* of ontological uncertainty, expressions of both Kansas and Oz.[34]

Although we may perceive no alternative, no one forces people to watch television or to drive, particularly on the freeway, or to go to the mall or to buy anything on display there or on television. But few indeed resist. One prescription for an aesthetic mode of resistance to consumer culture requires the passerby to remain bewitched on this side of the window, glass, or mirror, poised at the moment between perfection and lack, never cashing in desire for the disappointments of fulfillment.[35] But aesthetic resistance depends on an older disposition of the subject in relation to the spectacle of an imaginary world framed and discrete behind the glass. The cycle of consumption in a "highway comfort" culture is designed for maximum mobility and circulation of a consumer inside the imaginary world of images and objects. One of the successes of this system of interrelations is on one hand, the liquidity of images, objects, and commodities, and on the other, the ease with which the subject passes from one role to another—driver, passerby, and consumer—each requiring a different mode of attention and psychic investment in objects.

Such *convertibility* between these various systems of communication and exchange is necessary; freeways, malls, and television are not merely similar in form, they are systems constructed to interact in mutually reinforcing ways.[36] Each institution is a kind of sociocultural distribution and feedback system for the others: television (most obviously as mass-audience, network broadcasts) serves as the nationwide distribution system for symbols in anticipation and reinforcement of a national culture presented not only as desirable but as already realized somewhere else. The mall is a displacement and the enclosure of the walkable street and a collective site in which to cash in the promises of the commodities seen on television. The freeway is the manifestation of personal mobility at its most literal, its radius a lifeline that makes the consumption style of suburban living and shopping economically feasible as well as logistically possible. The auto on the freeway is a juncture between television and mall, a "home" and commodity fetish on wheels. Convertibility between systems means that values can be exchanged whether they are expressed as commodity objects or images, in two or three dimensions or in gigantic or miniature scale.

Just as the mall is a miniature suburbia, a figure of desire become literal and three-dimensional, the television box is a quintessential miniature, both as copy *and* prototype. Even in its gigantic form, the large screen projection, it is no bigger than a picture window or an alternative to wallpaper. Bachelard explains how miniaturization is an attempt to master and control the world, which one can then enter in one's imagination by making oneself very small (148–82). This *miniaturization* is responsible for the feelings of safety linked with malls, freeways, and television, what Susan Stewart in *On Longing* termed "feminization," as opposed to a "masculine" metaphor of the gigantic as abstract authority of the state in collective and public life. Miniaturization is a process of interiorization, enclosure, and perfection, one in which the temporal dimensions of narrative or history are transformed into spatial ones, a plenitude of description of seemingly endless details. This contraction of the world which expands the personal serves a process of commodification as well, the transformation of action into exchange, nature into marketplace, history into collection and property. The realm of the gigantic and exaggerated in public life, a collective body in pieces, has been shrunk into a perfect whole. Kowinski describes the technique of miniaturizing the shops and concessions in theme parks and malls as designed to evoke the nostalgic feelings the adult has when visiting the world of childhood, the once vast seen as tiny. The incomprehensible then comes near, no longer too far away or too foreboding: the distant and the exotic are sought in order to collapse them into proximity and approximation with the self.

However, once within the miniature, the universe looms endless, just as the stars shine through Benjamin's glass-topped arcades of nineteenth-century Paris. How are malls, freeways, and television as miniatures compatible with representation of the universal and the social? In *Learning from Las Vegas* Robert Venturi described a new kind of monumentality which began with the Las Vegas strip cut off from the surrounding desert and concluded within the darkened and low-ceilinged casinos, spotted with islands of activity, from glowing tables to garden oases. Rather than the tall and imposing, like the skyscraper as upended panopticon and symbol of coercive or (via reflective glass) impenetrable power, the new monumentality is long and low, without discernible edges or ends or secure locus in place, rather like mirages lifted above the grids of homes, shops, and offices. Indeed, the very lack of panoptical positions afforded within the wings and cubbyholes of the typical mall is responsible for its sense of endlessness and a sense of disorientation within it. The freeway is "long and lowness" incarnate, but it also offers "kinks in the road" beyond which one can anticipate the unknown, in which accident and death can lurk, as a prime source of the monumental within a highly controlled, otherwise predictable system. "Kinks in the road" on television are temporal in order, possibilities of irruption of the unexpected in a plot or a schedule within an endlessness of parallel worlds which go on whether switched on or not, whether we watch or not, a world which is a primary reference in daily conversation, which we may or may not be equipped to enter.

In principle, miniatures like the mall are conceptual units which are invertible: that is, a mall can be lifted off the page, a scale model can be shrunk or expanded and plunked down in a nowhere that is anywhere that suitable freeway access and (usually upscale) demographics prevail. This liquidity is certainly one of the secrets of commodity culture, allowing signs and images to become realized as objects of desire and also to circulate freely between different levels of reality. One still "unnatural" and hence disconcerting feature of postmodernity is the presence of glowing signifiers of desire realized in the midst of everyday life—images magnified into monuments (for example, Michel de Certeau speaks of New York skyscrapers as "letters") or the big world shrunk down to the miniature size of a theme park or a mall. This invertibility between language and reality, that is, world-to-image-to-world fit, is inherent in the performative aspect of language, or in the capacity to declare worlds into existence within designated and proper boundaries. But those boundaries now extend to cover much of everyday experience: perhaps never before has it been so opportune or so feasible to realize a symbol or idea dramatically in 3-D. This expansion of the performative, making the actual virtual and the virtual actual, is behind the most recognizable features of postmodernity as theorized in Boorstein's culture of the image and "pseudo-events," in Callois's description of an undecidable state between the animate and inanimate,[37] and in Baudrillard's "simulations." Beyond liquid worlds that readily convert into one another, we are now undergoing a process of gradual convergence of the analogy of television with television itself. In the mall, not only can television screens be found in department stores and passages, but the mall as an architectural form has begun to sprout "video walls." On the freeway, we can soon anticipate the appearance of the virtual video screen or "head-up display" that will float in a driver's field of vision like a freeway sign (Duensing 3).[38] It seems that soon one will have to speak of one great machine.

CONCLUSION

The nonspace of privatized mobility is not neutral ground. It is rather the result of the dominance of one set of values over other values held a little less dear. Those other values, loosely allied with the "public sphere," are represented but not included in a way which gives them substance. The dominance of the values linked with mobile privatization is also the result of a misunderstanding. Ideas in the marketplace, that is, words and images as markers of economic and social exchange, are not the same thing as the free marketplace of ideas; and correlatively, consumers are not the same thing as subjects of discourse. Broadcast and narrowcast ratings and cassette sales figures, for instance, are the measure of the first kind of marketplace, the pure exchange-value of language and images. To the extent that the stock of ideas is determined by pure exchange-value, the marketplace of ideas is diminished. (Deregulation and dismantling of obligation to a "public," however defined, are perhaps better understood as a "depublication" of transport, social, and media communication, the legal and regulatory surface of the general phenomenon of privatization discussed here.) To strengthen the second kind of values—those related to discursive exchange among subjects, community, and a shared commitment to the just as well as the good life—requires foundation work. First, a widely held sense of the difference between the market value and the discursive value of ideas must be established. Then, recognizing the extent and scope of an attenuated fiction effect in everyday life—an effect now largely unappreciated or considered trivial and hence subject to little vigilance—might already be a step toward bringing distraction within a controlled, psychic economy of disavowal. For distraction both motivates and promotes the "liquidity" of words and images in economic exchange by undermining a sense of different levels of reality and of incommensurable difference among them.

However, the analysis of the situation advanced here suggests how difficult such a project has become. First, the means of advancing such notions are largely restricted to those very venues of privatization and distraction which work against them. Furthermore, older concepts of liberation in everyday life based on "escape attempts" (see Cohen and Taylor) and figurative practices are no longer viable in a built environment that is already evidence of dreamwork in the service of particular kinds of commerce, communication, and exchange. Indeed, older notions of the public realm and of paramount reality have been largely undermined, and a return to a pretelevisual world of politics, the street, or marketplace is unlikely.

Not that there is nothing outside of the built environment of freeways, malls, and television. There is indeed a heterogeneous world of local values; the decaying world of the city and town left beyond the enclosures is also becoming a gentrified and lively realm of privilege and experimentation. Because the realms of privatization present a facade of self-sufficiency and self-determination, means of change are easier to imagine as coming from those realms outside than from within. Thus a prime strategy that has been devised for changing television is one of penetration of these enclosed worlds with other public and private voices.[39] What is ultimately at stake in puncturing everyday enclosures for low-intensity dreams are the rights and responsibilities of subjects in the public realm, a once gigantic, now shrunken terrain to be reclaimed from everyday life.

However, when included within television, the public and private worlds outside are distanced ontologically under several other layers of representation. That is why inclusion in representation per se is not enough to open the television apparatus out into the public world—for the privileged sites of subjectivity on television are first, those allotted to the enunciation of televisual utterances and the interests those utterances serve; and second, to those subjects in passage represented in the utterance, shifting between a relation to the viewer and relations to embedded object-worlds. That is, the very formats and conventions that have evolved in U.S. televisual representation work against dialogue with the "other," the excluded outsiders. Or the past and otherness are included by proxy in a way that blunts the sense of an outside and of other possible worlds.

Furthermore, even the embedded narratives or dramatic segments under the plane of discourse are not conducive to the representation of change, either formally or at the level of social content. Narrative that embraces change, heterogeneity, and historical reach is undermined at a global level by the underlying serial organization of televisual representation per se: the notion of a linear sequence with a beginning, a middle, and an end, in which "something happens," is limited to the microlevel of the segment. The spatiotemporal organization of narrative on television can be compared with Bakhtin's analysis of the "road" chronotope in Greek romance. That is, the road was not a place where a change from one state or condition to another could occur—it was rather an obstacle course which merely delayed the eventual reunion of two characters who were destined to be lovers. These characters neither change, nor develop, nor age in a journey governed solely by fortuitous incident. Like the romance, television narrative often manages to combine a sense of passage with an ultimately static situation. Like itineraries in the mall or the freeway, these stories are highly segmented en-chainments that have largely given up any pretense of development. The itineraries of viewing will always pass by representations of cul-tural goods of various kinds, over and over, but the system of combina-tion seems impervious to change.

So when the dominant principles of alternation on television work against both the narrative process of change in characters and a rhetori-cal process of argumentation, how can they then challenge or encour-age change in the mind of the viewer? Differentiation by means of lifestyle and disposable income must be distinguished from the differ-ences between subjects in "local" and "heterogeneous" outside realms. That is why the proliferating venues for ever more demographically segmented audiences for audiovisual representation bode well only if they also bring about formats that allow for the entry of new subjects from the outer world at the primary level of discourse. However, con-sidering that this primary level of discourse is itself a fictional represen-tation of discourse and part of a process that transforms outsiders automatically into insiders, the problem of representing discourse is one of degree. At best one can present a somewhat more intersubjective fiction of discourse and an only somewhat different kind of celebrity and momentary fame.

Yet, models of "penetration" and discursive exchange are necessary and useful precisely because the power relations of mobile privatization are the conventional expression of a kind of legal and social fiction based on widely held values. Changes in shared fictions, values, and beliefs occur over the long term, slowly and incrementally, not merely because once-shared values are discredited or may be no longer viable, but because alternative values and their constituencies have labored to mark themselves in discourse. I believe the criticism of television can serve cultural change where it keeps such long-term goals in mind.

FIVE

What Do Cyborgs Eat?
Oral Logic in an Information Society

"Well, I'll eat it," said Alice, "and if it makes me grow larger, I can reach the key; and if it makes me grow smaller, I can creep under the door; so either way I'll get into the garden and I don't care which happens!"

—Lewis Carroll[1]

For couch potatoes, video game addicts, and surrogate travelers of cyberspace alike, an organic body just gets in the way.[2] The culinary discourses of a culture undergoing transformation to an information society will have to confront not only the problems of a much-depleted earth, but a growing desire to disengage from the human condition. Travelers on the virtual highways of an information society have, in fact, at least one body too many—the one now largely sedentary carbon-based body resting at the control console that suffers hunger, corpulence, illness, old age, and ultimately death. The other body, a silicon-based surrogate jacked into immaterial realms of data, has superpowers, albeit virtually, and is immortal; or rather, the chosen body, an electronic avatar "decoupled" from the physical body, is a program capable of enduring endless deaths. Given these physical handicaps, how can organically embodied beings enter an electronic future? Like Alice, this requires asking ourselves if and what to eat.

Some theorists in future-oriented subcultures who have wholeheartedly embraced technology (or who, as critics, at least speak from its belly) have posed the union of machine and organism as the hybrid meld, the *cyborg*, a "human individual who has some of its vital bodily processes controlled by cybernetically operated devices."[3] However satisfying such an imaginary blend might be, the actual status of the cyborg is murky as to whether it is a metaphor, a dreamlike fantasy, and/or a literal being; and its mode of fabrication and maintenance is, practically at least, problematic.

Consider such a mundane and practical problem as this: what do cyborgs eat? After all, the different nutritional requirements of silicon- versus carbon-based intelligence of the mammalian persuasion are not negotiable in material reality. The alimentary process and its beginning and end products, food and waste, tie us inextricably to the organic world. Both the need to eat and the pleasure of eating are part and parcel of the condition of mortality which electronic beings are spared. It is unlikely that the very notion of "breakfast" (or lubrication cycle? power feed?) would have much meaning for the relatively immortal and virtual parts of a creature that might suffer obsolescence, silica fatigue, and sudden crashes, but not hunger or death. Willing the cyborg into being appears to be the equivalent of wishing the problems of organic life away. Yet unless the human is erased entirely, food and waste will enter the cyborg condition.

The more immediate question then is: what do humans who want to become electronic eat? For we are no longer talking about metaphors or electronic prostheses that extend organic body functions (in the way Marshall McLuhan understands the media, for instance), or even about Frankensteinian reassemblage or Tin Man–like displacements of the organic body part by part. In this more *mechanical* sense, cyborgs with heart monitors, organ implants, and artificial limbs already walk the earth. The contemporary fantasy is rather how, if the organic body cannot be abandoned, it might be fused with electronic culture in what amounts to an *oral* logic of *incorporation*.

In the first section of this admittedly speculative chapter on food—or rather *nonfood*—in the context of body loathing and machine desire, I introduce the oral logic of incorporation into the electronic machine— for instance, that of eating/being eaten or of being covered by a second skin. The second section, "Post-Culinary Defense Mechanisms," describes modes of culinary and corporeal negation, including the psychological defense mechanisms of repudiation, denial, and disavowal.

In a context in which "fast" and "fresh" food ideologies have failed their democratic promise of health and abundance for all, and when food itself can be considered unhealthy, *nonfood* also has an odd relation to the discourses of health and nutrition. It is this cultural context of ideological failure and the desire to become (not merely to have) electronic machines in which food per se can be—at least symbolically—refused. Indeed, body loathing entails food loathing, which manifests itself in food which negates its value as such (that is, as *nonfood*) as well as in other ways of purifying the organic body from "meat."[4] These defenses are means of purification from the organic associated with culinary phenomena in cyberpunk fiction, virtual reality, artificial fat, and smart drinks and drugs.[5]

In closing I consider the inverse process, that of contaminating the electronic body and the virtual world with the organic—for example, by vomiting, that is, turning the body inside out. Reversing the alimentary continuum is the mark of a largely misunderstood and recently controversial strand of "excretory" art. Smearing the body with food waste/simulated bodily fluids puts the inside on the outside, as if turning the body inside out in a symbolic rendering of *abjection*. Ultimately, the strategy of inversion also promotes a different cultural agenda. Insofar as it is the electronic body that is smeared, the electronic machine is enveloped in a second skin of human waste. That is, rather than making cyborgs by accommodating the organic to the electronic, the eater (cyberculture) becomes the eaten, in a symbolic initiation of the cyborg into the human condition.

As she withered, sucked of energy, he became more alive and animated. When she brought our tea, her face was clouded and dark, her shoulders bunched and turned in. He had eaten her alive. I sat amazed watching this psychic cannibalism.

—William Patrick Patterson[6]

ORAL LOGIC: THE DIALECTICS OF INCORPORATION

While the process of identification paradoxically depends on distance,[7] the fusion of oral incorporation is a more-than-closeness: it involves introjecting or surrounding the other (or being introjected or surrounded) and ultimately the mixing of two "bodies" in a dialectic of inside and outside that also can involve a massive difference in scale. Bodies in oral logic can range from very small (usually, but not always, the eaten) to the immense (often, but not always, the eater). The body of the other can be as large as an intrauterine-stomachic-intestinal interiority or virtual void within which one is "immersed" (consider, for instance, encapsulation of the body in virtual reality), or as small as a smart pill one ingests. There also appears to be a dialectic between eating/being eaten and the sucking out, piercing, and fragmenting of the body (as if into food) versus resurrecting it into wholeness or preserving it in an incorruptible state. Note that unlike identification, incorporation does not depend on likeness or similarity or mirrors in order to mistake the other as the self; in an "oral-sadistic" or "cannibalistic" fantasy, the introjected object (electronic machine or human body as other, depending on who eats whom) is occluded and destroyed, only in order to be assimilated and to transform its host.

Eating

One method of cyborg construction is that of introjection and absorption. That is, in the words of Laplanche and Pontalis, "the subject, more or less on the level of phantasy, has an object penetrate his body and keeps it 'inside' his body":

> [Incorporation] means to obtain pleasure by making an object penetrate oneself; it means to destroy this object; and it means, by keeping it within oneself, to appropriate the object's qualities. It is this last aspect that makes incorporation into the matrix of introjection and identification. (212)[8]

That is, *pace* Brillat-Savarin, you are what you eat or introject. Therefore, to become a cyborg—a partly human, partly electronic entity—a human must eat the stuff of cyborgs. Indeed, cannibalistic fantasy plays a great part in this oral logic "marked by the meanings of *eating* and *being eaten*" (Laplanche and Pontalis 287).[9] As J. G. Ballard's aphorism on "Food" proposes, "Our delight in food is rooted in our immense relish at the thought that, prospectively, we are eating ourselves" ("Project" 277).

Currently, when we want to introject cyborgs, "smart" drinks and drugs will have to do. Built along the analogy of smart appliances, houses, and bombs, the adjective *smart* attributes some degree of agency and, at times, of human subjectivity to the object world. "Smart" pill and powder cuisine consists of vitamins and/or drugs, laced at times with psychotropics and aimed directly at the brain.[10] To the cyberpunk culinary imaginary, these chemicals are decidedly utopian, a kind of lubricant or "tuneup"[11] for wetware that breaks the blood-brain barrier, makes neurons fire faster, and encourages dendrite growth, *not unlike* the networks linking the electronic channels along which information flows.

But the more fundamental, albeit speculative answer for humans who want to transcend the organic body and its limits—that is, those who want to be cyborgs—is to eat *nonfood*, food that negates the very idea of the organic or "natural" value of food. Vitamin gels and chemical soups qualify precisely *because* they blur the categories of food and drugs, anticipating the advent of what futurologist Faith Popcorn calls "food-ceuticals" (66–67).[12] Capsules of what are tantamount to brain chemicals condense "intelligence" into a magical essence or fetish for transforming the human brain into a high-performance electr(on)ic machine.

Smart drugs are chemically targeted at the brain, but they are considered efficacious at bringing the flesh at the console along for the ride. For instance, despite the fact that he reports spending "all my time lying flat on my back on my waterbed with my computer," Durk Pearson of Durk Pearson and Sandy Shaw® claims to have "good muscles," thanks to smart nutrition ("Durk and Sandy" 32). Thus the strategy is not only to feed the mind but in the process to *purify* the body of organic deterioration. For would the ideal cyborg, an electronic *kouros* or imaginary of machine/human perfection, have any need of flesh? To become cyborg, one does not eat the apple of the knowledge of good and evil, but something more like the body of the deity, the host of disembodied information.

Being Eaten

On the other hand, the fusion of organic and electronic must also logically include the possibility of being eaten by electronic machines.[13] Some scientists of artificial intelligence anticipate such an event as ecstasy. For instance, Hans Moravec, author of *Mind Children*, foresees leaving the organic body behind like an empty shell after what amounts to having the brain scooped out, emptied bit by bit by one's own advanced robot mind-child. Brain cells or wetware would be displaced with silicon, byte by byte:

> In a final, disoriented step the surgeon lifts its hand. Your suddenly abandoned body dies. For a moment you experience only quiet and

dark. Then, once again, you can open your eyes. Your perspective has shifted. The computer simulation has been disconnected from the cable leading to the [robot brain] surgeon's hand and reconnected to a shiny new body of the style, color, and material of your choice. Your metamorphosis is complete. ("Universal Robot" 25)

(This fantasy is elaborated at length in Harry Harrison and Marvin Minsky's 1992 science fiction novel, *The Turing Option*.) "Downloading consciousness" into a computer, achievable according to Moravec by the mid-twenty-first century, would simulate brain functions but at an incomparably faster speed. Gerald Jay Sussman, a professor at MIT, once reportedly expressed a similar desire for machine fusion as the wish for immortality:

> If you can make a machine that contains the contents of your mind, then the machine is you. The hell with the rest of your physical body, it's not very interesting. Now, the machine can last forever. Even if it doesn't last forever, you [notice this logical lapse or, perhaps, metalepsis] can always dump onto tape and make backups, then load it up on some other machine if the first one breaks. . . . Everyone would like to be immortal. . . . I'm afraid, unfortunately, that I am the last generation to die. (Quoted in Rifkin 246; from Fjermedal 8)[14]

Far more recently, Larry Yeager's confession of why he "fell for artificial life" expressed a similar desire to "live on inside the chips."[15] Yet in O. B. Hardison's concluding image of humanity's immersion in or engulfment by the machine in *Disappearing through the Skylight*, remnants of the organic body are nonetheless retained within the greater body of technology and silicon-based intelligence, much as the mitochondria within human cells remind us of our origin in the sea and in asexual reproduction.

Compare these images of incorporation *within* machines—be it as enthusiastic vision or warning—with the image of disembodied, artificial intelligence in the Romantic imagination; a miniature artificial man, the homunculus, was a created product of mind kept in a bell jar. His greatest desire was to dissolve himself in the ocean, perceived as a female realm of pure body, in a kind of death wish of erotic fusion with undifferentiated nature itself.[16] In contemporary discourse about the future with its various degrees of hostility to organic life, intelligence which breaks its corporeal container is seen as simply joining its like in a great digital sea of data. So the virtual realm is tied symbolically to *immersion* and all its attendant hopes for transcendence and, in this case, *inorganic* rebirth. However, death-wishing and repudiation of the organic body—insofar as they apply to this and not some afterlife or spiritual plane—adopt a kind of psychotic and fatal reasoning, only to be haunted by the very parts of the organic world they fail to register. For of course the scientist only apparently usurps motherhood with the extrauterine development of the robot-child; his subsequent immersion in a sea of data is implicitly a symbolic return to the first inner space, the womb, much as the fantasy of being eaten by machines evokes fantasies of being eaten or destroyed by the mother.[17]

Melanie Klein's descriptions of the preoedipal fantasies of infants and very young children, fantasies which largely take the interior of the mother's body as their *mise en scène*, bear a striking resemblance to such imagery of immersion. Klein's model also explains fantasies of aggression within what amounts to intrauterine space. The mother's breast, split into good and bad part-objects, is also to be found (in a sort of strange loop) in its interior; in the oral-sadistic phase, the bad breast must be pierced and punished, only to be restored and made whole again in the depressive phase, echoing cannibalistic fantasies of the breaking up and then resurrection of the body.[18]

This fantasy of being eaten by machines which are, in some confused or unspecified way, part of the natural world is graphically visualized in the controversial (and hence widely censored) industrial music video, "Happiness in Slavery" by Nine Inch Nails. A man (and by implication another man, ad infinitum) is shown "submitting to ritualized sadomasochistic relationships with devouring machines" (publicity release). The man is played, significantly enough, by Bob Flanagan, a recently deceased performance artist with cystic fibrosis whose larger subject was illness, pain, and sadomasochistic pleasure.[19] In the video fantasy, the man's nude body is pierced by pinchers and grinders, put into "some kind of disposal system" (publicity release), and ultimately "ground into meat" (*Hollywood Reporter* 25 Nov. 1992). Oddly enough, this strange kind of bachelor machine is "servicing the MAN's desires" (evidently for castration, penetration, death, and complete fragmentation). The result appears to not only mix machine and human fluid but to nourish the natural world which appears to consist largely of writhing worms (or, at another level, geometrically multiplying castration symbols):

> Blood and semen mix with oil. Quick cut closeups of gears grinding flesh intercut with smooth sensual moves to convey the sensuousness of this encounter. The MAN writhes in complete ecstasy. Blood spatters to the floor and is greedily consumed by the garden. The

garden appears to be a part of the symbiosis between MAN and machine. (publicity release)

In spite of most waking experience to the contrary, the ecstatic affect and the symbiotic relation of nature and machine are not articulated— they are just there. This is not a proposition about reality, but a fantasy which reaches back into experiences in infancy. In "Happiness in Slavery" the posture of the devouring machine leaning over the reclining, restrained body of the man to take a bite is a reminder of the archaic mother and the wish for self-annihilation to which she is ultimately linked. In this case, the oceanic feeling and ecstatic transcendence of the body occur by means of pain—and in a way that Flanagan's installation suggests is specific to this culture and its denial of illness and death.

Second Skins

In this highly reversible logic in which subject and object are not clearly differentiated, rather than being eaten one can try to *become the other* by "getting into someone else's skin." That is, the cannibalistic fantasy of introjection has a counterpart in the reverse gesture, that of covering oneself with the other as a means of self-transformation. Entering this skin envelope also suggests that where the space is not already void, one is scooping out or evacuating the other either from without or within. That is, the issue is not one of replication or cloning of bodies, but rather a struggle for sovereignty over the same body as host of identity and subjectivity. In this instance, what was once "other" (machine) becomes the "self" and vice versa. In the process, identification shifts toward the electronic.

In some historical societies where ritual involved human sacrifice, the "skin ego," or envelope of identity and self, could literally be transferred by flaying a human victim and wearing his or her skin. In one record describing Aztec ritual, for instance, prisoners who were made to impersonate gods were then flayed. In the account of Diego Durán, cited by Tzvetan Todorov, "Other men donned the skins immediately and then took the names of the gods who had been impersonated. Over the skins they wore the garments and insignia of the same divinities, each man bearing the name of the god and considering himself divine" (158). Todorov contrasts such Aztec sacrifice of victims who are socially very much like themselves with the societies of massacre associated with the conquistadors, whose cruelty grew in proportion to the distance from the observation and control of their own culture. Literalized skin symbolism has a sad counterpart in the flaying and facial mutilations which accompanied genocide in Bosnia-Herzegovina, inflicted on people who are only partly other, who belong to essentially the same language and ethnicity but to a different religion and culture. The desire to literally cut away or obliterate the outer identity or "skin ego" of an other—not to mention destroying that close other from within via hunger, rape, and torture—owes something both to sacrificial rites and a society of massacre.

When political boundaries fall apart, ego and identity are also threatened with fragmentation, and they must be radically fortified. Even for an individual in the relative calm of the post–Cold War United States, an ordinary skin may no longer be enough to contain the ego or to protect bodily fluids from escaping or pollution and irritants from the outside world from entering. Consider the announcement of a new product, a transparent SmartSkin™ or "ultra-high-molecular-weight cellulose polymer," which is permanently electrically charged so that it firmly binds to the skin surface, now made slick, smooth and, as a result, youthful. When used with BETAMAX CAROTENE+™, a melanin layer (or "suntan" without the sun) is also produced, in effect marrying body and techno-chemicals into what is literally a second, fortified skin.[20]

However, skin egos are usually less literal, though there is always some sensuous element or other that envelopes the body—for instance, the muscular skin earned through weight training (also accompanied by a preferably sunless tan) or a symbolic skin applied via tattooing or writing. The flayed female skin in *Silence of the Lambs* (both the novel and the film) is literal only at the referential level, though it is materially borne as fiction via skins of paper or of film and its enveloping halo of light and darkness. The ultimate in second skin is electronic, as in the data suit, helmet, and gloves of virtual reality. Under an electronic skin one can adopt virtually any persona and experience a written world of images and symbols *as if* it were immediate experience. Indeed, it is as if the body were immersed in unframed symbols themselves, without need for distance or reference.

Immediacy and Ubiquity

Such introjecting and enveloping responses do depend on a sense of presence and participation (what the Lacanian tradition calls the *imaginary*) but in a way in which "the distance necessary to symbolic functioning seems to be lacking" (Todorov 158). Oral logic can be as archaic and *immediate* as an infant at the breast or as immersive as the fetus in the womb. However, the expressed belief that virtual reality provides an unmediated or "postsymbolic" experience of externalized mind is an illusion fostered and supported by an oral logic of incorporation. In the state of immersion, it seems that one doesn't symbolize flying, one *does* it, just as virtual objects *are*, albeit only via an electronic skin. However, this illusion is possible only because the second skin (or "interface") that mediates the virtual world can also conveniently mask the very apparatus of that mediation. (Walter Benjamin noted similarly that the film image is the only place in which the technological apparatus is invisible, because it is carefully organized to be out of frame.) In both cases, mechanical and electronic, this absence of the apparatus from awareness furthers psychic regression—on one hand, in the form of disavowal and the classical fiction film, and on the other, as various strategies of negation which I will discuss in the second part of this chapter.

While "cannibalistic fantasy" may have its prototype in infancy, it is far from restricted to the past or to infantile or regressive aspects of life. One could call both "eating"/"being eaten" and "enveloping"/"being enveloped" deep metaphors that pervade even the most advanced cultures and the highest art forms. Perhaps not surprisingly, the imagery of piercing and engulfment is ubiquitous in the technological realms of laboratory-created immersive virtual worlds, as well as in high-tech war. But even certain philosophies could be lambasted by Jean-Paul Sartre for introjecting the world into the "rancid marinade of Mind." Sartre's disgust with "knowing as a kind of eating" (387) is a lucid polemic against oral logic which has much in common with Brecht's attack on the "culinary" aspects of illusionistic theater.[21]

Although oral logic is conceived as a stage of development in the infant and child before the development of language, it evidently coexists with the logics of other stages of development into adulthood and throughout culture in general. Furthermore, oral logic is hardly restricted to the thematics of food, just as food is not exclusively "oral," but rather participates in the constitution of a full range of oral, imaginary, and symbolic subjectivity. Considering that food itself is the liminal organic substance at the boundary between life and death, need and pleasure, it is also the symbolic medium par excellence. A particular cooking process not only transforms nature into culture (as elaborated in Claude Lévi-Strauss's work in structural anthropology), it also offers the means of exchange or communion between the body, the world, and other human beings and defines a culture per se in its specificity. There can be wide differences in the perceived immediacy or degree of mediation of the body in relation to food, from the fully enculturated eating of an organized meal with utensils to feeding at the breast (or inversely, the imaginary of being devoured by the mother), to imagining oneself inside the mother's body or immersed in oceanic oneness. This range is comparable to the different degrees of convergence of self and other, from symbolizing the other to "interfacing" with it, or wearing brain probes and "jacking in" or being "immersed" in a digital sea. Thus subjectivity includes processes of incorporation, identification, and symbolization, and oral logic is a constant part of that range of subjectivization.

However, when fragmentation and fortification of the ego become strongly thematized, it suggests a situation of cultural distress. The contemporary prevalence of the imagery of horror and disintegration—fragmented, dismembered, or, for that matter, mismatched, multiple, or decaying bodies and lost parts (namely, the cannibalistic fantasy of the body treated as food)—suggests that something fundamental is "eating" our culture. Perhaps because we live in a situation of epochal cultural change, the envelopes of cultural identity—the body image and skin ego—seem to have been torn beyond repair. But how can the body be resurrected when it is so loathed? We are in a strange situation when the desire for fusion and wholeness presupposes, at least in representation, the repudiation or disavowal of the body and the negation of food itself.

As the dark mirrors of Cold-War identities shatter and the power of the Face (which is implicitly white) wanes,[22] we stand at the beginning of an epochal change—for which, of course, we need (non)bodies to match. Our imagery is no longer one of confrontation with the other at well-defined borders, but a confusing zone of shifting culinary and symbolic boundaries. That a cultural boundary has been crossed is often not signaled by lifted gates from without but by nausea from within, when, perhaps unbeknownst, taboos or even rhythms have been violated or the native flora of microbes are wiped out or displaced.

The answer of electronic culture to a vision of confusion and waste is largely one of "purification" or disembodiment. However, this option may be of limited value, for how can the response of culinary and corporeal negation afford to be more than a minor and transitional phase when food confronts cultural change? Food is at once a symbol system and organic fuel; thus there are limits to *nonfood*—we humans have to eat or perish. However, a tacit assumption of the contemporary technological fantasies to be discussed later is that we perish *because* we eat. The desire for an evolutionary transformation of the human has shifted focus from the preparation for the journey into "outer space" from a dying planet to the virtual "inner" space of the computer.

The Fast, the Fresh, and Food Loathing

The failure of a food discourse can be read in terms of survival of a population; the body itself is the surface written and sculpted from within in terms of well-being or in terms of eating disorders, disease, and death. Which is to say, food ideologies and the symbolic order have an ineluctable organic limit that might be thought of as the intervention of the *real*. The consequences of the sociopolitical and ideological dimension of food can be seen in malnourishment for some and over-abundance for others that cannot be blamed on nature. To an outside observer, the most striking American culinary metaphors might be too little and too much. On one hand, there is lack of food for significant populations of children, the working poor, and the homeless for at least part of each month and poor quality food for the rest of it.[23] On the other hand, the significant numbers of overweight Americans suggest a perverse situation of unwanted abundance.

In America, "fat" is a stigma and the sign of the self-indulgent behavior of people who have "let themselves go." Yet the fat body has an intimate and causal link not only with a poor quality, fast-food diet (shared even by a quickly labeled fast-food President Clinton, counseled to freshness by celebrity chefs and schoolchildren), but also with the lifestyles of an information society. Consider, for example, the link between a massive increase in pizza deliveries in Washington and the high-tech planning for virtual war in the Gulf. But the link is even more direct: recent research shows that just watching the tube can put on weight.[24] Perhaps, as Michael Sorkin suggests, writing on the future of design, Walter Hudson, the 1200-pound Guinness Book record holder for body weight who died Christmas Eve 1991, "was the ideal citizen of the electronic city,"

> not for his bulk but for his immobility. Surrounding his bed was a kind of minimum survival setup—refrigerator and toilet, computer, telephone and television—a personal pod. The system had Hudson exactly where it wanted him, fully wired in, fixed in location, and fully available to both receive signals and to provide a stream of negotiable images. . . . we are all at risk of becoming so many Walter Hudsons, well-wired lumps of protoplasm, free to enjoy our virtual pleasures, mind-moving and disembodied, unable to get out of bed. (75, 77)

By embracing the results of today's sedentary lifestyle and a fast, high-fat diet tongue-in-cheek, Sorkin's ironic image of the future confronts the hypocrisy of a society which does one thing (or actually nothing but small motor movements) and values another (the body as perfect man-machine).

While fast-food restaurants have begun to respond to health criticisms by lowering fat content—without much commercial success—a recent PBS documentary on the industry, *Fast Food Women* (1992), suggests the social cost of cheap, albeit addictive food: repetitive work that is not only unsatisfying to perform but which does not return a living wage. In fact, employment in the fast-food industry has become the emblem for a postindustrial trend toward the downskilling of the labor force and an expansion of a low-wage service sector; at the same time, there is a counterdevelopment of a highly educated and skilled information elite of what Robert Reich calls "symbolic analysts." Cheap, fast food seems to generate the social disparities its accessibility appears to heal. The addictive power of drug-food ingredients also enhances disengagement from unpleasant surroundings, not unlike other phenomena of electronic culture, from virtual personas to smart drugs.

For while the once utopian food counterdiscourse of *freshness* in America still retains many of the populist and progressive aspects it had in the 1960s (such as engagement in practical issues of healthful ingredients, pesticide use, and small farm production), in the 1980s it evolved into an elite restaurant culture of "foodies" grazing on tiny portions. The social failure of the "fresh" is a sad one that includes food critics as well, who rarely address what a homeless person eats for breakfast or what is being offered in school lunches today. (Certainly, one of the fundaments of human intelligence, not to mention social justice, is having enough food to eat of sufficient quantity and quality.) Meanwhile, technological advances have produced simulated "fresh" food that virtually can't rot, via irradiation and genetic engineering. Now there are ex-"foodies" concerned enough with health and intelligence maintenance to have, insofar as possible, stopped eating unhealthy and, at the extreme, dangerous substances (namely food) from depleted and often polluted soils largely lacking in the trace minerals and electrolytes needed by the brain.[25]

Since food is a lived metaphor of culture itself, it should not be surprising that a culinary system could emerge in the United States that has many analogs with the computer. After all, the television/microwave and food/word processing have been image supports of the "fast" and "fresh," the two great food ideologies of the post-World-War-

II era.[26] But the computer and cyberspace have come to be reference points for what amounts to a postculinary discourse. Perhaps, as opposed to Alice's "very small cake, on which the words 'EAT ME' were beautifully marked in currants," an electronic culture virtually confronts us with the directive, "DO NOT EAT." For what cyborgs eat (and what evidently incorporates people into cyborgs) negates the very idea of food as mediation between the organic body and the natural world.

POSTCULINARY DEFENSE MECHANISMS

The *negation* of the organic body, its nourishment, and all that it stands for can occur in many different cultural fields and adopt many different means—for instance, forms of psychic defense such as *repudiation*, *denial*, or *disavowal* (I am basing my discussion here on the useful distinctions offered by Elizabeth Grosz). Furthermore, the body-machine relationship can be inverted, much as the body may (at least in fantasy) be turned inside out in surrender to the collapsing boundaries between the symbolic and meaninglessness, as in Julia Kristeva's concept of *abjection*.

These modes of negation are at work in contemporary phenomena such as cyberpunk fiction, simulated food, virtual reality, smart drugs, and finally, "excretory" art. However, such texts represent or present cultural phenomena with varying degrees of distance to what they portray—from critique, irony or cynicism, and positive engagement to a perverse kind of heroic idealism. What we are dealing with here is not the psychic defense itself, but its use in a *symbolic* coming to terms with cultural distress. Here is a playful realm of the subjunctive in which the fundamental mode is disavowal, or split belief: I *know* it's just a story (a fake, an optical illusion, a fetish, a performance), but *nevertheless* . . . it is primarily the literal, serious manifestations of such phenomena that can be dangerous, for good or ill. First I describe some of the purification strategies at work in these texts. I then turn to the counterstrategy of contaminating the electronic with the organic.

Purification Strategies: Repudiation and Cyberpunk

Repudiation is the "rejection of an idea which emanates from external reality rather than from the id. It is a failure to register an impression, involving a rejection of or detachment from a piece of reality" (Grosz 45–46).[27] What certain cyberpunk fantasies fail to register is the organic body itself. If, according to Allucquère Stone, *cyberspace* is "a physically inhabitable, electronically generated alternate reality, entered by means of direct links to the brain—that is, it is inhabited by refigured human 'persons' separated from their physical bodies, which are parked in 'normal' space" (see Stone, "Virtual Systems" 609n2)—the next question might be, how does an organic body "park"? The answer of William Gibson's sci-fi novel *Neuromancer*, the bible of cyberpunk, is to submit the body to pseudodeath in the coffins and loft-niches of the desolate landscape of Chiba. While the surrogate Case travels cyberspace, his organic body is evidently in a state of suspended animation, neurally sustained by a fantastic pharmacopeia (67).[28] The junction between the human brain and the computer ("a graphic representation of data abstracted from the bank of every computer in the human system" [67]—note slippage between computer/human) seems to consist of electronic impulses between implanted chips and brain chemicals enhanced by drugs. In terms of oral logic, machine penetration of the brain allows the fusion of electronic-human chemicals which in turn allow the virtual traveler to be enveloped in the electronic skin of cyberspace—at the cost of leaving the meat behind.

But the flesh is left gladly. The desire to repudiate the body that pervades the novel—a desire which, of course, can't succeed in reality without a fall into a completely psychotic state—is marked by revulsion at the very thought of "meat." Even the description of sex reads like a SCSI port docking. As for food, in *Neuromancer* there *is* a restaurant called the Vingtième Siècle where steak is served. But Case isn't hungry despite Molly's cry that "They gotta raise a whole animal for years and then they kill it. This isn't vat stuff" (137–38). Why? Because his brain was "deep-fried" and the "aftermath of the betaphenethylamine made [the steak] taste like iodine" (138). (Corpulence will never be a problem for this hero.) Ultimately (im)mortality and the (in)capacity to love become the principal issues in the novel, though not in the way they might in Chiba, but rather in the ethers of cyberspace, suggesting that for virtual bodies (and, by extension, for cyborgs) the limits of organic life are not evaded, they are merely displaced.

Beyond Operation Margarine: Simulation and Olestra

Denial is a way of negating the corpulence-prone, mortal body (that is, "the piece of reality") at the *symbolic* level. Grosz describes it thusly: "By simply adding a 'no,' to the affirmation, negation allows a conscious registration of the repressed content and avoids censorship. It is a very economical mode of psychical defense, accepting unconscious contents on the condition that they are denied" (45). Of course, *denial* as Roland Barthes identified it in his well-known "Operation Margarine" can also work at a far more conscious level of willful public and self-delusion. In *Mythologies* Barthes described the process of denial at work when confronting unpleasant cuisine like artificial fat—at a time when the "natural" was preferred. (Today, of course, a preference for the artificial prevails among many initiates of an information society.) First, the fact is affirmed (that is, *yes*, it is margarine), then denied (*but* it is, in effect, butter) in an act which inoculates the discourse against the artificial, after which the fact may be ignored without embarrassment.

On the other hand, Olestra, a synthetic fat product patented by Procter and Gamble, does Barthes's margarine one better: "It [sucrose polyester] retains the culinary and textural qualities of the fat, but in a form that the body is unable to digest. Result: a fat that passes straight through the body" (Woolley 1). As a result, one needn't even try to negate or repudiate the body—its cravings have no consequences for health or mortality. One can "let oneself go" or "carry on" as before and nonetheless be pure, because Olestra is not merely artificial (like margarine—which remains a fat, with all its consequences for the body). It *is* the simulacrum of food—a solution to the fat accumulating on this side of the television screen and computer monitor that requires no change in lifestyle to purge the flesh. It is this process which makes junk food—itself already a concoction of artificial food ingredients plus sugar and fat—subjunctive or contrary-to-fact food, that is, "Junk Food That's Lean and Healthy?" (title of a report by Calvin Sims, *New York Times* [27 Jan. 1988: 30, D6]). (Though Procter and Gamble's Olestra was approved by the FDA in early 1996, it remains controversial and is said to make a percentage of those who eat Olestra products sick.)[29]

Interestingly, this "fat-free fat," another guise of nonfood, is the opening metaphor for artificiality per se in Benjamin Woolley's introduction to *Virtual Worlds*. For Woolley, this culinary bypass operation raises the issue of what remains real in an increasingly artificial world. Unfortunately, his argument resorts to denial in another mode; for Woolley eventually finds reality itself to reside not in a visible material and physical world, but "in the formal, abstract domain revealed by mathematics and computation" (254). The capacity to mathematically model or *simulate* what is otherwise beyond human perception is thus more real than whatever passes for reality itself.[30] So on one hand, there is a "food" which treats the body like a cyborgian steel conduit, but allows us all the incomparable pleasures of junk food; on the other, there is Woolley's implicit rejection of the visible and manifest (here the "flesh" and its problematic nourishment) in favor of truth in pure mathematics—an act of denial. Neither Olestra nor math ultimately evades the effects of the real.

Virtual Reality and Telepresencing: The Body Disavowed

In virtual reality, the "meat" body is not "parked" but rather mapped onto one or more (or even shared) virtual bodies; at the same time, the organic body is purified by being out of the frame, hidden from view for the virtual traveler, in favor of a cartoonlike graphic world. It is as if Walter Hudson were able to shrink down to whatever shape he desired and enter his TV, transformed into fully rendered, life-size three-dimensional space filled with virtual objects (and possibly other virtual personas) with which he could interact. To "enter" or "stick your head in" such an immersive artificial world with a technological second skin—or helmet and gloves—simultaneously blinds the virtual traveler to the world and obscures from view his or her organic body *and* the machine apparatus which sustains the virtual world. Meanwhile, an organic finger merely points inside the dataglove and the surrogate body flies at great speed through an artificial world, promoting an impression of disembodied superpower and almost omnipotent thought in a persona that is freely chosen, not contingent and limited by flesh.

It is as if the apparatus of virtual reality could solve the problem of the organic body, at least temporarily, by *hiding* it. Yet the organic body as problem has not been eluded: it has only been made momentarily invisible to the user. According to Michael Naimark's "Nutrition" segment of the tongue-in-cheek video documentation "Virtuality, Inc.," virtual reality even has application as a diet tool (and, I might add, in a way not unlike Olestra): while a helmet with television eye-screens blinds the woman immersed in virtual reality to what we as spectators see are actually nutritious crackers, she munches with moans of pleasure at virtual cherry pie.[31]

The seduction and playfulness of virtual reality are based on this very disparity between organic and virtual bodies—its power to erase the organic from awareness, if only partly and just for a while. To the degree that the duality of worlds (a reversal of the everyday situation of mental invisibility and physical visibility) remains conscious to the one immersed in a world in which she or he possesses superpowers, the situation is one of *disavowal* or split-belief ("I know it's just a computer-generated display, but nevertheless . . .").[32]

IMMERSION IN IMAGE WORLDS

A dieter in a head-mounted display eats crackers but sees virtual cherry pie in the spoof "Virtuality, Inc.," a video produced by Michael Naimark with students at the San Francisco Art Institute, 1991. Frame grab courtesy of Michael Naimark and Interval Research. By permission of Michael Naimark.

However, once one switches point of view from the internal to the external, from the virtual to the organic world, virtual reality takes on a wholly different guise. To the observer on the outside, the improbable gustatory moaning of the eater of the virtual cherry pie resembles a regression to infancy; similarly the flailing motions of "flying" (or other virtual locomotion) suggest an actual situation of helplessness and vulnerability in physical space.[33] Indeed, immersion in the artificial realms of information presupposes not only an electronic skin, but also a womblike fortress of safety from the physical world before the user can enjoy apparent invulnerability.

This link and disparity between the two worlds can serve virtual play. But the two worlds can also be electronically linked to cause real effects in other distant (or microscopic) parts of the physical world via *telepresence*, as in, for instance, long-distance robotic brain surgery or precision bombing. Organic bodies in the referent world (that is, those without access to the virtual system who are to be operated on, bombed, and so forth) need to be prone, anesthetized, or otherwise disempowered in order to be vulnerable to the actual remote operator of any robotic agent. It is as if persons with material bodies were confronted with phantoms; or as if they were put into a story as characters within which other characters are surrogates of the author and enjoy his or her special privileges and ultimate invulnerability. The danger in the electronic divide between "symbolic analysts" encapsulated in global cyberspace and those outside is a kind of willful blindness that supports that maldistribution of power (not to mention calories and culinary capital) that is ultimately a negation of the social contract.

Furthermore, responsibility for the organic consequences of remote action are all the easier to deny. Consider the virtual conduct of the Gulf War and the many opportunities it offered for denying the connection between war and human suffering. Yet even for relatively invulnerable warriors beyond the phantoms and under the technological superskin, the temporarily invisible flesh that suffers hunger and that needs to go to the bathroom is still there, its demands merely deferred.

Smart Fetishism: Do Not Eat

Smart drinks and drugs are the ultimate fetishes for initiation into the cyborgian condition. Like tiny introjected phalluses (that is, undecidably organic/electronic and thus both), they offer a kind of magical thinking, the promise of human transcendence, with the alibi of science. This imaginary ideal nourishment is a technofood reduced to its byte-sized chemical constituents like decontextualized data for intake into a brain conceptualized very much like a computer.

At present, smart concoctions actually consist largely of vitamins and drugs developed for the treatment of Alzheimer's, Parkinson's, AIDS, cancer, and other diseases. This suggests that their deepest rationale is fear and their modus operandi is the preemptive strike. Some people who once preferred baby vegetables now eat choline and other amino acids, minerals, herbs like ginkgo biloba and ginseng, drugs like Piracetam, Deprenyl vinpocetine, aniracetam, pramiracetam, oxiracetam, pyroglutamate, and other cognitive enhancers such as AlC, caffeine, Lucidril, Al721, DHEA, SMAE, Ferovital, Hyderine, Idebenone, Phenytoin, Propranology hydrochloride, thyroid hormone, vasopressin (pituitary gland hormone), vincamine, vitamins B, C, and E, Xanthinol nicotinate, essential fatty acids, selenium, L-Dopa, RNA, human growth hormone, and the neurotransmitters norepinephrine, NE PRL-8-53, and ACTH4-10.[34] Such a chemical litany also serves the deniability factor: what is smart isn't (but then again it is) really food.

In addition to ex-"foodies," people in cyberpunk circles and technomusic clubs have made the smart (and the psychedelic) the beverage of choice, in lieu of snacks, alcohol, and cola. The odd result is a mix of the discourses of health, space exploration, and junk food. No wonder smart drugs enjoy an at-best quasilegality (but then so should barbecue potato chips). In youth culture "raves" and technomusic clubs, smart drinks and drugs (or "nootropics," which provide "desirable qualities of cerebral stimulation without the negative side effects of ordinary psychoactive drugs" [Pelton 318]) enhance the effects of psychotropics like XTC and MMDA, extremely fast beat technomusic, and the psychedelia of image and light shows, whistles, and special glasses to create a communal sense of oneness and high energy in a self-sufficient and completely engrossing present tense. While the psychotropics are on the Food and Drug Administration schedule one (that is, they are illegal), the nootropics or smart drugs have had a hazy legality when ordered for personal use without prescription from England or Switzerland under a hard-won circumvention of FDA rules via AIDS activism. However, the FDA's recent raids on vitamin dealers have put even smart drinks largely composed of vitamins on notice. Perhaps, as with rock culture, this semioutlaw status serves the ethos of "smartness" as a counter-discourse with a program for, if not social, then evolutionary change out of the human condition.

There are certain recurring features in the very limited literature on smart drinks and drugs in how-to books, manifestos, and ads in *Mondo 2000*: a) smart nonfood tastes bad—medicinal, in fact; b) smart drugs are better than nature, once one achieves the right "fit" between brain and chemicals; and c) they result in better performance of mental tasks. To at least one countercultural theorist, smart drugs, insofar as they are psychotropic, are in fact "food of the gods," at once archaic and post-historical tools toward the next phase of human evolution toward colonizing the stars.

Bad-Tasting Medicine

Once we have entered a realm of negation and nonfood, we have left behind as cultural values the voluptuous effects of food on the "gastronome's body" of a Brillat-Savarin or the sense of "well-being" Roland Barthes describes as *cenesthesia*—the total sensation of the inner body or bowels (*Empire*). For if food is the manna of fullness and pleasure, nonfood is bad-tasting medicine that—precisely because it is disgusting—can be eaten with pleasure, much like the ecstatic response to devouring machines.

While an April 1991 cover story on vitamins in *Time* stressed their supplemental character and claimed that "real food is here to stay" (if nothing else, for reasons of obscure nutrients—for example, phenols, flaveins, and lutein—and for "hunger and the savoring of good food"[35]), other prophets of food-ceuticals as longevity enhancers described with particular relish one of their concoctions (arginine and cofactors) that not only didn't taste good, it smelled like "dog vomit" (Pearson and Shaw, "Durk and Sandy" 32).[36] Pills as electronic metaphors for firing synapses may not taste very good. Evidently, savor and taste are not the primary issue when "smartness" or health is at stake.

The underlying image may be a mixture of medicine and the future-food of aerospace and astronauts, but at stake is *not* the legendary unpalatability of K-rations or MREs. Rather, ingesting this space-age concoction is part of the magic of preparing for a future in which more and more demands will be made on mental performance. While or even because smart drugs are not so very good to eat, they may be literally good to think. Smart-drug discourse vacillates between medicine that is "good for you," an ascetic or virtuously masochistic negative desire to transcend the body, and a cerebral high that invokes a body image of wholeness and perfection at one with the future.

Better Than Nature

Smart discourse how-tos are largely about the right dose and the proper *fit* between chemicals and the brain. Of course, "fitting" the various entities, reality statuses, and modes of electronic culture together is the general practical problem a global information society must solve in order to come into being; composing cyborgs is but an especially difficult instance of it. Note that the cyborgian direction of fit between organic and electronic is heavily weighted toward the latter.

Smart drug "fit" is not based on existing "natural" quantities—neurochemicals are too costly for the body to make in beneficial amounts (Pearson and Shaw, *Life Extension* 168). However, according to Terence McKenna, nature has offered psychoactive drugs, which are not merely smart but which he claims have spurred human mental evolution, in abundance. In *Food of the Gods*, McKenna explains,

> My contention is that mutation-causing, psychoactive chemical compounds in the early human diet directly influenced the rapid reorganization of the brain's information-processing capacities. Alkaloids in plants, specifically the hallucinogenic compounds such as psilocybin, dimethyltryptamine (DMT), and harmaline, could be the chemical factors in the protohuman diet that catalyzed the emergence of human self-reflection. (24)

McKenna views the fifteen thousand years of cultural history in between the archaic period and the present as "Paradise Lost," a dark age of ego-imbalance to be abandoned, along with "the monkey body and tribal group," in favor of "star flight, virtual reality technologies, and a revivified shamanism" (274). Again, the archaic and the electronic are united.

Smart Performances

It is informative to consider what "smart" means in the context of this drug discourse, where "learning" is defined as "a change in neural function as a consequence of experience" (Ward and Morgenthaler 206). In descriptions of the drugs, smartness implies more effective neurotransmissions. However, in drug testimonials by users, "smart" is not described in terms of higher cognitive processes but as the ability to retrieve trivial or obscure information in the context of school or work. This information recall is prized largely for its exchange-value or as evidence of performative ability and instrumental reasoning capacity: a secretary given a raise by her boss to buy smart drugs becomes "more alert, and intelligent acting and she smiles more. She is overall a much better employee." A student is enabled to become a math major and get a job in Silicon Valley. A graphic artist is able to work all night and present her work the next day with a smile. A father in his forties is given Hydergine by his son, and to the son's amazement, the father recalls "family vacations, picnics and holidays" that happened in his twenties (!).[37] (Note how often "smartness" is something desired of someone else.)

Smart drugs also reportedly rejuvenate sexual performance a good twenty years.[38] Yet often, however facetiously, descriptions of sexual and keyboard activity are mutually substitutable or are metaphorically intertwined: "It started so innocently: just a snort of vasopressin before sex, or before getting down with your keyboard" (St. Jude 38). So, smart drugs may enhance cognition and sex (or they may not), but many of the motivations the discourse implicitly suggests for taking them imply a situation of stress and fear for the future, plus wishful thinking. My reading of the connotations of smart drugs extends beyond the personal utopian quest for health and longevity to include loss of faith in our ability to survive a toxic natural and social world without medicinal help, as well as guilt and despair with the arrangement of our social-communal world. The half-secret and intensely shared present tense of a "rave" is a substitution for such communality. Capsules of "information" are at once a kind of sympathetic magic which allows the body to converge with computers and apotropaic magic which holds all sorts of plagues now loose in the world at bay.

Contamination Strategies: Excremental Art and Cyborg Initiation

If nonfood is a cuisine of lack *or* waste, either nothing or excess to be received with loathing, then rather than being taken in, nonfood may be something that is spit out. And rather than purifying the body into electronic wholeness, the negation of the organic may wreak a transformation via waste and defilement, in which bodies are violently implicated, torn open, their inner linings exposed to the world, allowing bodily fluids and food waste to smear the boundary between inside and outside, and between self and other.

Such deliberate violation of the surface of the body or skin affects the symbolic order as well by undermining the boundary which produces recognition, identity, and meaning by separating it from a ground of meaninglessness: namely, a deliberate evocation of what Julia Kristeva has theorized as *abjection*. In *Powers of Horror*, she describes the primordial experience of abjection as food loathing—in her case, disgust at the skin forming on the surface of a glass of milk. Spitting the milk out establishes a limit, a notself, but at the cost of expelling a substance, food waste, that is ambiguously self and notself. Kristeva writes: "I expel *myself*, I spit *myself* out, I abject *myself* within the same motion through which 'I' claim to establish *myself*. . . . It is thus that *they* see that 'I' am in the process of becoming an other at the expense of my own death" (3). Beyond food loathing, other examples of abjection include the sight of bodily fluids or corpses. She concludes, "It is thus not lack of cleanliness or health that causes abjection but what disturbs identity, system, order. What does not respect borders, positions, rules. The in-between, the ambiguous, the composite" (4). To symbolically embrace the abject is to evoke horror and to call forth this disturbance and this death, in order to become something else, now shapeless. (That is, one identifies not with the body, but with the waste.)

Excretory art is a genre of photographic, performance, and installation art of defilement characterized by the media of smeared foods and the simulated ooze of bodily fluids. The notion of impurity (that which is transgressive or forbidden) is central to the use of such outlandish or impolite materials by a wide range of contemporary artists from Piero Manzoni and Cindy Sherman to Mike Kelley and John Miller.[39] Certain of these works have inspired the condemnation of conservative politicians, most notoriously Andres Serrano's crucifix immersed in urine and Karen Finley's smearing of simulated feces (actually chocolate) over her body.[40] The voluptuous effects and gustatory pleasure of eating are inverted into disgust and food loathing. The gastronome himself has become the artist as homeless person, as displaced woman, as border creature, homosexual, and plague victim. Using apparent food waste and bodily fluids as media simulates exposing the inner lining of the symbolic to light, in a kind of writing on the margins that can't yet be deciphered. At stake in the arts of disgust are the symbolic itself and the generation of new subjects, tongues untied.

No wonder the unerringly conservative Senator Jesse Helms introduced legislation that would have prevented the National Endowment for the Arts from funding any art works describing or representing sexual or excretory organs or activities.[41] This genre of expelled secrets and exposed linings is a whipping boy for iconophobic politicians, who mistake symbolic acts or statements for the cultural instability and decay to which they allude. This child being beaten is a stand-in for many others in a culture undergoing epochal change.

A recent monumental sculpture by Judith Barry takes the contamination thematic one step further: Barry used complex digital technology—the capacity to turn images into electronic information or pixels—to mix the images of two live models (one male and one female) together into an undecidably gendered huge human head projected on four sides of an eight-foot-high cube.[42] (The top of the head was also projected onto the cube when the sculpture was first shown in the group show "The Savage Garden" at the Foundation Caixa des Pensiones in Madrid in early 1991.) The majestic scale, geometric purity, and luminosity of the video head make it seem sublime, like an ancient sculptured head of Athena; yet what we hear is the more and more labored breathing of the "being," a mysteriously androgynous and lifelike electronic persona or cyborg trapped within.

Barry's title, "Imagination Dead Imagine," was borrowed from the title of Samuel Beckett's last novel, "possibly the shortest ever published," perhaps because what it tersely describes is the end of stories, a cycle between extremes where nothing else conceivable could happen next. In a scene of geometric purity, light and heat that pass into dark and cold and back again, a male and a female suffer the cycles of light and dark aligned in matching semicircles; their gazes never meet except once, at the beginning. Barry's "Imagination Dead Imagine" distinguishes itself from its Beckett namesake through its lack of closure: "dead" takes on the connotations of whatever exists beyond secure trajectories and boundaries: male/female, alive/dead, human/electronic.[43] At an elegiac pace, the digital being is repeatedly anointed with disgusting substances. In each of the eight three-dimensional video sequences (in a shoot that required three days, five cameras, a ten-person crew, and a professional special effects technician), what appear to be "bodily fluids" (urine, blood, feces, semen, or vomit) or substances associated with corporeal decay (bugs, worms, or sand) are poured over the head and allowed to gush or trickle down its face, sides, and back. (The actual fluids that were used turned out to be relatively inoffensive—honey, soup, crickets, and beet juice, among other things.) Each substance flows down the head in sensuous, even disturbingly erotic colors and patterns, whereupon the head is "wiped" digitally clean in order to suffer the next indignation. The video cycle takes about fifteen minutes to demonstrate eight varieties of dreck. Almost heroically the head suffers humiliation after humiliation, remaining impassive but for the eyelids closing to protect itself against each deluge. The only sound is the magnified sound of breathing and

IMMERSION IN IMAGE WORLDS

A cyborg doused with a series of simulated bodily fluids, crickets (14),
and worms suffers abjection in Judith Barry's five-screen video projection
"Imagination Dead Imagine" (1991). The installation is 114 x 96 x 96 inches.
Frames grabbed from the "face" video sequence.
By courtesy of Judith Barry.

the noise of each anointing—the blood spatters, the crickets chirp, and the earth makes a falling sound.

Barry was also influenced by Antonin Artaud's essay "All Writing Is Pigshit," which suggests that the stains and blotches of bodily fluids could be a kind of writing that we can't read yet, a language in pain, caught before it can come into shape. In eight untitled drawings (each $28 \frac{3}{4} \times 20 \frac{1}{2}$ inches) that accompany "Imagination Dead Imagine," Barry defiles words rather than the undecidably human/electronic. Each drawing consists of a series of words, each in a different typeface drawn in pigment on handmade paper, then rubbed and stained to the edge of legibility with dirt and insects, meal worms, soup, blood, tea, glue, beans, and vinegar. The words are chosen from the semantic range of awe and horror, such as: "exalt," "gag," "bilge," "engross," "spew," "defile," "refuse," "transgress," and "ameliorate." Together these terms build a growing sense of excess, which is amplified by the way their lines and edges are nearly obliterated, in graphic expression of ecstasy and abjection, caught in the pain of becoming.[44]

The bizarre worm sequence of "Imagination Dead Imagine" also points to a transition from one state to another: the filthy face deluged with worms that writ(h)e and crawl over the electronic head is imperfectly superimposed over a clean face with fluttering eyelids. The result (simultaneously) suggests being buried alive and its opposite—resurrection. So the body in decay coexists with the body coming to life—a disgusting spectacle, like a horror film in the part we want to look away from but can't. Thus "Imagination Dead Imagine" covers the electronic with second skins of symbolic mortality.

Many historical and contemporary cultural rites throughout the world propitiate the spirits of the dead with food and libations. (For example, in Chinese rites humans may eat the delicious offerings to ancestors with gusto—in effect, incorporating them; other cultures prefer to leave the food and wine of the dead or of sacrifice to deity to evaporate and decay.) Considering widespread practices of making offerings to inanimate spirits, it is not so strange to subject immaterial projections or the ghosts in machines to symbolic exchange with death. What are these devouring ghosts but alienated human agency, otherwise locked out of ripeness and development in time?

Implicit in the very question of what cyborgs eat is an accommodation of the human to the machine. The better question could be: how can cyborgs incarnate the human condition? That is, how can cyborgs become meat?

PART THREE

MEDIA ART
AND
VIRTUAL
ENVIRONMENTS

SIX

The Body, the Image, and the Space-in-Between: Video Installation Art

But our argument indicates that [learning] is a capacity which is innate in each man's mind, and that the organ by which he learns is like an eye which cannot be turned from darkness to light unless the whole body is turned.

—Plato

The following hypotheses on video installation art are speculative answers to fundamental questions that someone rather new to video installation as an art form might ask. The answers posed here were based on research and interviews with artists and were conceptualized with the tools of cinema and television theory rather than with those of the discourse of art history. The basic questions—what is a video installation? What are its means of expression? How do these differ from the media per se and from other arts? What kinds of installations are there? What effects on a visitor does the art form promote? What cultural function does or could this art form serve?—are questions I would never have cared enough to ask had I never experienced a video installation. Such an experience, for instance of Bruce Nauman's "Live Taped Video Corridor" (1968–70),[1] can be stunning. To me it was as if my body had come unglued from my own image, as if the ground of my orientation in space had been pulled out

MEDIA ART AND VIRTUAL ENVIRONMENTS

A view down Bruce Nauman's "Live Taped Video Corridor" (1969–70).
Wallboard, camera, videotape, and two monitors. 975.4 x 50.8 cm (384 x 20 inches),
ceiling height. Panza Collection, Gift 1992. Copyright Solomon R. Guggenheim Foundation,
New York. (FN92.4165BN 17), copyright 1998 Bruce Nauman/Artists' Rights Society
(ARS), New York. By permission of The Solomon R. Guggenheim Museum,
the Artists' Rights Society, and Bruce Nauman.

from under me. Some installations jam habitual modes of sensorimotor experience; others operate at a more contemplative level, depending for their effect on the passage of images or conceptual fields through various dimensions rather than on the passage of the body of a visitor through the installation. Yet even then, the visitor is enclosed within an envelope of images, textures, and sounds.

We lack the vocabulary for kinesthetic "insights," for learning at the level of the body ego and its orientation in space. (Perhaps such learning principles might be considered "Deweyan," a "figuring within" as opposed to the "reading" of literature or the "imagining" of pictorial art.) These hypotheses attempt to articulate this kind of experience, in a preliminary to a poetics of video installation art. Detailed description and interpretation of specific installations must reluctantly be left aside. The following sections address in turn (1) the conditions of existence of the art form; (2) its plane of expression and different levels within that plane; (3) the disposition of bodies and images in space; and (4) the temporal and experiential passage, reflections toward a metapsychology of closed-circuit and recorded video installation art.

THE CONDITIONS OF EXISTENCE OF
A NONCOMMODITY ART FORM

The designation *video installation* is not an accurate guide to what is undoubtedly the most complex art form in contemporary culture. However, the term does suggest much about this art form's conditions of existence: *installation* per se suggests that an artist must actually come and install the elements, including electronic components in the case of video, in a designated space. Such an activity presumes the support of an entity to clear and hallow the ground to be occupied, that is, most likely a museum, but sometimes also a gallery, an alternative, or even perhaps a commercial or public space. Thus, installation is a topsy-turvy art that depends for its very existence on museums or like institutions, whereas for commodity arts such as painting, the museum serves as the pinnacle of validation in a longer history of display.

Furthermore, the process of installing suggests a temporary occupation of space, a bracketed existence enclosed by a matching process of breaking down the composition into its elements again and vacating the site. Thus, installation implies a kind of art that is ephemeral and never to be utterly severed from the subject, time, and place of its enunciation.

In contrast, an object that can be completely freed from the act of its production, such as a painting, becomes displaceable and freely exchangeable, that is, commodifiable. In addition, this severance from the process of enunciation is what ordinarily allows a magical origin or aura to be supplied to objects of art. It is the tie to process, to the action of a subject in a here-and-now, whether loose or tight, which works against the installation as a commodity and also suggests why it is so hard to document. While an installation can be diagrammed, photographed, videotaped, or described in language, its crucial element is ultimately missing from any such two-dimensional construction, that is, "the space-in-between," or the actual construction of a passage for bodies or figures in space and time. Indeed, I would argue, the art is the part that collapses whenever the installation isn't installed.[2]

The frame of an installation is then only apparently the actual room in which it is placed. This room is rather the *ground* over which a conceptual, figural, embodied, and temporalized space that is the installation breaks. Then, the material objects placed in space and the images on the monitor(s) are meaningful within the whole pattern of orientations and constraints on the passage of either the body of the visitor or of conceptual figures through various modes of manifestation—pictorial, sculptural, kinesthetic, aural, and linguistic.

MEDIA ART AND VIRTUAL ENVIRONMENTS

Note that the artist vacates the scene in installation per se.[3] This allows the visitor rather than the artist to perform the piece. Indeed, she or he is *in* the piece as its experiential subject, not by identification, but in body. Thus, the installation is not a proscenium art. (Hence the choice of "visitor" over spectator or viewer.) It is not hard to see the relation of installation to other anticommodity art forms that emerged in the 1960s, such as conceptual art, performance, body art, earth works, and expanded forms of sculpture.[4]

But how does this noncommodity art survive? Sometimes an installation is commissioned by a museum, such as the Whitney Museum for its Biennial, or by the Carnegie Museum in Pittsburgh, or the Institute of Contemporary Art in Boston. In addition, like "single-channel" or narrative video, the form is generally dependent on corporate, civic, and charitable art subventions and the economic support of the artist in some other occupation. Provided an installation is site-independent and can be reerected in various places, a museum-sponsored tour can also generate rentals for the artist/installer.[5]

Because of the nature of its economic support, some artists decry the growing "bureaucratization" of the art: that is, funding a piece requires not only formal requests to corporations, foundations, and commissions, but the generation of detailed plans, models, and prototypes; improvisation is reduced to a minimum. But, however detailed a video installation becomes in conception, there remains an element of uncertainty and risk at the level of the material execution and installation of its elements conceived by the artist, and an element of surprise in the actual bodily experience of the visitor. Indeed, I speculate that exploring the materialization of the conceptual through all the various modes available to our heavily mediated society is at the heart of the cultural function of video installation.

In that sense, the "video" in video installation stands for contemporary image-culture per se.[6] Each installation is an experiment in the redesign of the apparatus that represents our culture to itself: a new disposition of machines that project the imagination onto the world and that store, recirculate, and display images, and a fresh orientation of the body in space and a reformulation of visual and kinesthetic experience.

While video installation as a form is not directly related to or dependent on the institution and apparatus of television, it is just as hard to imagine the art form without television as it is to imagine the contemporary world without it. Not only do we live surrounded by images, but our built environment and even our natural world have largely passed through image-culture before rematerializing in three-dimensional space. Thus, though they completely overpower the art form in size and reach, television broadcasting, cable, and the videocassette as usually consumed are each but one kind of video installation that is reproduced over and over again in a field of open and otherwise unrealized possibilities.[7] The materialization of other possible apparatuses allows us to imagine alternatives and thus provides the Archimedean points from which to criticize what we have come to take for granted.

The following section distinguishes video installation from proscenium arts such as theater and film, as well as from traditional painting and sculpture. Various modes and types of installation apparatuses are then discussed, drawing on examples from various artists, emphasizing first spatial, then temporal dimensions.

ONE AMONG THE NEW ARTS OF PRESENTATION

Explaining why the video installation is not theatrical or filmic does much to clarify other aspects, from its metapsychology to its modes of expression, which distinguish it from the other more illusionistic arts.

In the proscenium arts—and one can begin them with Plato's "Simile of the Cave"—the spectator is carefully divided from the field to be contemplated. The machinery that creates the vision of another world is largely hidden, allowing the immobilized spectator to sink into an impression of its reality with horror or delight but without danger from the world on view. The proscenium of the theater, and in its most ideal expression, the fourth wall, as well as the screen of film divide the here-and-now of the spectator from the elsewhere and elsewhen beyond with varying degrees of absoluteness. The frame of a painting likewise allows a painting not to be taken literally (as well as to be transportable and salable), and to allow a not-here and not-now to occupy the present. The visitor to an installation, on the other hand, is surrounded by a spatial here-and-now, enclosed within a construction that is grounded in actual (not illusionistic) space. (The title of the group installation exhibition and catalog, *The Situated In.age*, emphasizes that aspect.)

Video installation can be seen as part of a larger shift in art forms toward "liveness" that began in earnest in the 1960s, in a field that included happenings, performance, conceptual art, body art, earth works, and the larger category of installation art. If there are two planes of language,[8] a *here* and *now* in which we can speak and be present to each other, and an *elsewhere* and *elsewhen*, inhabited by people and things that are absent from the act of enunciation, then these new arts explore expression on the plane of presentation and of subjects in a here-and-now.

Art on the plane of presentation can be contrasted to art as representation, an evocation of absences that has been the focus of artistic exploration since the Renaissance. Representation invokes things apart from us, using language as a window on another world. In Western art, that world came to be represented as realistically as possible, using a variety of techniques such as perspective in painting and photography. Other techniques developed to suppress the here-and-now in which we inevitably receive representations, for instance, separation from the realm of reception by means of the aforementioned proscenium, frame, or screen. In photography and the cinema, the separation became absolute temporal and physical separation. Cinema spectators immobilized in darkness were like the prisoners in Plato's cave, not held in place by chains but by machines of desire, enjoying the impression of mastery over an imaginary world. We ordinarily think of fiction effect and illusionism in terms of these arts of representation.

While the cinematic machine or apparatus includes the cinema in which viewers sit and the projection room (not to mention the box office and the candy counter), "movies" are what appear on the screen, just as photographs and paintings are what appear in frame. Attention to this other plane, the here-and-now of production and reception beyond the frame, became a rich object of theoretical investigation and a critique of representation in philosophy and in cultural and film studies—as well as in art—in the 1960s.[9]

It is hard to imagine at first how much this new ontological status— presence, or here-and-nowness of art with the receiver of art—changes the rules of art making and receiving. In fact, from the beginning there were many who refused the work on the presentational plane the status of art. For one thing, if art and everyday life can share the same place of language, what distinguishes art from life? What happens when "experience" must substitute for "transcendence"? What does it mean to participate in art? At first, these questions may not have seemed complicated: a faith in perceiving things as they "really" are and a habit of confusing the present tense with reality and of equating experience with personal change, common to the 1960s, may have been useful in exposing the fictions of there and then and in exploring the apparatuses of the past. But the disconcerting discovery of fictions and manipulations that inhabit the here-and-now is on ongoing project of video installation.[10]

The impetus behind the artistic exploration of this plane of presentation and discovering its rules and limits perhaps began with utopian
desires to change society via changes in consciousness (see Rosler). But
the impetus was also apparently ontological—a new and virtually unknown postwar world had yet to be explored, a world mythically first
discovered for art in Tony Smith's cat ride along a newly constructed
New Jersey Turnpike at night. What Smith saw in the dark horizon
beyond the freeway has become in the intervening period a landscape
of suburbs, malls, and television in which everything, including the
natural environment, is either enveloped by the low-intensity fictions
of consumer culture or abandoned to decay. A subject in this everyday
world is surrounded by images and a built environment that are at
times hard to tell apart. Three-dimensional objects are no longer a prior
reality to be represented, but rather seem to be blowups of a two-
dimensional world. As I suggest in chapter 5, two and three dimensions
interchange freely with each other in a derealizing process so hard to
grasp that we turn to catchwords like *postmodernism* in desperation.

The arts of presentation and, particularly, video installation, are the
privileged art forms for setting this mediated, built environment into
play for purposes of reflection. Indeed, the underlying premise of
the installation appears to be that the audiovisual experience supplemented kinesthetically can be a kind of learning not with the mind
alone, but with the body itself.

While the new arts of presentation have been conceptualized as
"theatrical" (see Fried),[11] it is important to note the massive difference
between the two worlds of a traditional theater, in which the audience
receives the events on stage as happening safely in an "elsewhere," and
a theater in which events happen on the same plane of here-and-now as
the audience inhabits. It is as if the audience in this new kind of theater
were free to cross the proscenium and wander about on stage, contem-
plating the actors' makeup and props, able to change point of view, to
hear actors' asides, seeing both the process of creating an imaginary
world and—more dimly than before—the represented world itself. But
the difference can be even more radical, for in performance art, as
opposed to traditional theater, the body of the performer and his or her
experience in a here-and-now can be presented directly and discursively to an audience, which thereby becomes a *you*, a partner inhabiting the same world, possessing the capacity to influence as well as
respond to events.

Even sculptural objects could participate in this plane of presentations in a here-and-now: minimal sculpture in the 1960s, as Michael Fried perceptively noted at the time, offered a sculptural object, not as a monument or memorial of some world or time, but as an ersatz person that confronted the viewer *in his or her own space*. Indeed, the work consisted not just of an object, but implicated the physical space around the object and the play of light in it. The minimal object also required a subject capable of realizing the work, responding to the changing light and positions of a here-and-now, so that each time a work is perceived it is a different one.

Even the inevitably more narrative "single-channel" video art is part of this move toward exploring the presentational plane. While structuralist film was largely engaged in a modernist exploration of the unique properties of the medium, narrative video has long been engaged in exploring what it means to narrate stories, how stories are told, what cultural function narrative serves, and so on, so that the plane of presentation is represented over stories in a "messier," multileveled form.[12]

Instead of offering simplicity, the presentational arts are hybrid and complex. For instance, even though the plane of expression of presentational arts is essentially the present, it is possible to explore physically more than one tense—reference to the past and future can coexist with the present, provided that all are figured and grounded in the experience of here-and-now. Two types of video installation art can be differentiated by tense:

1. Closed-circuit video plays with "presence." A "live" camera can relay the image and sound of visitors in charged positions in installation space to one or more monitors. Shifting back and forth between two and three dimensions, closed-circuit installation explores the fit between images and the built environment and the process of mediating identity and power.

2. The recorded-video art installation can be compared to the spectator wandering about on a stage, in a bodily experience of conceptual propositions and imaginary worlds of memory and anticipation. A conceptual world is made manifest as literal objects and images set in physical relation to each other. That is, the technique for raising referent worlds to consciousness is not mimesis, but simulation. In general, the *mode* of enunciation in video installation in terms of speech-act theory is *performative* or *declarative* (see Searle and Vanderveken). Legitimated and contained by the boundaries of the art institution, a world is declared into existence. It need not match the world outside (that is, be constative), nor does installation video command the visitor nor commit the artist nor merely express some state of mind.

One could further divide this field of installation work into the referent world(s) that symbols made literal evoke. Yet it seems that these worlds are seldom cleanly one thing or one tense—they are rather a copresence of multiple worlds, linked like stories (Mary Lucier's "Ohio at Giverny," 1983), like sagas (Joan Jonas's "Iceland Naples Express [Icelandic and Neapolitan Volcanic Sagas]," 1985–88), like dreams (Rita Myers's "The Allure of the Concentric," 1985) and obsessions (Ken Feingold's "The Lost Soul," 1988) as condensations of public and private space (Muntadas's "The Board Room," 1987), or even as if they were a simile (Dieter Froese's unrealized "Eavesdrop") or syllogism (Francesc Torres's "Belchite-South Bronx," 1987–88). In this sense, multiple channels distributed over multiple monitors are but another way of setting copresent worlds in relation to each other. And from the beginning, installation video has been a mixed medium: closed circuit with recorded video, slides, and photography.

What ultimately distinguishes one type of installation from another is less tense or medium than whether or not the visitor spatially enters two as well as three dimensions or remains in "real" space. The ultimate question that differentiates among the arts of presentation appears to be, who is the subject of the experience? Performance, even where it has installationlike sets, differs from installation, because the artist occupies the position of the subject within the installation world. Interactive work differs in yet another way. Room is made for the visitor to play with the parameters of a posited world, thus taking on a virtual role of "artist/installer" if not the role of artist as declarer and inventor of that world.[13] In a larger sense, all installation art is interactive, since the visitor chooses a trajectory among all the possibilities. This trajectory is a variable narrative simultaneously embodied and constructed at the level of presentation.

THE PLAY OF APPARATUSES: PASSAGES IN
TWO AND THREE DIMENSIONS

Television as a kind of primordial video apparatus already encloses the viewer within a virtual space of the monitor in several ways: light from the screen (as emphasized in the title of another group video installation, "The Luminous Image") bathes surrounding space in shifting tones and colors. In addition, what is on the television screen typically begins by presenting itself as if it were a here-and-now actually shared by viewer and media presenters and personalities. That is, television has developed a mode of presentation that envelops the viewer

MEDIA ART AND VIRTUAL ENVIRONMENTS

Two channels alternate on seven monitors placed at various heights in Mary Lucier's video installation "Ohio at Giverny" (1983). Installation view Whitney Museum. By courtesy of Mary Lucier.

Sculpture: a single unit from Mary Lucier's video installation displaying burned vidicon tubes, "Untitled Display System" (1974/88). Whitney Museum at Equitable Center. Photo: Bill Jacobson. By courtesy of Mary Lucier.

and presenter in a virtual space of an imaginary conversation. This "fiction of discourse" or of presence is furthered by the habitual and distracted way in which we receive television.

If, however, the television apparatus were a video art installation and not a part of a habitual home environment, then awareness of the charged position in space in front of the television set (that is, the position of a virtual subject of address) would be part of the experience of the visitor. Furthermore, one would be aware of the television set itself as an object, with a shape and position in (living-room) space. One could walk around the "news" and note the back side of the "window on the world"—the annexation of our own three-dimensional world by the two-dimensional image would be obvious not only to our conscious minds but a part of our sensorimotor experience (see my "Architecture").

The development of video installation as an art form and the discovery of its parameters can begin, as in John Hanhardt's work on Wolf Vostell and Nam June Paik, with the use of the television set itself as sculptural object. To become aware of its sculptural aspects, this object had to be freed from its context, as in Paik's displacement of the monitor into clothing for the (female) body (Charlotte Moorman's "TV Bra for Living Sculpture," 1969) or as in his reorientation of television sets into "TV Clock" (1968–81; described in Paik), in a literalization of the temporal order of television programming. The displacement of TV sets into a natural setting in "TV Garden" (1974–78), on which "Global Groove" (1973), tape compiled from all over the world, was played, demonstrated an image world as natural and international environment. That is, our image-surround no longer represents a world apart; it is our world. The computer processing of images, in which Paik played a pioneering role, is another indication that images were now themselves our raw material, the natural world upon which we exercise our influence as subjects.

Rather than pretending to timelessness (see Kraus), these early TV sculptures were subjected to the processes of mortality, in a literal kind of deconstruction, submitting the object to destruction, decay, and disappearance as in the performance of physical burial in Wolf Vostell's TV "Dé-collage" (1961). The performance of Ant Farm's "Media Burn" (1975) comes to mind as well. Mary Lucier's closed-circuit installation "Untitled Display System" (1974/1988), displaying on a monitor the "live" image from a camera burned and scarred by light, is another example of the machine made mortal.[14] The contrary process (to the death drive) of building sets into greater and greater unities is exemplified in Paik's work, with his robot family, and continuing to such symbolic forms as "Video Flag X" (1985, in the collection of the Chase Manhattan Bank), "Video Flag Z" (1986, collection of the Los Angeles County Museum of Art), "Flag Y" (1986, collection of the Detroit Institute of Art), and "Get-Away Car" (1988, collection of the American Museum of the Moving Image).

The physical arrangement of television monitors into sculptural objects continues to be significant in installation video, though when an artist wishes to suppress the immediate reference to the primordial American video installation—the home TV set—that TVs and even video monitors inevitably bring to mind, then how to mask or distract the visitor from these connotations becomes a problem. Then, various housings and sculptural enclosures for monitors are part of a strategy for allowing other apparatuses to emerge.

Developing the parameters of video installation beyond the monitor image / object itself, video sculpture can present an act of inverting what is inside to the outside: for example, in Shigeko Kubota's video sculpture "Three Mountains" (1976–79),[15] it is as if the TV image of mountains were emptied out, its contents taking geometrical shape in the pyramids surrounding the monitors. These pyramids are then no longer imitations of mountains, but processed, so to speak, through our image culture and offered to us again as image ghosts and mental apparations in three dimensions.

But the act of inversion is not limited to image culture per se: Ken Feingold sees his installations as exteriorizations of his own interior mental life. Alternatively, as I interpret an installation by Mary Lucier, "Asylum, A Romance" (1986), the symbolic map of our culture with its dared and inadequate oppositions and boundaries is made manifest and undermined as obsolete (see my "Mary Lucier: Burning and Shining").

The interiority of such exteriorized images becomes most obvious, least anchored in materiality, in video projections, such as Peter Campus's "mem" (1975) (see Duguet 233–34). There is no monitor, only the visitor's body and perceptual system in relation to an image projection system, an interrelationship embodied in ghostly images, nothing but light. In contrast, this projection of interiority can be given massive form, equivalent to the very walls around the visitor, in Bill Viola's "Room for St. John of the Cross" (1983).[16] The saint's imagination is projected as the visitor's overwhelming subjective view of a risky flight over mountain peaks. (Meanwhile, an exterior surface of calm contemplation is presented within the interior of a hut with a still video image of a snow-capped mountain.)

There are also different degrees to which installation work occupies three-dimensional space, for example, the video wall, the kinetic painting, the relief, the sculpture, and the installation. Insofar as spatial positions outside the two-dimensional field are charged with meaning that is an essential aspect of the work, all these levels partake of the poetics of installation. The spectator thus enters a charged space-in-between, taking on an itinerary, a role in a set in which images move through different ontological levels with each shift in dimension, in a kinesthetic art, a body art, an image art that is rather an embodied conceptual art.

Once multiple monitors and multiple channels of video were used, other parameters for comparison and contrast came into play. In Ira Schneider's "Manhattan Is an Island" (1974), for example, an informational topographic map was created from video recordings taken at various height levels (a boat, a helicopter) and locations (downtown, midtown, uptown) of Manhattan.[17] In "Time Zones (A Reality Simulation)" (1980), Schneider attempted the same on a world scale, displaying a circle of twenty-four (recorded, but ideally simultaneous satellite) images, one from each zone. These pieces are technologically complex, but conceptually simple elaborations of the notion of place.

In their collaboration on temporality, "Wipe Cycle" (1969),[18] Frank Gillette and Ira Schneider used nine color monitors around which pretaped material, live broadcast television, and live closed-circuit television images from the entrance to the gallery were subjected to time delay and switching. Here the possibility for an image track to migrate from monitor to monitor was exploited, as well as a series of contrasts between three different types of "liveness" and time delay. In his own work, however, the serial contrasts Gillette makes are not restricted to the same conceptual realm. For example, in "Quidditas," a three-part installation from 1974–75,[19] images and ambient sound were collected in Cape Cod, Vermont, and New Hampshire, in a display that compared three different rates of "nature time." (Here, rather than establish equivalent series, the camera could establish rhythms counter to that of natural processes.)

Beryl Korot's "Dachau" (1974) was the first video installation to systematically explore the juxtaposition of the material on monitors, in a process that could be compared to serial music, or, as Korot noted, to weaving.[20] The spatial disposition of four monitors recreates a kind of broken proscenium space; it is the play at the temporal level that makes the piece, as intended, "impossible to put on television" (Korot, interview 1989) and that forces a viewer to watch the images differently. The ascetic, black-and-white video images show a rather banal tour of the contemporary concentration camp in Dachau, the Holocaust an absence like horror left unspoken. The monitors use architectural features in the image to create vertical and horizontal patterns. The images from two channels alternate across the monitors: a/b/a/b. However, the pattern is not true—there is a slight delay that puts every repetition across the visual field a little off. The whole reflects a complex relation to recording and memory, to images and what they do and don't convey.

I have come to think of this possibility for repetition, contrast, and migration of images across a shape as a poetic dimension of video installation; that is, it is a practice that deemphasizes the content of images in favor of such properties as line, color, and vectors of motion, with content of their own to convey. The choreography of these properties is another kinesthetic dimension of transformation.[21]

The transformation from monitor to monitor, from two to three dimensions and back again, is most visible when these ontological levels do not match and the conceptual is transformed in its passage through various material manifestations. Curt Royston's installations (such as "Room with Blinds" [1987] or "Flat World" [1987]) are like large paintings folded over, creating such mismatches at an optical level: two and three dimensions intersect—but the information one gets by examining the three-dimensional painting/relief/sculptural objects up close contradicts the (false) perspectival image one gets from a distance or by viewing a video monitor. (Note that Royston's video image can potentially include a visitor within the "painting.")

Several of Muntadas's pieces illustrate another kind of mismatching: that is, the conceptual realm of the installation is not contained within a gallery space, but spills over into public space. The "Board Room," shown in Barcelona at La Virreina (1988), is one example. In another piece, "haute CULTURE Part I" (Montpellier, France, 1983), a seesaw with a monitor at each end, tilted one way in a mall and the other way in a museum, makes an implicit comparison between the two sites. In "Part II" (Santa Monica Mall 1984) the difference between the two social-institutional spaces is virtually moot—one seesaw with monitors tilts slowly this way and that. These pieces suggest that an installation need not coincide with its container or exist in contiguous space; what unites an installation is the conceptual space that breaks unevenly over a spatial realm charged with social meaning. Another Muntadas technique, the evacuation of all the image material from the installation "Exposicion" (1985), leaving only the shell or spatial frame, is yet another exposure of the mismatch of realms ordinarily so liquid in our commercial image culture that the seams are virtually invisible to us. Thus, we learn that ideas and dreams are not utterly interchangeable with images nor are they exchangeable with bodies and objects.

EXPERIENCE IN ONE OR FOUR DIMENSIONS

If there is transcendence in the presentational arts, it must come not from elsewhere, nor in a controlled regression to a preconscious state via identification with the not-self as self. These arts address the wide-awake consciousness that we call experience. Such a realm is not immune from its own fictions and intensities, nor does it lack spirituality; play, ritual, and revolution are part of this plane of presence. Experience implies that a change has taken place in the visitor, that he or she has learned something. This learning is not a kind of knowing better but nevertheless . . . , nor is it knowing unleashed from the habitual realm of a body that never learns but rather endlessly repeats. Rather, it exploits the capacities of the body itself and its senses to grasp the world visually, aurally, and kinesthetically. If the first kind of transcendence in the arts is the kind denigrated in Plato's "Simile of the Cave," the second kind of transcendence, while not a peripatetic philosophy in motion through the groves of academe itself, could be compared with the trajectory of a prisoner in motion from the darkness to light. (If it is possible to do so, I would prefer not to adopt Plato's idealism or his hierarchy of values along with his simile.) An installation without this intertwining of corporeal and conceptual transcendence would be nothing more than an exhibition, a site for learning knowledge always already known, transmitted by the authorities who know it—governments, corporations, schools, and other institutions of all kinds.

To describe the things we can learn from installation art requires interpretation of each experience itself. These things are left to the detailed treatment they deserve in other venues, but the range of subjects treated in installation art is easy to summarize as vast—from the spatial and temporal notions of identity, to the exploration of image culture, reaching from the technological sublime to institution of art itself, to mourning the loss of the natural world and the desire for the renewal of a spiritual dimension in material reality.

"YOU HAD TO BE THERE": THE LIMITS OF VIDEO INSTALLATION

Beyond whatever failures there might be in specific installations that, for whatever reason, might offer visitors an experience of puzzlement or boredom rather than insight, there are limitations intrinsic to the art form. Perhaps the most intransigent problem is the relation of video installation to temporality, a subject left virtually unaddressed until now: as a spatial form, installation art might appear to have escaped the ghetto of time-based arts into the museum proper, leaving single-channel video art to fend for itself. Video installation, however, remains a form that unfolds in time—the time a visitor requires to complete a trajectory inspecting objects and monitors, the time a video track or a poetic juxtaposition of tracks requires to play out, or the time for a track to wander across a field of monitors, and, one might add, the time for reflection in the subject her- or himself, that is, for the experience of a transformation to occur.

Temporal unfolding is commonly organized within video installations in repeating cycles that allow a visitor to enter and leave at any point. (Some installations cycle a kind of narrative instead.) There is a contradiction between cyclic repetition in the art form and the transcendence of repetition through experience that is the desired result—yet at the level of each individual visitor this contradiction may be moot. A more practical problem with temporality has to do with the dominant mode of perceiving in museums and galleries. However long the cycle, at whatever rate the installation unfolds, this unfolding is incompatible with taking in visual objects all at once, in a matter of seconds. If in response to this dominant mode, one were to reduce temporal unfolding to the barest minimum, what would happen then to the notion of experience or transcendence? This incommensurability of perceptual modes is of course related to the difference between the arts of presentation and the arts of representation, and the different planes of language that have come to cohabit in the museum.

In this light, the "museumization" of installation art can be evaluated in two diametrically opposed ways. In one way, installation art could be said to transform the nature of the museum itself, now a place fraught with problems related to the commodification of art and the penetration of corporations with economic agendas of their own into the command of the art world. Installation art in this setting reinvigorates all the spaces-in-between, so that the museum visitor becomes aware of the museum itself as a megainstallation, even to the point of self-critique: an installation full of spatial positions charged with power, full of fetish-objects transposable anywhere, a site that oils the fluid transpositions of concepts and commodity-objects between ontological realms.

On the other hand, installation art begins to partake in a long-overdue recognition afforded to arts of presentation. In the process, installation art itself could become more commodifiable, a prestige art, and its practioners a relatively closed elite. I personally see that there are intrinsic limits to the commodifiability of installation art that brake what some would see as its corruption as well as its acceptance. More problematic is the accessibility of the art form itself to a general public. "You had to be there" to know what an installation is. Even then, until recently a general lack of discourse on the arts of presentation has led to incomprehension or misunderstanding about the premises or goals of this art form as well. For instance, the experiments with feedback of sound and image in the closed-circuit video experiments of the early 1970s have been long been diagnosed as narcissism.[22]

Surely, narcissism is one moment in an oscillation at the threshold between gaining and losing one's own image. However, in retrospect the virtual relation between the body of the perceiver and the monitor image was precisely one of decentering. Remembering Nauman's claustrophobic "Live Taped Video Corridor" with which this chapter began underlines the possibilities for disturbing the relation to one's own body image. Unlike film, in which the camera, the optical printer, and the projector occupy the same position at different times, in live closed-circuit video, the monitor operates simultaneously with the camera and must be placed asymmetrically to it to some degree or other (barring putting the camera *into* the monitor). This decentering effect is hidden in the ordinary use of video as one-way television. The skewed relation between physical space and its representation on screen becomes apparent in live video feedback, most especially when the viewer's body in relation to his or her own image is involved. Splitting apart the symmetrical relationship of the body and the image breaks the illusion most fundamental to mass culture and to broadcast television—that serially produced merchandise or broadcast images are meant "just for you."

Aesthetic strategies for displacing that symmetrical and virtual relation between the body and the screen are at the heart of the closed-circuit video installations of Bruce Nauman, Peter Campus, Dan Graham, and others. Single-channel videotapes by these artists as well as by Joan Jonas, Vito Acconci, and other artists of the period experiment with shifting relations between the body of the artist, the camera, and the monitor.

While "Vertical Roll" (1970) is her best-known performance video of the period, Joan Jonas's profoundly simple "Left Side Right Side" of the same year (seven minutes, black-and-white) uses a mirror and a monitor to demonstrate the fragmentation and multiplication of the self-image. At first, with the constant refrain of her voice and her finger pointing, "This is my left side, this is my right side," we find that the mirror image (which divides the body into parts and reflects them in symmetrical right/left inversion) doesn't at all match the video image, which is a replica of the body image. Furthermore, the video replicant is free to wander, no longer tied to a mirror position; once recorded, it is unleashed in time as well to enjoy its semiautonomous but ever so repetitive existence. When seen in the same frame together, the mirror image and the replicant image produce confusing inverted symmetries. Peter Campus's video and glass installation "Interface" (1972) allows the visitor to experience this division and multiplication for her- or himself by projecting the visitor's video image onto the same glass on which reflected light produces a mirror-reflection. The double image that results is inverted right and left and can overlap or divide, according to the visitor's will. This theme of overlapping and superimposed right-left inversions of the self-image is played to its conclusion in Peter Campus's 1973 performance video "Three Transitions" (six minutes, color). The first transition superimposes video feedback of the other side of a paper screen on a closed-circuit image of Campus seen at the screen from the back. As Campus is shown slitting the screen and bending through it, the image of his body is seen from both sides of the screen in a complex rotated, inverted, and converging symmetry, as if he and his alter ego were scooping each other out. Thereupon Campus climbs entirely through and tapes up the wound in the screen, leaving only the bandaged paper in view. In the second transition, as Campus smears himself with a chroma-keyed color, his own closed-circuit image appears in the matte created by the smears. However, his live superimposed image does not quite match his face—yet it is as near as one could ever get to an identity. The image inside the mask trembles, in fact, in a disturbing rendering of the conscious creation of one's own presentation of self. The third transition burns the paper on which Campus's own feedback image has been keyed, eventually leaving

The Body, the Image, and the Space-in-Between

Joan Jonas demonstrates the difference between her mirror image and the replicant in the monitor in the video "Left Side Right Side" (1970). By courtesy of Joan Jonas.

"This is my right eye."

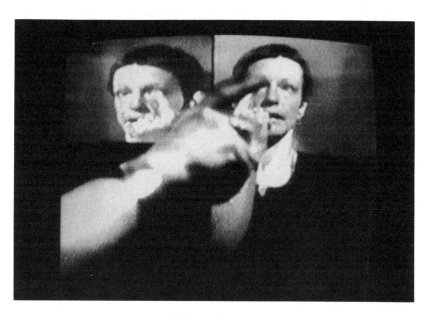

"This is my left eye."

The artist, Peter Campus, confronts his reflected image and his video replica on the glass in "Interface," a closed-circuit video installation, Bykert Gallery, New York 1972.
Photo: Nathan Rabin. By courtesy of Paula Cooper Gallery, New York.

A visitor encounters her anamorphic closed-circuit projection in Peter Campus's "mem" (1975), a video installation in variable dimensions. Installation: Kölnischer Kunstverein, Cologne, 1979. (Private collection, Hamburg.)
By courtesy of Paula Cooper Gallery, New York.

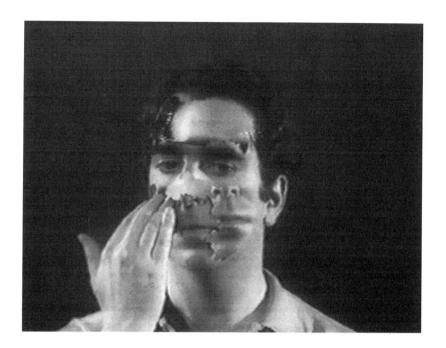

The second and third transitions in progress, from "Three Transitions" (1973)
by Peter Campus. Frame grab by Electronic Arts Intermix.
By courtesy of Peter Campus.

nothing but empty screen space. Here is the subtext of the closed-circuit work of the period *in nuce.*

In an example of aural and audio feedback, Richard Serra's video "Boomerang" (1974) allows the viewer to witness the confusion that results from the overlap of Nancy Holt's live speaking voice with its playback at an approximately one-second delay. As Rosalind Krauss describes it, "Because the audio delay keeps hypostatizing her words, [Holt] has great difficulty coinciding with herself as a subject. It is a situation, she says, that 'puts a distance between the words and their apprehension—their comprehension', a situation that is 'like a mirror reflection . . . so that I am surrounded by me and my mind surrounds me . . . there is no escape'," from what Krauss calls "the prison of a collapsed present" (Krauss, "Narcissism" 181). However, nearly two decades and much cultural experience later, the problem appears not to be the hypostasis of one unbroken and continous "now" without connection to the past, so much as it is a proliferation of "nows" in hybrid "heres" and a displacement of the self that results in a multi-plication of personas or "me's."

The most elaborate environment for exploring temporal and spatial disjunction and the multiplication of mirror reflections and video replicants is Dan Graham's closed-circuit installation "Opposing Mir-rors and Video Monitors on Time Delay" (1974). The configuration is chiasmic: two monitors face toward mirror walls across from each other; each monitor is fed by a camera on the opposing monitor. Fur-thermore, one monitor is on time delay, meaning that one might be able to stand in front of the camera, cross the room, and possibly glimpse oneself in the monitor on the opposite side. However, there is no dearth of images of self or of other visitors: one might focus on one's mirror reflection or the mirror reflection of one's mirror reflection; or one's image reflected in the mirror in the monitor, and so forth, or for that matter, see any other visitor in one of these permutations. The inability to master the spatiotemporal situation is figured in monitor images themselves: each monitor displays an infinite recursion or *mise-en-abyme* of the opposing mirror image of the room with the other monitor in it with another room and monitor in it. However confusing, the situation inspires collaborators to send signals to visitors on the other side of the room in improvised mirror-monitor play. In fact, with few exceptions, live feedback pieces benefit from the cooperation of other visitors; if one cannot have one's own image, one can at least be recog-nized by exchanging it with someone else.

The Body, the Image, and the Space-in-Between

The emphasis of the art of the period on the moment of absence or loss of the image must be seen in the context of mass culture and its emphasis on fostering the impression of presence. Under such conditions, to cultivate a taste for exhilarating disillusionment and breathtaking loss is to call the foundation of mass consumer culture into question.

In this decade, techniques have evolved for producing ever more involving and encompassing perceptual illusions. In an era when cameras can travel under the surface of the skin, the desire to experience, interact, and even touch the image in an apparently unmediated way refuses to stop at the screen itself. As a culture, we want to break through to the other side of the screen and enter inside the image itself. It is as if we could break into the computer monitor, and, like a traveler, explore a virtual space of stored audiovisual information.

SEVEN

Cyberscapes, Control, and
Transcendence:
The Aesthetics of the Virtual

Cyberspace. A consensual
hallucination experienced
daily by billions of legiti-
mate operators, in every
nation, by children being
taught mathematical
concepts. . . . A graphic
representation of data
abstracted from the banks
of every computer in the
human system. Unthink-
able complexity. Lines of
lights ranged in the
nonspace of the mind,
clusters and constellations
of data. Like city lights,
receding.

—Gibson, *Neuromancer* 51

THE NONSPACE OF THE MIND: SPATIAL GENRES OF VIRTUALITY

Cyberspace is the manifestation of what some call the data sphere in perceptible and metaphoric forms—a symbolic system supported and maintained by machines. The concept of "space" applied to computer- and other machine-generated virtual realms is itself a metaphor that invokes something quite different from the fundamental experience of being in a location in the physical world in a body rooted to the ground by gravity, in view of a horizon. Gibson's famous description of cyberspace as "nonspace of the mind" suggests the enigmatic qualities of a space of dreamlike condensation that doesn't take up actual room. This novelistic cyberspace fudges the difference between the mind and the computer, just as it confuses the level of digital objects made from data stored as ones and zeros and their display.[1] For instance, is the "space" of a virtual object in a computer program? Even if it can be quantified as data in megabytes or ultimately in bandwidth or pixels, the virtual object itself remains an imperceptible potentiality that occupies no space at all until it is accessed and displayed.[2] Can one even say the object is "inside" the opaque casing of the computer or hidden under the obscure machine language of programming? Even if one could break into the black box or extract and analyze the program, one wouldn't expose the virtual object, only the mechanism that has the potential to produce it.[3] Yet once displayed, the virtual object is a symbol in a realm subject to cause and effect, albeit disproportionate to what we are accustomed to in physical space.

Cyberspace can be experienced in various degrees of person and immersiveness and in different symbolic modes. It is virtually embodied metaphor into which the flesh (or meat body) can't go, but which allows disengaged spectral bodies and multiple personas to be inducted, fly and interact, alone or in an electronic crowd. Of course, "flying" or locomotion of any kind in cyberspace is also a metaphor. The cyberscene itself can move and is responsive to the user in ways which promote performative and/or magical experiences, loosely covered in scientific and socioeconomic alibis.

That is, electronically produced virtual realms and induced experiences are only superficially about technology. They are about transcendence (even when in degraded forms of sex, shopping, high-speed driving, combat, and so forth). Some of the organizing metaphors of cyberspace (frontier, highway, spaceflight, cave, net, theater, game) and locomotion within it are propositions which should be scrutinized carefully as to the way they define the control, access, reality status, and experiences assigned to the virtual and symbolic realms which are increasingly our everyday world.

The following distinguishes various aspects and genres of cyberspace that extend from coherent *virtual worlds* and the dispersed spatiality of *networks* to *virtualized* physical space. Indeed, virtualities are inevitably linked to materiality and physical space, be they in terms of the body or the technological apparatuses that generate virtual images or the geographic localities over which they are mapped.

Virtual environments can signify *liminal* spaces, sacred places of social and personal transformation like the cave or the sweat lodge, if only by reason of their virtuality—neither imaginary nor real, animate, but neither living nor dead, a subjunctive realm of externalized imagination wherein events happen in effect, but not actually.[4] In his treatment of the features of postmodernist fiction in literature, Brian McHale identifies "opalescence" with uncertain ontological status, a place where worlds overlap. The quality of "opalescence," or what Robert Kyr called "shimmering" sound in his description of gamelan tunings played together with electronic music, is prominent in many examples of cyberspace as art. Consider the wavering path of global positioning satellites traced by Laura Kurgan in marking the location of her installation at the New Museum in New York, suggesting the play of the oscillating satellites above the earth (as well as inexactitudes introduced into GPS data by the Defense Department). This trembling quality is visible in Toni Dove's pulsating and glowing images of girls in Dove's and Michael Mackenzie's "Archeology of a Mother Tongue." In "See Banff!", Michael Naimark's simulation of a kinetoscope evokes both a period before the cinema and after it (comparable to limited computer-animation such as "quicktime"); the flicker of noticeable intervals between frames is simulated as well, when the stop-motion stereoscopic images of touristic Banff are "cranked through" the machine. Three of Naimark's time-lapse or what he calls "temporally undersampled" segments are especially ghostlike: the spectral jogger on the Fenland Trail, the fleeting appearances of tourists on the Athabasca Glacier, and the thin stalks of the grasses glowing nearly transparent in the sun on "Head-Smashed-In Buffalo Jump," perhaps as much a result of the instability of stereoscopic vision itself as of the haunting images in unreal time ("Frame Rate" 34–35). The landscape in both pieces is bathed in the opalescence of worlds not quite coalescing. The spectral, "shimmering" aspect of cyberspace draws forth the enigmatic or transcendent reality status of the virtual.

However, drawing on signs of transcendence, especially when understood as a cultural relation to another realm beyond this mortal life, has disturbing implications, because unlike prior illusion-producing modes of expression, cyberspace is a means of enchanting not only liminal realms, but everyday life. The technological ability to recreate the acoustic space of a medieval cathedral in one's living room, or to merge movie stars and tourists into the same image and have them interact, merely exploits the ability to superimpose the virtual over physical space: it is entertainment. Of course, the spiritual potential and powerful metapsychological effects of immersion can easily be abused as a seductive force in the more mundane, instrumental uses of cyberspace. Art can, however, distinguish itself from cyberspace per se and its instrumental and entertainment uses as both an aesthetic statement and as a kind of metacommentary on cyberculture and its desire to transcend the material world by entering another realm of "nonspace."

Enthralling Spaces: Virtual Worlds

Virtual worlds are the solely virtual or immaterial realms with which one interacts to varying degrees in varying modes of personhood. While virtual worlds can seek to reproduce natural landscapes, there is a thrill of transgression in entering a symbolic landscape or metaphor of what would otherwise be inaccessible and impenetrable—from the inside of the body, of the atom, of the black box to the outsides of our galaxy and our universe, and of other worlds entirely that have no counterpart except in fantasies and dreams. For the most part, to be inducted into a three-dimensional virtual environment is to seem to go where people can't go but computers can, into a landscape that is nano-, macro-, or otherwise out of human scale or which would otherwise be invisible beyond opaque surfaces of material or skin. To enter the virtual environment itself is like being able to walk through one's TV or computer, through the vanishing point or vortex and into a three-dimensional field of symbols. It is as if one were immersed in language itself or as if the symbols on a map were virtually embodied as landscape. The virtual landscape in question might be imaginary because it never existed or never could exist or once existed and is now lost, lost, lost. (Salvage anthropology which seeks to preserve disappearing behaviors and decaying or dispersed artifacts has found its appropriate medium.)

My first visit to a demonstration of virtual reality—a cartoonlike "Virtual Seattle" at VPL Labs in California a number of years ago—indicated that for me at least, the great attraction was not the lure of computer technology or of interface devices, which included a cumbersome helmet ("eyephones" or HMD: head-mounted display) which put little video monitors over my eyes. The neon-colored artificial world coarsely rendered in real-time in which I had the illusion of being immersed was not a convincing imitation of the physical Seattle, or for that matter, any other landscape which could possibly have drawn me in. The allure of this cyberscape was the impression that it was responsive to me, as if my gaze itself were creating (or performing) this world and that I was to some extent enunciating it according to my own desire. My most abiding memory was of an exhilarating ability to fly through the artificial world at great speed simply by cocking my hand like a gun—"navigation" is a poor metaphor for this experience. Best of all, I had a sense of the weightlessness and superpower that I had imagined in childhood and had read about in myths and comic books, but had never before experienced, not even in my dreams. (My childhood friends in first and second grade and I tried fruitlessly to fly day after day by flapping blankets while jumping off walls and out of trees.) It is this feeling of transcendence of the mortal body and the gravity of earth that for me is a key to the desire and media attention which have been focused on "cyberspace" and the subculture that has grown up around it.

In effect, while the visitor to the virtual environment moves in a very circumscribed physical area, his or her motion is tracked and the appropriate shift in his or her point of view within a vast virtual landscape is constructed instantly. With my "eyephones" and dataglove I did not need to leave the spot to travel. In actuality, however, my field of view in the virtual world was constantly being reconstituted in "real time" by a computer from a digital store through devices which tracked the position of my head and hand. ("Simulator sickness" and the disturbing experience of "lag" between head motion and image formation are clues to the inexact fit between a cyberscape and the body in physical space.) Despite its futuristic connotations, a "world" like "Virtual Seattle" belongs to the most traditional kind of virtual environment and may even be considered the last gasp of Renaissance space. However, the spectator's station point is *inside* the projection of an image, transformed from a monocular and stationary point of view into mobile agency in a three-dimensional space. Of course, this visual three-dimensionality is supported by sound—the most potentially immersive and virtual medium of all.

I was fascinated with being both *in* the picture and having *control* over it. That is, though I was virtually inside the scene or story-world in cyberspace, I also enjoyed the choice-making privileges about the order, direction, and the pace of what happened next. So, my role lay somewhere between that of a character inside the virtual environment and a narrator outside the virtual space. Furthermore, I could hear the voice of a controller/programmer/author leaking into my world from fur-

ther "outside" while others nearby could see my fly-through of "Seattle" on a monitor. I could chase a whale or follow restaurant sounds to
the Space Needle landmark, whatever took my fancy, and when I got
tired of it, I could tell the operator at the computer, "Give me another
world!" (Choices at VPL included "Virtual Kitchen" and a toy world
with a quacking duck in a virtual plastic pond.)

Despite these mundane examples and the fact that "hype" or inflated
publicity about them far outstrips technological developments, future
transformation does seem to leak from cyberplaces. The term "cyberspace" may have lost its novelty, and much of the practical discourse
about the "information superhighway" or "infobahn" is about disap-
pointment and disenchantment. Yet the lure of cyberplaces remains in
the hint they give of something that is not quite there, at least yet—an
escape or a change, but in any case, a response to the directive, "Give
me another world!"

The uncanny and more sinister implications of my first flight occurred to me later: a virtual space is not just the ground or background
or the landscape at which I look, or even that my look calls forth—that
space looks at me, like Lacan's sardine can bobbing in the harbor,
following my every move. Indeed, space constituted itself in response
to various indices of my intention, for instance, the vectors of my gaze
and the motion of my body or head. That is, in a virtual world, not just
objects but *space itself is interactive*. Cyberspace is not merely space as a
scene where things could happen, it is also the artificial intelligence or
agency that puts the virtual scene in place. This intelligence can even be
invested with aspects of personality, challenging the rational distinction between space versus agency or landscape versus character in the
process. As a consequence the virtual environment that surrounds the
visitor itself can appear to be something "live" or animate, that sees us
without being seen.[5]

One implication is that cyberspace has the potential to be the most
powerful and effective means of surveillance and social control, not
merely of the user in cyberspace, but of the external material world, yet
invented.[6] Then far from being neutral, the point of such an imaging
system is, the words of N. Katherine Hayles, "to reconstitute the body,"
and we might add, landscape, "as a technical object under human
control" ("Seductions" 173; see also Nichols). As discussed in chapter 1,
the Gulf War revealed the implications of machine vision that is blind to
the actual world, viewing only its simulation on an image display.
Symbols manipulated in a virtual landscape matched to physical space

can be used to kill or obliterate the actual referents of undesirable symbols in real space. The worlds of video game entertainment, while not actually deadly, commonly depend for a sense of finality and realism on building in the option of "killing" the symbols for one's opponents in the form of "finishing moves"—decapitation, tearing out the heart, blowing up, eating, and so forth—into the game.[7] Death is apparently the guarantee that the joystick controls the image and that the map controls the territory, while "death" is the measure of mastery in the game, just as the material body and its ultimate death is the warrant for all the personas and avatars that lurk and wander through the net.[8]

Ivan Sutherland exposed this logic at its most extreme at the inception of contemporary work in virtual imaging systems nearly thirty years ago with his "ultimate display":

> The ultimate display would, of course, be a room within which the computer can control the existence of matter. A chair displayed in such a room would be good enough to sit in. Handcuffs displayed in such a room would be confining, and a bullet, displayed in such a room would be fatal. With appropriate programming such a display could literally be the Wonderland into which Alice walked. (508)

Sutherland's Wonderland is remarkably sparse: a chair and a pair of handcuffs suggest one chained to the chair somewhat like a prisoner in Plato's cave. The room also possesses a fatal bullet and by implication, somewhere inside or outside it, a body—it's not clear whose. Note that the realism of the ultimate display does not depend on appearing like reality or verisimilitude or *referential illusion* (that is, convincingly invoking another world elsewhere) but on the power of language or the display to make reality itself or *enunciative illusion* (that is, when speaking a word or drawing a symbol appears to call a world forth into existence, or what is known in linguistics as a performative). This power of the symbol or the word to give life is paradoxically demonstrated or confirmed only by a performance that puts a body (a real body?) really to death. Beyond such deadly performatives there are more gentle displays that neither represent nor kill the "real" world as we know it, though they may change it socioeconomically and culturally.

The often-mentioned desire for photographic resolution in virtual displays may also have as much to do with the goal of controlling physical objects and events as it does with aesthetics. An art of virtual spaces that simply aims toward realism of fit or of appearance with a physical landscape may then risk merely serving the instrumental or

hegemonic purposes of military and business interests in an information society. Though art that surrenders to the allure of the mysterious
or that seems to offer transcendence may find—like Icarus—the wax
that holds its feathers together melted by the sun, art that serves the
seamless operation of cyberculture and the production of realistic virtual worlds may be flying so low as to be dragged into the sea.

However, the very notion of *immersion* suggests a spiritual realm, an
amniotic ocean, where one might be washed in symbols and emerge
reborn. Virtual landscapes can also figure as liminal realms of transformation, outside of the world of social limits and constraints, like the
cave or sweat lodge, if only by reason of their virtuality—not entirely
imaginary nor entirely real, animate but neither living nor dead, a
subjunctive realm wherein events happen in effect, but not actually. It
might seem that the limits of the body and material existence might
be transcended within such a subjunctive realm. *Neuromancer* is explicit
in this connection: the hero Case's meeting with his dead wife toward
the conclusion of the novel is followed by an encounter with a boy. In
response to a question about his name, the boy answers:

> "Neuromancer," the boy said, slitting long gray eyes against the rising
> sun. "The lane to the land of the dead. Where you are, my friend. . . .
> Neuro, from the nerves, the silver paths. Romancer. Necromancer. I
> call up the dead. But no my friend," and the boy did a little dance,
> brown feet printing the sand. "I *am* the dead and their land." He
> laughed. A gull cried. "Stay. If your woman is a ghost, she doesn't
> know it. Neither will you." (243–44)

Note that in this excerpt, "Neuromancer" wavers between referring to
a computer-produced spatiotemporal realm within which Case and his
dead wife meet, the artificial intelligence that produces that realm, and
a persona standing for it and acting within it—not to mention Gibson's
book itself. So cyberspace, beyond its business uses, can invoke a parallel and sometimes a transcendent or spiritual world that revives the
dead or the spirits of things in the limbo of the possible. This world may
be mixed up in an undecidable way with reality itself. Just as the
mysterious telegraph and the telephone were also once thought able to
contact the other world, cyberspace is also an underworld in which to
meet one's Eurydice.

Sometimes a work of art can function much like a metaphor for the
metaphoric realm of virtual reality itself. In the process, the desire to
become disembodied and to enter an immaterial world is shown to be
historical, in contrast to the mantra of "never-seen-before-ness" that

MEDIA ART AND VIRTUAL ENVIRONMENTS

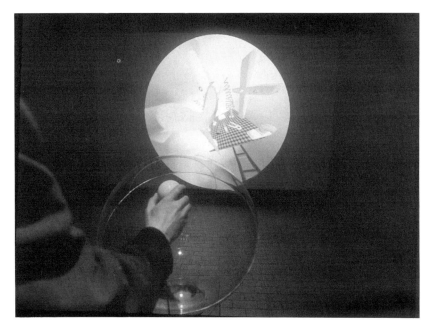

Agnes Hegedüs's "Handsight" (1992/1993). Programmers: Gideon May and Richard Holloway. Collection of the Zentrum für Kunst und Medientechnologie Medienmuseum Karlsruhe. By courtesy of Agnes Hegedüs.

puts technologies like virtual reality outside of sociohistorical continuity and thus beyond criticism. In Agnes Hegedüs's "Handsight" (1993), the visitor's hand moves a spherical sensor into the opening and around inside an empty transparent globe, both sensor and globe reminiscent of the eye. These hand motions are translated into a moving point of view within a virtual world, like an "endoscopic eye" (*endo* = within, e.g., capable of penetrating an interior space). This virtual worldview is displayed on a spherical screen beyond the globe. The 3-D computer graphic virtual world is modeled on the interior of a very beautiful "passion bottle," that is, a narrow-necked nineteenth-century Hungarian folk art bottle, into which—as if miraculously—a crucifixion scene has been set. What the colors and geometric shapes so typical of computer graphics lack in beauty, the scene in the virtual bottle makes up through its strange and precipitous spatial relationships, quite unlike "real" or perspectival space. Thus the piece sets the virtual world in the screen-projection display, the interface (the "eye" and container), and the folk art into relation as expressions of the desire for transcendence.

Networks and Webs as "Space"

Where is that noplace in which, for instance, two people talking by telephone meet? Where is the room and where is the display in which the hundreds who belong to the same MUD (Multi-User Dimension) or MOO (MUD, Object-Oriented) may gather? Space is ordinarily conceived of as continuous or at least, at its most abstract, as a homogeneous void. Yet a unified virtual nonspace or cyberspace can be *distributed discontinuously* over physical space. Networks as linking devices that create virtual realms of greater and greater, albeit ephemeral unity are understood, paradoxically enough, as "spaces" composed of maze-like vectors and links. Netspace includes text-based on-line networks, MUDs and MOOs, telecommunication satellite links and cables, but also railroads and highways as protocyberspace in networks that unify physical space. Furthermore, physical separation between the users and objects of physical space need have little bearing on the seams that separate and link virtual spaces. Virtual space as "nonspace" need not occupy ground, nor be a continuous linear extension, area, or void, nor even constitute the interval between things; and, unlike the material *Lebensraum* of earth, it need not be perceived as limited or scarce. The discontinuous yet communal virtual space of isolated computer network users can expand ad infinitum, like the text-based "rooms" which make up a MUD.

The additive aesthetic principle of the Internet, the global network of networks, is an extremely elegant, nonhierarchical, rhizomatic global web of relatively independent yet connecting nodes. Though it was conceived out of militaristic considerations, it might be compared with Panofsky's analysis of the Gothic cathedral. This comparison is not trivial, for combined as an infrastructural and virtual entity, the Internet is among the greatest architecture the world has ever known, far greater than the material reference point of the information highway metaphor, the freeway system. More intriguingly, the use of computer networks is susceptible to crowd movements of far more variety and speed than can usually be studied in material space and ordinary temporal durations: the rise of a topic on the Net, its ebb and flow, the attractors and repulsors of exchange are at a scale that is cosmic or social at the supraindividual level and in any case not encompassed by traditional aesthetic principles. Such virtual environments of discontinuous and overlapping jurisdictions would tax any political imagination capable of ethnic cleansing or of resolving ethnic conflict by dedicating bounded areas to one homogeneous culture. If virtual space were our model of political space, there would be no struggle for nationhood as a geographical entity. What would remain a nagging material problem is opening wide the material gateways of induction into the virtual realm.

While cyberspace per se is an exclusive realm, its production depends on the material space beyond its interfaces. Cyberspace is real estate in terms of data space on computer disks and in mainframes, personal space in seats in front of computer workstations, frequencies on the broadcast spectrum, satellite space off which to bounce signals, and room in the bandwidth of fiberoptic cables that global corporations struggle among themselves to own and control. The scarcity and costliness of these material gates of entry limit the number and types of subjects we can find in the virtual gathering spaces of cyberculture. Yet even those who assemble the chips may not have access to the worlds computers engender. Since electronic networks involve a choice about who will be connected and who won't, a network consists of its holes as well as its links and nodes. There is a negative or shadow cyberspace that is material and devoid of technological resources that those who seek to understand electronic culture must take into account. Relations to cyberspace as nightmare and/or utopia are understandably related to one's position in this economy and the mode of access to it, if any—the data-entry worker is different from the programmer, the cultural entitlement of a little girl to cyberplay is not the same as a little boy's. The subsistence farmer's life, if not status, could not be more different than the fast food worker's, but they will nonetheless be ultimately related in a global system of integration and exclusion, like the strands and negative space of a net. That is why those who are technologically barred from the networks of cyberspace are nonetheless discursively and actually a negative part of this system; they can offer valuable and enlightening views about the material shadow of virtuality in what must be a truly global dialogue with local positions.

Artists and cultural activists—for instance, Paper Tiger/Deep Dish and Ponton—have also not forgotten the issue of public access to the material and technical level where information is processed, stored, and transmitted or, like "The Fileroom: An Interactive Computer Project Addressing Cultural Censorship" initiated by Muntadas and produced by Randolph Street Gallery (1994), the practical level of interdiction of

Cyberscapes, Control, and Transcendence

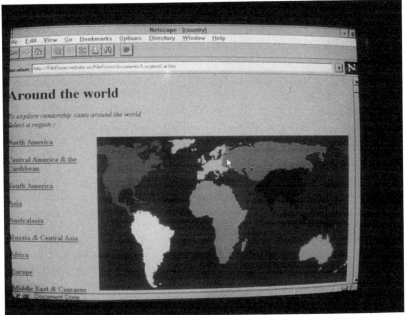

Muntadas's "The Fileroom: An Interactive Computer Project Addressing
Cultural Censorship" was produced by Randolph Street Gallery and seen as
an installation of file cabinets and on-line monitors at the Chicago
Cultural Center (1994). The public is invited to add to an
open-ended database on censorship.
By courtesy of Muntadas.

the first uses of the Internet and the World Wide Web as conceptual art (http://fileroom.aa.uic.edu/fileroom.html). Student researchers gathered an open-ended database of instances of censorship over five centuries to which members of the public are invited to add their own examples. In contrast to its subject matter of repression, the piece itself foregrounds the Internet and the Web as on-line public spheres and sites of intersubjective exchange at a time of privatization, when the right of free speech is in danger, and invites the public to speak and be heard on-line.

Agnes Hegedüs's "Televirtual Fruit Machine" uses networks to enact a metaphor of global cooperation. I experienced the piece in Karlsruhe in 1993, connected to another player in Tokyo. Each of us had control over one hemisphere of a hollow globe, the exterior of which was texture-mapped with fruit. Both hemispheres were projected on a screen and we two players were visible to each other by videophone. Our goal was to unite the globe virtually like 3-D puzzle pieces using our track balls, thereby unleashing symbolic values of coins and candy. As silly as it sounds, I discovered how erotic it was to share this task with a very skillful and seductive player, who would whisk his side of the world away just as I was about to connect, making our eventual virtual union its own reward.

This virtual realm of links and networks invites the study of transitions between spaces and conditions and of crowd movements in and between worlds. Such investigation finds its inspiration in the representation of the crowds or group protagonists, in, for instance, films by Eisenstein, Buñuel, Jansco, Akerman, and Altman (though Riefenstahl's are too predictably regimented to be of much use in comprehending spontaneous movement and agency of groups), in the satellite experimentation of early video, and the use of time-lapse studies, flocking algorithms, and the statistical flows and ruptures of chaos theory for the purposes of art.

The compression of crowd flows over centuries of space and time finds an exponent in Jeffrey Shaw's interactive installation "Revolution." The user's effort turns a monitor on a turnstile, simulating a grindstone that churns out pictorial representations of hundreds of social revolutions in the historical record onto a video monitor. "Revolution" is then not a representational space of linear histories or of geographical areas but the presentational space of a metaphor and its recurring metahistorical patterns. The visitor to the installation stands

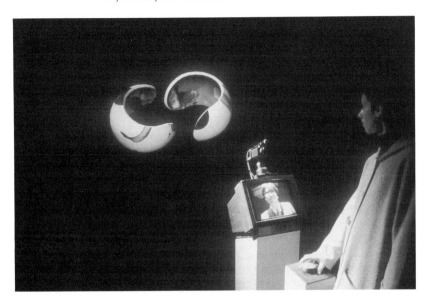

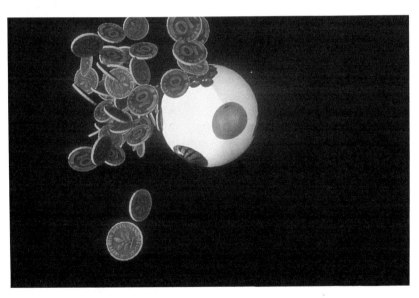

In Agnes Hegedüs's "Televirtual Fruit Machine" (1993), the visitor at the podium controls half of a graphic world/ball with fruit symbols (reminiscent of a slot machine). Meanwhile, she can see and hear her distant partner by means of a videophone ISDN connection. Once the two players have successfully reunited the fruited sphere, it spews forth symbolic riches in coin. Programmer: Gideon May.
By courtesy of Agnes Hegedüs.

for the protagonist and motive force of this social phenomenon, a spontaneously acting group called at times the "mass," the "crowd," or the "people." Then the vocation of an art of the kind that reflects on electronic crowds and networks is not the representation of the visible world, but the visualization of what is otherwise inaccessible to perception and is difficult to imagine because of its cosmic or microscopic scale, its discontinuity in space and time, or its impenetrability—from the insides of the body, the atom, or the black box to the outside of our galaxy and our universe.

Virtualized Physical Space

In response to a question about cyberspace today, William Gibson answered, "It's where the bank keeps your money" (Rosenberg). Cyberspace serves and is shaped by the needs of postnational and postindustrial corporations: knowledge decontextualized and digitized as information is stored in databases and manipulated. However, whatever the interests and applications involved, for the vast majority of users, information must be displayed as symbolic forms and made perceptible—cyberspace proper, so to speak. In fact, for an economy based on virtual money to work, as in the artist Jeff Schulz's model of the credit system (159–63), the system of exchange-value seems to demand passage from the conceptual to the virtual to the material and back again, crossing through a variety of reality statuses. In the process, virtuality also enters the world of material objects and environments that have been invested with computer-supported agency (that is, delegated human subjectivity) or which have been given the skins of other times or places. Artifacts and even space itself can be "cyberized" by programming that simulates some other space, time, or agency (see chapter 1 and Bolter). Physical reality can also be "virtualized" with or without the help of a computer. Before the advent of information society, the nonspace of derealized mall and freeway landscapes served mass consumer society in a process described in chapter 4. Mass touristic destinations have similarly become the hyperreal symbols of themselves in global touristic exchange. Street lighting might also be considered protovirtualized physical space, changing night into artificial day.[9] In such ways, physical space has been transformed into the "nonspace of the mind."

In the same way, an electronic and virtual art may work through metaphors that are realized across different degrees of virtuality and materiality.[10] This means to me that art should not be ghettoized into the electronic and/or virtual environment versus traditional genres. David Rokeby's "A Very Nervous System" (1991) is simple in technology, but illustrates space that has been veiled with a layer of virtuality and machine agency. Here, however, it is a magic realm of musical sound brought forth out of thin air through the visitor's corporeal gestures and dance.

The level of technology achieved in a piece of art can even be in inverse proportion to the usefulness of the piece as metacommentary. Take, for example, Perry Hoberman's interactive installation "Faraday's Garden" (exhibited at "Machine Culture" Siggraph 1993, as were the next two pieces discussed), a playful meditation on technological obsolescence that allows the visitor to bring a graveyard of outdated appliances to life. Through stepping or even dancing on sensors in a mat on the floor, the visitor can control a symphony of hums, whirs, and buzzes of dated can openers, clock radios, 8mm film projectors, and so forth, brought back from the wasteland where machines wind down. This machine-human interaction is decidedly conscious and humorously empowering in demystifying the domination by technology of everyday life.

We may even interact with robotic agents and machine personas, which seem to share our here-and-now and to communicate with us, largely by responding to our position, as well as to the position of other robots, via "flocking" or other algorithms. In Kenneth Rinaldo and Mark Grossman's "The Flock," three large robot arms entwined with grapevines hung from the ceiling. The robot arms had sensors which tracked each other's and any visitor's position; they could respond by moving together in a pattern. The use of metal and natural materials suggests the status of "flocking" as both animal behavior and as algorithmically governed artificial life. The robots also "talked" together in indecipherable machine sounds, again suggesting autonomous lifeforms and independent agents capable of true interaction.

However, whatever the apparatus and the degree to which the visitor can intervene, the impression of interaction with machines actually consists of nothing more than machine feedback that simulates presence and agency of one kind or another. Which is to say that ultimately we are interacting with the "second selves" of every human who has contributed to the development and programming of the apparatus. Far from being posthuman, the capacities for communication and learning which have been displaced onto this machine and others should be

MEDIA ART AND VIRTUAL ENVIRONMENTS

Visitors to Perry Hoberman's "Faraday's Garden" (1993) can incidentally compose musique concrète and dance outdated appliances briefly to life by stepping on the right place in the mat that feeds each appliance the juice.

judged by the standards governing human-human interaction—is it reciprocal? Is it generous? Is it evocative?—but with one proviso: at least in the realm of art, we are dealing with a metaphor or a meta-interaction, if you will, not the thing itself.

Martin Spanjaard's "Adelbrecht" was a mumbling robotic ball and machine pest which could use its gyromotor to run back into anyone who tried to push it away. (In the artist's catalog description, the ball's behavior is charming.) While "Adelbrecht" met none of the standards of intersubjectivity—underlining that art can make any apparatus or mode into metacommentary—"he" does foreground the fictitious nature of "interaction" with machines; he can intrude and interrupt, but, like a psychotic personality, he is a "living" demonstration that in actuality knows nothing of us. Yet we can learn and enjoy "Adelbrecht" precisely because "he" is not a psychotic, but a robotic ball and a metaphor realized.

Luc Courchesne's "Family Portrait" offered another kind of symbolic exploration by allowing the visitor to reconstruct a network of virtual relations among nine people. Visitors could enter a space and see four of the nine people seem to hang in space where they might have

Cyberscapes, Control, and Transcendence

This installation view of Luc Courchesne's "Family Portrait" (1993) shows the apparatus
of four computer stations where each visitor responds to one of nine characters
respectively reflected on half-mirrored glass from a monitor hung above. While the
visitors are oriented away from each other, the spectral presences that hang in space
respond to one another as a constellation of intimate relations, more or less
talking through as well as with the visitors in between.

stood in life. These hypertext "portraits" were staged in a very effectively modified monitor-mouse apparatus: four monitors were hung
from the ceiling in a square and reflected in half-mirrored glass. To
"talk" to any one of the portraits, one would select one of two or more
options on a monitor in front of each image: one option usually consisted of a question virtually directed to the portrait; the other offered a
polite way of ending the "conversation." Continuing questioning simulated increasing levels of intimacy. However, any one portrait could
not only virtually respond to a visitor's question, but via well-aimed
"looks" left, right, or across the square, could virtually address another
portrait, more or less talking through the visitors in between.

The piece achieves a feeling of lifelikeness and richness in what Luc
Courchesne calls "a metaphor for an encounter" in a number of ways:
the greetings and parting exchanges built into the piece are polite
rituals and protocols that one does not usually owe to machines or
recordings. These portraits address us virtually as if present in our
physical space; but, they also behave autonomously because they have

a mutual history which supposedly began long before we came in. Furthermore, it continues without us even in our own physical presence. Why the apparent autonomy of virtual lives indeed has charm, here and elsewhere, is a matter for speculation. However, artists who foreground "interaction" and "life" as metaphors make the links and fissures between the material and the virtual perceptible rather than seamless. Technological control of the body and the landscape seems neither inevitable nor absolute.

Translating Culture between Two and Three Dimensions

So far at least, there is no direct translation or transparent membrane between the cultural forms of the mechanical age and the developing forms of the information age. So it is not as technically easy as one might think to simply transfer the immense cultural capital of image culture into virtual fields intact. What could mediate between the vista of a specific site, the representation of it as a framed landscape in two-dimensional, photographic (that is, analogical and indexical) realism and a three-dimensional, digitally produced, utterly symbolic virtual environment?

The primordial virtual world is an utterly empty display, unlike the physical world, which is always "full" and ready-made. So far at least, immersive virtual worlds are sparsely stocked with metaphors, now largely constituted from scratch with considerable graphic effort. Once these graphics are out of sight, it is easy to get lost in a void that is uniformly colored (usually black) and that wears infinity at its edges if not at a vanishing point. My first flight revealed "Virtual Seattle," like most other virtual environments, to be relatively void but for a crude symbolscape of geometric objects. I remember my panic at flying through and out the swimming pool–like image-space of Puget Sound and getting lost in utter emptiness. (I have also flown too far from the landing strip metaphor of a Wall Street stock market program and have fallen off the checkerboard world of "Dactyl Nightmare." The stock market program has an arrow function that points the way back to civilization.) What a comfort it was to find the traces of the human imagination in the spacescape near me again.

On the other hand, why are these cybertraces, the externalized imagination of electronic producers, filled with so little of our cultural legacy?[11] I am thinking of metaphorically and graphically impoverished architectural flythroughs or crude male-centered fantasies of pornotopia ("Virtual Valerie") or a pseudoprehistoric past wherein the only activity is relentless killing (for instance, the aforementioned "Dactyl Nightmare"). One task of art that commodity culture apparently eschews is to resituate the disengaged space of virtuality into a sociohistorical context. For instance, Jeffrey Shaw's interactive city installations, such as virtual New York or Amsterdam, are richly symbolic, suggesting how the built environment may be refigured in image-space as a kind of three-dimensional alphabet. Multiple and interlacing historical narratives are traced in a kind of writing motion over the display area via a bicycle interface, revealing streets as narratives in print.

One reason for the relative cultural emptiness of cyberspace might be that the record of the past *is* stored in two-dimensional print and images. An immersive culture that wishes to retain the past requires techniques and strategies for translating this legacy into three dimensions. Michael Naimark's demonstration tape "Panoramic and Moviemap Studies in Computer 3-Space" (1992) is a description of the process by which Naimark sought to meld photographic space and cyberspace. His videotaping forays produced three segments: a panorama of the Banff river valley, a depth or z-axis move through a recreational vehicle park, and a traveling shot of a Rocky Mountain vista from a moving car. Then, he selected specific frames from each field study and texture-mapped them over one of three different wireframe geometric shapes floating in a cybervoid. Despite being wrapped over sculptural shapes, the photos which compose the virtual world retain their two-dimensionality, appearing more as stacks or fields of photographs than as a convincing landscape. The results are paradoxical, in that the effect of this incongruent mixture is to undermine the illusion-producing capacity of both the two-dimensional photographic and the three-dimensional immersive modes of spatial representation. In effect, Naimark solved the problem of the flatness of photographs when introduced into a three-dimensional virtual world by underlining their two-dimensionality. (Compare the "graphication" effect described in chapter 3.)

For instance, the video panorama was taped by a stationary camera moving systematically like an apple peeler in a circular axis around the landscape, then texture-mapped over a stationary hollow sphere that the visitor to virtual space can navigate in and around. Seen from outside, the resulting landscape is like a design on a ball; from inside the sphere, it is a partially immersive virtual landscape—partial because it also conveys the sense of being a paste-up of flat photographs.

MEDIA ART AND VIRTUAL ENVIRONMENTS

Frames from "Field Recording Study #1" (1992) in Michael Naimark's "Panoramic and Moviemap Studies in Computer 3-Space" (1992), produced at the Banff Centre.

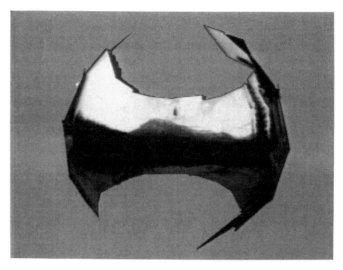

A panoramic video made of 360° rotations at different heights is recomposed out of individual frames and mapped over a wire-frame sphere.

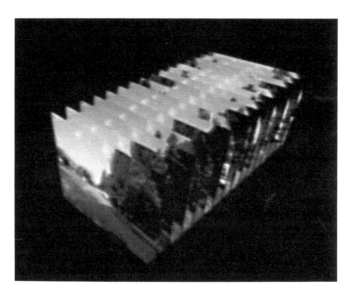

Individual video frames are digitized and arrayed like postcards on a skewer in order to simulate a z-axis move in depth.

The effect might be compared to one of David Hockney's photo collages, except that Hockney's pieces actually *are* a paste-up of photos spread over a flat surface.

The second field study of a z-axis move through a campsite is texture-mapped onto a stack of flat images lined up like sheets of photographic paper on a spike, or in Naimark's description, "an exploded deck of cards." Virtually "driving" through image after image in quick leaps and jerks is like a subjective view of a skewer assembling a shish kebab, breaking through card after card. (See chapter 3 on movement through stacked images as a transitional device on television.)

The final segment, a traveling shot out the window from an automobile driving screen right, produced a particularly confusing image for viewers of his video documentation, according to Naimark. The reason why is easy to understand: by laying his selected images end to end in cyberspace like a filmstrip, the "temporally undersampled" trees and other features on the landscape in the foreground pop up and disappear left and right in frame, effectively violating the rules of film continuity. Meanwhile, despite the fact that the foreground images and the vector of motion travel to the right, the image of the huge mountain range in the background remains relatively constant. Thus the image undermines the notion of a stable landscape over which one travels, not to mention the sense of traveling itself as covering ground. It is this study which suggests how paradoxical "travel" can be when movement that makes sense in physical landscape is translated into the disparate imaging technologies of video and the computer.

Toni Dove and Michael Mackenzie learned, while designing and producing the interactive virtual environment "Archeology of a Mother Tongue" in residency at the Banff Centre in 1993, that they required entirely different ways of editing narrative in space than the cinema. The virtual objects they created for the demands of real-time imaging were either wire-frames without texture maps or flat images that were animated to oscillate or vibrate in space. The landscape itself was continuous, without cuts or edits. It was the gaze of the visitor with a head-mounted display, scanning the landscape that selected what would be seen on the monitors in the helmet and projected on a screen for a larger public. Duration, or the pace of the narration of the story, was individual and variable, depending as it did on the curiosity of the visitor and his or her skill in releasing narration from objects in each of four different worlds. (For this reason, an experienced "driver" ran the piece in public exhibition. All narration was stored digitally and triggered by programmed cues.)

On the other hand, there is another editing problem that cinematic realism rarely faced—the passage between one virtual world and the next. It can take an instant, but it must nonetheless be symbolically marked and motivated. The figural conventions that ease the passages between virtual "worlds" have drawn on architectural conventions or the vortex. The solutions in "Archeology" are motivated by the narrative: we pass through a drain hole or vortex into the first world of dreams and, in the second passage, we are "flown" toward a "city" in wire-frame fuselage that is also an enormous ribcage. The port of immigration to the city is also a gate to the underworld that divides natives and strangers. The last passage is a blackout or simulated power failure of the machine that seems not only to maintain but to *be* the city. To push restart is to enter a different world. (As with a computer, there is short-term memory loss.)

At present, virtual environments are in the stage of aesthetic experimentation, in which solutions are found rather than rules obeyed. Virtual environments are produced like packages that are designed without knowing what they might hold on the inside. In a field where the lore of veterans is nonexistent and where conventions are invented ad hoc as one goes along, even the artists, as Toni Dove explained, could not be sure what to expect once the "machine" or environment they had spent months at the computer building was finished and they could step inside. Only after their piece was inaccessible to further tinkering and on display for a public could the artists assess how much of a difference it makes whether a visitor occupies the role of activator-driver or passenger, how much exposition was needed to make the piece gel, whether the variable order of segments within a narrative scene changes the story itself in any significant way, or what the appropriate pace is for the stories to unfold and how interactivity affects timing.[12] The massive computer power needed to drive the piece meant it was erected for two brief periods at Banff as full-fledged cyberspace. Like other virtual worlds, this piece exists largely as a memory, as a video documentation, and as information on disk.

The following is an exploration of the implications of movement through a landscape, once both landscape and movement through it are virtual. The section begins with a discussion of the meaning of travel and tourism as a cultural practice and then turns to three specific examples of virtual voyaging.

While our sense of the natural world has always been encumbered by our sense of human culture and history, there was a time, not long ago, when you get out of your car at a curve on a scenic road and admire the view on something resembling its own terms.

—Wilson[13]

CYBERSCAPES AND TRAVEL: FROM TOURISM TO ART

According to Alexander Wilson, to view the natural landscape in the mid-twentieth century was to see a world largely blanketed over with information. Dean MacCannell's *The Tourist* provides an explanation of how such information in the form of a "marker" or label produces a "sight."[14] In such a way, the picture postcard and its legend become not so much a way of framing and capturing the natural world as a way of producing an image and a set of connotations, which the natural world, when visited, is expected to respectively resemble and evoke. That is, the landscape is no longer blanketed with signs; even naked before the eye it virtually is a sign.

The social practice of travel is driven by romantic desire for transformative symbolic experience in an *other* place, preferably a paradise, from which one could return renewed. Tourism converted secular pilgrimage into a commodity marketed in two-dimensional images; mass tourism reconstituted the three-dimensional landscape itself into a "technical object under human control."[15] The dynamic through which a natural site becomes a theme park of its own ideal image can eventually destroy the attractiveness and aura of authenticity which first drew crowds to it. Put most drastically (and possibly controversially), the touristic sight invites the look that kills, albeit slowly, in a deadly spiral of development in which the virtual has been implicated from the start.

Travel through a physical landscape was once both a practice and a metaphor that served to constitute the self: "Subjective identities themselves were grounded in narrational journeys" (Pinney 422). To traverse the actual referent of the picture in physical space adds, according to Homi Bhabha, "that dimension of depth that provides the language of identity with its sense of 'reality'; a measure of the 'me' which emerges from the acknowledgement of my inwardness, the depth of my character" (6).[16] Then we might say that surrogate travel through a virtual environment simply realizes virtually what is already constituted as the goal of the journey—being there *in* the image. It is but one step more in this logic for the sight itself to become a landscape composed entirely of information, a virtual graphic realm sustained by computer into which the visitor enters virtually.

However, according to Christopher Pinney, "the phantom worlds and pseudo worlds of cyberspace could also destroy (have also destroyed) the quiet inner narrative on which the nineteenth and twentieth century self was built" (Pinney 423). How can just one story "quietly" unfold in the linear and coherent way stories were supposed to once the reader or viewer becomes a *visitor* immersed in virtual reality? He speculates that the identity of a subject with a mobile perspective and multiple narrative paths would splinter and fall apart (422). Perhaps the opposite is true—the multiple aspects of person in cyberspace and "agency" of the landscape, like the "second self" in the computer, are part of a long-term cultural trend (of which television has been the greatest exponent until now) in which the task of enculturation that produces subjects out of human beings has been delegated to machines. Then there may be more of a continuity between the experience of the physical, the electronic, and the virtual environment than the fragmentation thesis accounts for, and the many aspects of person available to the user of a virtual environment offer more possibilities for subjective integration and control, not less. The cybersubject, no longer socially determined by a physical appearance, is free to proliferate personalities—but is still linked for now to one physical living body. Yet what subjectivity will become in information societies is still an open question and an issue for struggle. Meanwhile, that material body, tethered to a tracking device, much like Ulysses bound to the mast, hears the Sirens "inside" on display, while the oarsmen made deaf to their song continue rowing.

Surrogate travel may—as some people fantasize—replace tourism in physical space entirely. (Consider how the fragile cave paintings of Lascaux have been put off limits in favor of their simulation.) However, it is more likely that cultural symbols (be they of self or other) will continue to be expressed across a continuum of cyberized "reality"— theme parks, two-dimensional images, and virtual landscapes. Could a reflection on tourism be staged without reinstigating its self-destructive process or enticing more footfalls onto fragile paths? The problem for the artist is the perennial one of how to employ the very mechanisms and apparatuses of vision that support the practice on which one wishes to reflect.

The Virtualized Landscape: "See Banff!"

Michael Naimark has long been involved in projects for surrogate travel using "Realspace Imaging" and "moviemaps" of photographic images of a particular landscape: an interface and a screen or monitor allow one to see, for instance, Aspen by "car" (with the Architecture Machine Group, MIT, 1978–80), San Francisco Bay by "air" (with the San Francisco Exploratorium, 1987), or Karlsruhe by "tram" (with the Zentrum für Kunst und Medientechnologie Karlsruhe, 1990–91). However, the surrogate "driver" or "pilot" is capable of moving at far faster speed and backward as easily as forward on a grid of predetermined paths—what Naimark calls "browsing."

Michael Naimark's kinetoscope simulation depicting the touristic destinations around Banff began with the aforementioned field studies. Then fifteen stereoscopic sequences (plus credits) of virtual journeys in the Canadian Rockies were selected from over one hundred for display through a peephole for one individual viewer. However, "See Banff!" is not a nostalgic reproduction or scenic postcards come to life, but a condensation of features from different eras in the history of tourism as it has been shaped by the photographic image—the kinetoscope, the stereoscope, the movies, and now surrogate travel or "Realspace Imaging" in a virtual environment. The vistas are at once hyperreal in depth and temporally unreal in a simulation of the flicker of animation—as noted earlier in the discussion of opalescence. "See Banff!" does not produce a smooth and coherent world, but rather a flipbook with bits of virtual space in between. The most typical move in the series is the z-axis or motion in depth into the image along a trail, for instance, to Johnston Falls. Oddly enough and by Naimark's choice, the z-axis reveals very little of the landscape and much more of the trail and the traffic on it. The viewer is implicated in the space of the virtual image not only through stereoscopic perspective and as voyeur or nature junkie, peeping at postcards of the Canadian Rockies, but also as a surrogate traveler *in* the image, cranking the pace of his or her own motion faster or slower, backward or forward at will down an obligatory trail hardwired not only into Naimark's program, but into the earth. Repeating a sequence over and over or moving the crank back and forth produces rapid and surreal appearances and disappearances of swarms of tourists in Brownian motion: it does not support a sense of subjective experience, rather it conveys the effect of an anonymous mass in a ritual with strict itineraries. Even the spectacular vista of Lake

MEDIA ART AND VIRTUAL ENVIRONMENTS

Tourists on Athabasca Glacier in one frame of the stereoscopic image series "Field Recording Study #3: See Banff!" produced with the Banff Centre and Interval Research (1993). By courtesy of Michael Naimark.

Louise must be glimpsed through the real subject of the segment—the ordinarily taboo image of the displaced urban bustle of tourists in the picture, which is no longer pure and "just for me" and all the less picturesque or sublime therefore. The cumulative effect of innumerable shades of tourists past haunting the trails and icefields in virtual space and time is discomfiting; subjectively experienced unreal time reveals a supraindividual process that threatens the picture postcard perfection one has come to see.

The series reflects on the tourist's look itself as a trajectory and a subject position that we all occupy at some time or another, by repressing the touristic sight as much as possible from view. We are invited not to look at the "real" landscape, with all the cultural baggage that implies, but to see seeing as a historical and social practice figured in a virtual landscape. In the process, we become aware of how coarsely the material world is sifted through "realspace" imaging technology, how ill-fitting the landscape is that different historical imaging apparatuses piece together, and how the underworld leaks through.

The Virtual City: "Archeology of a Mother Tongue"

The narrative lure of "Archeology of a Mother Tongue" that moves characters and the driver/navigator/viewer through a series of four worlds is the cause of death of a girl in an unnamed foreign "city" that seems to be a condensation of Third-World geographic locations. The opening premise of the piece is that a coroner is flying to this foreign city in order to examine the child's body. Yet this is not a murder mystery nor is the enigma it poses to be answered by this one body—there are other bodies involved. This is rather a "posthuman" oedipal journey in which the question ultimately to be answered is not where do I, or more accurately, where does my body come from? (the enigma of sexual difference), but am I human or machine? And, am I alive or dead? (the uncanny question for the information age). Two different narratives are told by the voices of two persons or entities—a coroner (Toni Dove's voice) and a pathologist (Michael Mackenzie's) that evoke bodies as extensions of a virtual and material city.[17]

The entire passage from world to world begins to resemble a journey through a wire-frame city that is also a machine and an enormous body seen from inside. The virtual landscape as a shape-shifting entity gives animistic, folkloric, or poetic attributions of agency to the earth and to features of the landscape a virtual sphere of reference. We know the characters of the coroner and of the pathologist largely as voices expressing different aspects of personhood. The coroner speaks subjectively as "I," while the pathologist has a voice in tone like the graphic "computer readouts" we see on screen, as well as another that becomes progressively more personal. The identity of the huge wire-frame/skeletal form comes to absorb into these characters and into virtual landscape itself. Is that body/city/landscape living or dead? The fundamental situation is not unlike the underworld of *Neuromancer*. The last world reveals an enormous wire-frame skull—a death's head, as if the body traveled upward were Mantegna's "Dead Christ."

The narration is released in each world by touching virtual objects (for example, a "girl," a "violin") with a dataglove. The "driver" directs the point of view by means of a handheld tracking device housed in a plastic toy camera. In the screen-based version of the piece (as opposed to the head-mounted display for one individual), the audience is passive, along for the "ride," not sure how far the limited and operational visual point of view of the "driver" role reflects the coroner's or another character's vision. The piece, and perhaps "interactive narra-

Toni Dove and Michael Mackenzie's interactive narrative "Archeology of a Mother Tongue" (1993). Produced at the Banff Centre. Frame grabs by Toni Dove. By courtesy of Toni Dove.

Spectral girls haunt the wire-frame architecture of a virtual city modelled on Piranesi. When the "driver's" glove selects a girl, another unit of the first story-world unfolds.

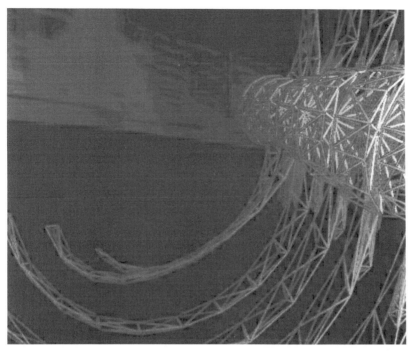

The wire-frame fuselage in which the coroner enters the city
is transformed into an immense rib cage.

The path of the coroner and the pathologist through the fantastic body
of the city culminates in a gigantic death's head.

tives" more generally, is unresolved as to whether it is offering the experience of a narrative or of the *act of narration* to the visitor.

The coroner's narrative concludes with a cognitive shift from alienation to a recognition of this enveloping machine/body/city as a kind of corporeal womb which produced her as an infant only to adopt her out as a body for sale. The foreigner is actually coming home to a dangerous, if no longer alien place, ripe for rebirth. The final narration (on laser disk, as was the opening segment) also tells us that the pathologist (as evidenced by his unacceptable error level)—and thus perhaps the city/body/cyberspace itself—is not a machine, but human after all. This narrational journey is one of transformation of a relation to virtuality itself as something we might recognize from our prehistory and somewhere we might be at home. However, in the visual field, the skeleton of the virtual city remains fleshless and unredeemed, a dreamlike condensation in an aural envelope of voices.

Immersive Fantasy: "Osmose"

Char Davies describes the immersive virtual space "Osmose" (first exhibited at the Museum of Contemporary Art in Montreal, September 1995) as a spatiotemporal arena, wherein mental models or abstract constructs of the world can be given virtual embodiment and then kinesthetically (i.e., via motor perception) and synesthetically (i.e., via a mixture of visual, auditory, and motor perception) explored through full-body immersion and interaction. That means that visitors are "immersed" in symbols that we can experience corporally and possibly emotionally from inside. While most of the virtual environments I have experienced use the metaphor of flying to move the visitor through virtual and symbolic space, Davies uses the metaphor of deep-sea diving in which we move between worlds organized largely in terms of up and down. We also hear sounds derived from sampling a single male and female voice. As we float through the dozen virtual world-spaces in the piece, we have as much access to the interior of transparent objects as to their exterior surface. The visitor uses a head-mounted display with tiny monitors over the eyes to virtually enter inside the piece; the tracking device is a "motion capture vest with a balance sensor," which is to say, the way to move up is to expand the chest with deep breathing; to go down, one contracts the chest circumference by breathing out. Davies herself and many visitors to the piece have had profound expe-

Char Davies, "Osmose" (1995). A view of the pond from below, looking at the tree.
Programmer: John Harrison. By courtesy of Char Davies/Softimage.

riences related to the worlds themselves and the use of breath and balance to explore them.

I, however, experienced several of the worlds in the piece as an occasion for panic. Like many asthmatics, being underwater makes me deeply and instantly afraid. Evidently, even when the water is symbolic, I experience it viscerally as water and as everything smothering that water means to me (see also Rutledge). Consider also that I have a math phobia and that one of the worlds in the piece consisted of machine language which scrolled upward faster than I could escape it by breathing in more and more. As I got more and more panicky, the programmer John Harrison revealed that the way out of machine language world was to surrender and sink into it. Despite my own reaction, I could understand the intention of the piece, to "encourage the immersant to effectively 'let go'" in a meditative experience that reconnects the body and the world. The piece also underlines that we can and do experience symbols viscerally and emotionally and that these symbols do not have just one meaning, but many potential and experientially determined ones.

If empathy (or "feeling as") is the capacity to visualize and experience the world from the position of the other, to walk in another's shoes, so to speak, then the distinguishing characteristic of a virtual environment—that you as a visitor experience an artificial world from inside—can function quite literally as an invitation to empathize, to see a world from another position and with other eyes.

I see a growing concern with the nurture of artificial life as a kind of exercise in the practice and refinement of empathy. Take Christa Sommerer and Laurent Mignonneau's "Interactive Plant Growing" (1992), in which visitors "grow" an artificial plant world together, through nearing or touching four different biological plants by hand. All the visitors influence the piece together, though one of them can "kill" off all the plants in a mutually created world. Thus, interaction with artificial life is a communal responsibility, but it is also a pleasure, since the results of group decisions are immediately to be seen in rewardingly beautiful graphic form. (Ken Goldberg's "Telematic Garden" exhibited at the 1995 Interactive Media Festival works through similar issues using a physical garden that is watered and planted via on-line instructions from the public.) Here, as in other examples of communal nurturance of organic or artificial life, the success or failure of a visitor's interaction becomes a metaphor for the human relation to a fragile biosphere as well as a metaphor for sociality itself. In the artists' "Phototropy" (1995), using a flashlight on a screen brings virtual insects to life. Enough light allows the insects to fly into the beam, flourish and reproduce, but too much light causes them to burn and die. The visitor must decide how many insects to bring to life and learn to temper the light they receive with infinite care. This piece also teaches us to value darkness: turning off the light is not necessarily an evil act of insect genocide, nor does it mean to create a void, since darkness holds the potential for regeneration and metamorphosis. So long as it is understood as metaphor, artificial life displaces these events into self-evolving patterns or "emergent social behavior" which compresses generations of time into minutes, enriching our impoverished social imagination in the process.

The nature of the virtual environment as a symbolic field or externalized imagination suggests why action within it is neither free nor lacking in emotional and social consequences. Nor is one so very or completely disembodied in a fully immersive virtual world as is commonly believed: awash in what amounts to a meaning system, at minimum one retains a felt body which is mapped quite differently than the seen body—as Catherine Richards's video "Spectral Bodies" demonstrates. The spectral body in the virtual realm is kinesthetically linked as well to the felt body. That is why a virtual persona can be violated and why there is a relation between cyberdeath and psychic annihilation (see Dibbell 36–42 and Rheingold 32–37). Thus, the liminal and virtual realm in the machine is far from immune from moral issues or the ultimate questions of life and death. And, finally, although a virtual environment is an invention and a simulation that is prepared in advance, we (and even its designers) cannot fully anticipate what it means to experience that realm until we are "inside."

Notes

1. Virtualities

1. The imaginary (prevalence of the relation to the image of the counterpart), the symbolic (structured like a language), and the real (a third but inaccessible order) are essential orders of the psychoanalytic field, as developed in the work of Jacques Lacan.

2. Simulation is pejoratively identified with the loss of referentiality by Jean Baudrillard. Here, simulation and referentiality are neutral terms and occupy different planes of discourse, one oriented on the speaking situation, the other on the world evoked by the utterance. The epochal cultural change that Baudrillard has observed, analyzed, and addressed in many different texts, is, differently interpreted, also the subject of *Virtualities*.

3. To paraphrase John Perry Barlow of the hacker-oriented activist group, the Electronic Frontier Foundation.

4. For popular as opposed to scientific definitions of virtual reality and other technical terms, see Rucker, Sirius, and Mu. Computers are the main source of virtual realities in the strictest sense. See Binkley. "The Virtual Environment Workstation" developed at the NASA Ames Research Center is an example of an utterly virtual world. A similar wide-angle stereoscopic display was marketed as the "eye phone" and dataglove by VPL Research. See also Cornwell.

5. According to Gamson, unlike our family, friends, and neighbors, celebrities "literally have no power of any kind over audiences. . . . What matters to celebrity watching play is that celebrities do not matter." Games with celebrity are "deep play," which mediates between the hierarchy of personal distinction and democratic equality. Freedom to gossip and play with the lives of others is possible precisely because the celebrities are not entirely "real" and the discourse about them is trivial and without consequence (184). It disturbs Gamson that "rationalized celebrity culture" has spread into the news and politics, as these are arenas that do matter and in which discourse can effect a "lived difference." What amounts to the semifictionalization of discourse as spectacle "signals a severe alienation from the democratic process that is very difficult to change" (193).

6. Gérard Genette has applied Benveniste's distinction between story and discourse to genre theory in "Boundaries of the Narrative," and Roland Barthes

has applied the model in "Historical Discourse." See Chatman on this distinction in print fiction and film. Barthes points out that the historical utterance is actually a "false performative"; that is, it calls forth into existence rather than represents.

7. Consider the perverse situation of CNN reporters in the Al-Rashid Hotel during the initial bombing of Baghdad, January 16, 1991. Despite the historical comparisons to Edward R. Murrow's radio reports from the midst of the London blitz, the first twenty-four-hour-a-day "live" report of the war on CNN was a truly novel situation. Hotel reporting of the police action in Panama might be more apropos as comparison, but even here there was a new wrinkle—the hotel was in enemy territority under bombardment, a strange loop, if not a short circuit in the news. Just by reporting where they estimated the bombs to have struck, the CNN reporters at the El-Rashid were providing real-time intelligence information to bombing strategists.

8. For instance, Tom Ray's "network-wide biodiversity reserve for digital organisms," one of the works featured at the Interactive Media Festival, June 4–7, 1995, in Los Angeles, was inspired by the disappearing rain forests and the desire to understand the generation of diversity in the Cambrian era. Ray has enlisted CPU cycles or computer-processing units at rest from other tasks to explore complexity and diversity evolving over countless generations. It should be emphasized that artificial life as a critical tool depends on treating it as a metaphor. For an introduction to the tenets of artificial life research, see Stephen Levy. For a survey of the science of artificial life or theoretical biology, see Emmeche. Hayles (1996) critiques the equation that researchers have made between the models or simulations of artificial life and life itself.

9. Examples and biting criticism of Gulf War graphics and symbols can be found in the "Designing War" chapter of John R. MacArthur's *Second Front: Censorship and Propaganda in the Gulf War*.

10. O. B. Hardison, Jr. on Myron Krueger: "Man is 'acquiring powers once reserved for the gods' and finds himself 'not the final goal of evolution but its conscious agent'. Krueger's 'conscious environments' are a metaphor for the fact that there is no longer anything than can rationally be called 'natural reality'. Nature has disappeared. What remains is reality created or structured consciously by man for human purposes" (228–29). Krueger's own "artificial reality" apparatus does not, however, cover the eye, unlike virtual reality. The American military arsenal offers another instance of total occlusion: "Simnet places tank crews in exact simulations of an M-1 tank. The tank can sink in the mud, fire shells, and be hit. In the latter case, there is a powerful crashing sound and the 'windows' that provide video simulations of the outside world go blank. Thomas Furness III, a designer of simulations systems, has been working since 1982 to create a 'Super Cockpit' for the F-16 in which the pilot will have the option of blanking out the real world and relying entirely on images supplied by a 'virtual world generator'" (226).

11. For example, the anti-Scud defense of Saudi Arabia and Israel was conducted globally by triangulating Defense Support Program satellites in geosynchronous orbit to cue Patriots to the trajectory of Scud launches. Then, the Saudis had first consented to American (and Western/Arab) multinational occupation after the invasion of Kuwait, persuaded by overhead satellite pho-

tos of the Iraqi army poised "like a sword ready to strike at the Saudi kingdom" (Woodward).

12. "Today it is already possible via satellite to determine what a man on the streets of Baghdad is reading in his newspaper. It will soon be possible to beam through the clouds and then the houses that receive reflections, and transfer them into images. For greater vividness the satellite perspective will be translated into that of a young boy who is cleaning the man's shoes while he reads his newspaper on the Baghdad streets" (Farocki 77).

13. There was one body that did appear on television at the end of the Gulf War that has since refused to go away—the body viciously beaten by four Los Angeles police officers on March 3, 1991. The video of the beating of Rodney King provided the body in contact with suffering and the possibility of death that was largely missing from the image of the war itself (see Doane 222–39). The King video was shown, obsessively, night after night, at the flimsiest provocation during the first war to be conducted and presented by digital graphic visualization systems—a war reportedly conducted with surgical precision, to excise evil without the usual consequences of human suffering and death. To show such violence on the actual enemy was taboo, yet the referential lure is something that our presentations evidently cannot do without.

14. The man Scott Fisher imagines in the year 2001 composing a model for a new pharmaceutical in virtual space seen from outside, is crawling on all fours, as if "miming a wrestling match with himself, or recapitulating his infancy" (423–24).

2. The News as Performance

1. Max Weber developed this religious concept for sociology. Richard Dyer, in his section on "charisma" in *Stars*, discusses Weber's concept of charisma as one means of legitimation of political order (34–37).

2. "You know it's Tom, Dan, and Peter. . . . Sometimes I think they're all the same guy. They must move from studio to studio." Reese Schoenfeld, speaking on PBS in 1984.

3. Beyond literally upstaging the news anchor, the East Coast feed of the ACT UP protest in front of the CBS news set had a visually demystifying effect of making the space of the set itself seem shallow and artificial. The event is reported in Hall and elsewhere.

4. Bush's words include: "None of this is what we wish to think of as American. It is as if we were looking in a mirror that distorted our better selves and turned us ugly. We cannot let that happen. We cannot do that to ourselves. We've seen images in the last 48 hours that we will never forget. Some were horrifying almost beyond belief."

5. Hallin finds that journalism's responsibility as "the major institution outside of the state which performs the function of providing political interpretation and critique" accounts for its conventions of representation, including a greater tendency to frame and interpret, the use of narrative structures, and extensive use of visual images and their integration into the semantic structure of the story (124–25).

6. There are at least three established formats for television talk—night, day, and the political or public service interview or roundtable—that are inflected in myriad ways. For a description of the classic "Tonight" show format with Johnny Carson see Morse, "Talk, Talk, Talk."

7. The best-known instances include the shooting to death of the "blunt" talk radio host Alan Berg at the curb of his Denver home in 1984, the breaking of Geraldo's nose on his television show in 1988, and the murder of Scott Amedure three days after the disclosure of his secret love on the March 6, 1995, taping of *Jenny Jones* by Jonathan T. Schmitz, the "humiliated" object of his affection. See Freeman.

8. "While there was a strong sense that the Soviet Union had probably lost the cold war, few [of the American public interviewed] were willing to say the United States had won." In a series of interviews with the public, the opinion, "We're just not a superpower anymore," uncovered apprehension "as if the fading of the Communist threat only illuminated other perils, especially the specter of sharpened economic competition with the Germans and the Japanese" (Schmidt 1).

9. Du Brow's critique of television news finds it good on the breaking story, but "increasingly shallow and trivial . . . combining to create an audience that is turned off by lengthy discussion and depth," and conditioned by "the new priorities of TV news—drama, extreme brevity, instant gratification, anything to prevent the viewer from zapping." Another critic, Michael Oreskes, wrote:

> Television was originally viewed as a democratizing force. It did help break down party machines and let candidates speak directly to the electorate. Now another result is becoming clear. . . . As America's democratic visions and values seem to triumph around the world, an unhappy consensus has emerged at home that domestic politics has become so shallow, mean and even meaningless that it is failing to produce the ideas and leadership needed to guide the United States in a rapidly changing world. . . . Instead of responding to changes in the world, the officials elected to lead the nation say they live each day in fear of the four horsemen of modern politics: televised attacks by their opponents, intense personal scrutiny by the press, cynicism on the part of the public and the need to raise huge sums to buy television time to combat the attacks, scrutiny and cynicism. (Oreskes, "America's" 1, 16)

See also Oreskes, "Political" on "the swamp of photo opportunities and sound bites."

On the other hand, Christopher S. Wren's book *The End of the Line,* among others, stresses the subversion of Eastern regimes by the technological revolution in the West, and "the photocopier, videocassette recorder, computer, and satellite dish."

10. Elihu Katz and Daniel Dayan see live media events on television as symbolic performances designed to celebrate the common identity of the audience. While disparaged as "pseudo-events" in Daniel Boorstein's *The Image: A*

Guide to Pseudo-Events in America, the raison d'être of televised ceremonial occasions is to issue declaratives bringing forth alliances, proclamations of faith, and statements of conviction sanctioned by social position. Performative speech as a form of action that brings forth new conditions in the world can and does take place without television; however, its power to bring forth and celebrate the common identity of the audience can be effectively multiplied into the millions by means of spectacle masquerading as participation. Furthermore, the institution of television itself seems to supply the legitimacy that performative speech acts, according to J. L. Austin, require. Television seen as a discourse is not a medium or a message, but is there in and of itself to constitute or more often to ratify a particular kind of reality.

11. Since every conjuncture resulting in social change is overdetermined, all three are appropriate at different times, in relation to different protagonists.

12. Louis Marin describes the historical development of the relation of spectacle and power. As for opulent privacy exposed, in Noriega's case some of the incriminating or humiliating leavings were apparently planted, the revolution was an invasion, and the palace a more modest dwelling.

13. Paul Willemen's concept of the "fourth look," the outside gaze that can bring shame and humiliation to a voyeur, suggests that television often plays this role, especially in the creation of international opinion. Televisual events suggest that the power of the gaze is far more unstable and reversible than in Mulvey's model of gender in film narrative and spectacle.

14. "Indeed, it was a Yugoslav report that 4,000 people had been killed in a massacre Dec. 17 in Timisoara that touched off the Romanian revolution. That death toll probably was inflated by 1,000 percent, but the fact that it was picked up by foreign stations and broadcast back into Romania was enough to light the fire" (Longworth A12). Robert Cullen, in "Report from Romania," lays more emphasis on the Hungarian program, "Panorama," as the way in which the Rev. Laszlo Tokes's plight in Timisoara became known even in Timisoara itself (94).

15. The property of televisual being-in-the-world consists of an interrelation between the television screen and "real" space that is rarely one of mutual confirmation, or a double effect. This doubling or coming together of two parallel worlds, in which television reality is validated in real space and vice versa, has been described in other situations as bringing a shock of recognition to the viewer / agent. See Rath 199.

16. Though Elena Ceauşescu was very briefly demonized on U.S. television as another Imelda Marcos (CBS News, 11 Jan. 1990).

17. Gaps in the original version screened on Romanian TV in December edited out the other visible parties in the trial, and the gaps were covered by holding still images of the Ceauşescus over the continuing sound track of the interrogation. The missing footage was apparently restored by French broadcasters TF-1 and A-2 and aired the last week of April 1990. The circumstances remained "as clear as mud" (*Variety* 2 May 1990: 293, 304) as to whether the Ceauşescus were executed by firing squad or summarily shot hours before the pictures in question were shot.

18. "At some lost moment in our history, journalism became identified with, defined by, breaking news, the news flash, the news bulletin. When that hap-

pened, our understanding of journalism as a democratic social practice was impossibly narrowed and our habits, of reading, of attention, of interpretation were impaired. Journalists came to think of themselves as being in the news business, where their greatest achievements were defined as being first rather than best, with uncovering the unknown rather than clarifying and interpreting the known" (James W. Carey 195).

19. CSPAN is a cable channel that transmits speeches largely from legislative bodies, now including British Parliament, and free speech from the public via telephone. A use in crisis of duration on the networks would be Senate hearings, such as the Army-McCarthy hearings, Watergate, the Bork nomination to the Supreme Court, and Iran-Contra hearings, forums that notably brought down McCarthy, Nixon, and Bork, and made a hero of Oliver North. While the hearings occurred at significant junctures in the creation and maintenance of faith in national leaders, I would argue that televising these hearings in total allowed a play of discourse with unforeseeable consequences to take its course. In other words, discourse unfolding in duration in the validating institution of television acts as a kind of fate, distributing not so much justice as popularity and belief.

20. This masked discourse also marked reports on the June violence, after the evacuation of the main square, when Romanians refused to be seen on camera and reporters spoke for them. One miner could be seen blocking off the television lens with his hand in WNN coverage that appeared on all networks and CNN, comparable to segregationist hands that blocked the camera lens during the civil rights movement in the early 1960s in the U.S.

21. A study by the Center for Media and Public Affairs concluded: "The birth of reforms and new freedoms for Eastern Europe might be assumed to have a positive effect on all involved. However, *television news coverage featured mostly negative assessments of the effect the region's reforms will have on both the Western Allies and the Soviet Union.* Out of 16 sources who assessed the economic, political and military effects on either the East or the West, only one was positive. *No sources assessed the effects on the West as positive, while all stressed the downside* [i.e., unemployment in the U.S., fodder for hardliners in the Soviet Union]." (Emphasis in the original; Center)

22. The lead story on ABC News of December 22 was a remarkably thorough report in headlines in four minutes and twenty seconds on fighting in Romania (with a three-minute wrap-up on Romania and Panama), noting the collusion of Western governments with a showpiece regime that had paid off its foreign debt. Thereafter, the corruption theme prevailed, suggesting that prior symbols of purity, like sport and childhood, not to mention spunky rebellion against the Evil Empire, had unexpectedly been despoiled.

23. While it has since proved to have had greater consequences in civilian bloodshed, in comparison, the contemporaneous U.S. invasion of Panama produced largely official U.S. government pictures and reporters doing standups from hotel balconies, relieved only at times on CNN by camcorder battle close-ups of unknown provenance. American soldiers have since been shown to have died largely under "friendly fire."

24. Tjebbe van Tijen's contribution to the conference on the Romanian Revolution in 1990 in Budapest, "Projecting the Television Image Back in Time—an

Iconographic Study of Three Centuries of Revolutionary Movements," suggests the main features of this revolutionary narrative. Jeffrey Shaw's interactive sculpture "Revolution," in the shape of a hand-turned mill grinding out historical images, was a collaboration with van Tijen.

25. According to Mary Ann Doane, catastrophe coverage enjoys the normal attributes of TV: immediacy, urgency, presence, discontinuity, the instantaneous and the forgettable: "The death associated with catastrophe insures that television is felt as an immediate collision with the real in all its intractability—bodies in crisis, technology gone awry. Televisual catastrophe is thus characterized by everything it is said not to be—it is expected, predictable, its presence crucial to television's operation" (238).

26. See Howard Rosenberg on "the process" as the news story in Gulf War reporting (57–59); see also Mimi White, who links "the process" to the significance of the effort to maintain signal.

27. The unofficial VHS format camcorders in question were not amateur, but rather the private tools of professionals from film and television studios for making money on the side. The documentarists selected material on the first five days of the revolution from December 21, 1989, choosing from about 120 hours of live coverage archived in the Culture Ministry of Romania (see Lovink 59–60). The untransmitted footage of Ceauşescu's failed media event was included in this documentary.

28. The fundamental analysis of such tactics as news can be found in Barthes's *Mythologies* in the section on "Myth Today" under "balance" and "neither-nor-ism."

29. Compare Newcomb and Hirsch.

30. For a discussion of the history and theoretical ramifications of two-way and interactive television, see Allen; Carey and O'Hara; and Tafler.

31. New media artists and curators have also made this historical connection. The electronic art on exhibition in conjunction with the International Symposium of Electronic Art in Helsinki 1994, curated by Erkki Huhtamo and others, emphasized the precinematic connection in pieces by Rebecca Cummings, Lynn Hershman, Toshio Iwai, Paul de Marinis, and Michael Naimark.

3. Television Graphics and the Virtual Body

1. Logo or logotype is used specifically as a type of corporate symbol while tacitly playing upon the biblical connotations of *Logos*. "The word" is used in the widest possible sense to refer beyond the linguistic system to the symbolic system. Both *Logos* and "the word" are performatives, that is, they bring the world or worlds into existence. "Graphics" is often used here in an expanded sense that includes pictographs and other symbols as well as letters and numbers. According to Philip Meggs, graphic design has long ceased to refer to typography and printing alone and now includes visual communication of all types. Because its raison d'être is display, graphic design is an intrinsically hybrid sphere in which words and symbols are also images.

2. John Caldwell's "televisuality" addresses excessive stylization of the 1980s in mainstream television as an industrial response to the challenge of

cable and camcorder that appropriated what were once avant-garde stylistic techniques—not as a protocyberspace. His many specific examples offer an interesting comparison and contrast of how a common concern with aesthetics and cultural change can be focused quite differently regarding the scale of the historical trend addressed and the locus of close analysis, thus leading to different but not necessarily contradictory interpretations and conclusions.

3. Douglas Merritt offers a practical categorization of television graphics by dividing them into the following: titles and end credits, graphics for program content, on-screen promotional material, station or network identity, and graphic props for set dressings. See also Merritt's *Graphic Design* 46–74.

4. Golden reportedly wanted to change the logo after a year of exposure, while Frank Stanton favored a strategy of familiarity through repetition.

5. Laughton also describes experimentation with 3-D letters and cleverly lit mobiles. There was also an abundance of three-dimensional letter forms before the development of a "universal tv graphics style" (6, 14).

In examples of nineteenth- and early-twentieth-century display graphics one can find many of the features—other than motion—associated with the depiction of bodies in space: three-dimensional letter shapes, the use of light sources and drop shadows, as well as instances in which the picture plane, graphic objects, and the point-of-view of the observer are at oblique angles from each other.

6. Merritt cites *Computer Basics* for the time frame of his periodization. The character generator or what the writer calls an "electronic typewriter" is described as newly in use in Hurrell 33. Merritt also notes that there was some use of electronics to generate test pattern signal, color bars, and Bernard Lodge's 1963 title for *Dr. Who* (9). The more versatile digital graphics generator improved on the character generator.

7. See Meggs 425. As this chronicler of graphic design explains, after World War II "large industrial and commercial organizations were becoming aware of the need to develop a corporate image and identity among various sectors of the public. Design was seen as a major way to shape a reputation for quality and reliability" (424–25). Saul Bass is the most celebrated designer of the period with his breakthrough 1955 film title sequence for *The Man with the Golden Arm*. See also Laughton 7; and Herdeg 144–47.

8. Dorfsman was still active in that position in the mid-1980s when I had the opportunity to meet with him briefly. See Hess and Muller's homage, *Dorfsman and CBS* (104–105), for photo sequences documenting several of Dorfsman's logo designs. Dorfsman wasn't confronted with the constraints of digital media when he designed his version of Didot. Matthew Carter, cofounder of the first electronic type-foundry in 1981, is extolled by John Plunkett for creating an electronically more legible version of the classic serif typeface, Waldbaum, on commission from the magazine *Wired* (Plunkett 126–27). The postmodern format of *Wired* makes legibility problematic—reminding one of the constant trade-off between attention-gathering display and the classic conventions which make type seem to disappear, transparently revealing signifieds—much like classic film editing makes the film disappear in favor of a story that seems to tell itself.

9. Harrison's contribution was unearthed by Woody Vasulka and Steina

Vasulka, artists who produced an exhibition of synthesizers and other electronic machines from the period of 1969–75 for ars electronica in Linz, 1992, along with an exhibition catalog. The section on "Lee Harrison," written by Jeff Schier, describes how the "bone generator," or Animac (hybrid graphic animation computer, 1962), "was converted into a transistorized version and numerous patents granted for its underlying processes. To commercialize on the scan processing experiments, the animated cute springy character transformed itself into a means for moving logos and high contrast graphics about the screen. . . . These modifications combined with its new commercial function, were named in 1969: SCANIMATE. The company went public and was renamed Computer Image Corporation" (95). According to Woody Vasulka, the heyday of Harrison's logo animation process was about 1971. While Harrison had no pretensions to art, features of his work anticipated the work of later artists, including Nam June Paik.

10. See Merritt 23–24 for a description of the TV Globo title. Pacific Data Images produced forty-five seconds of computer animation for it, which took twenty days to generate. See Baker 3–13. Baker briefly describes how largely defense-supported academic research into computer technology became the computer graphics industry of today. "While [the Lucasfilm Computer Development Division founded in 1978] began researching how to apply digital technology to filmmaking, the other studios began creating flying logos and broadcast graphics for TRW, Gillette, the National Football League and *The NBC Nightly News* and *ABC World News Tonight*" (6). Baker contrasts the successful small business of PDI, founded in 1980 by Carl Rosendahl, to the failure of Digital Production's supercomputer production strategy. PDI's four flying logo spots and show openings for TV Globo are cited as a landmark, along with animated openings for "Entertainment Tonight" 1983, the Winter Olympics 1984, and four years of ABC sports.

11. Goldberger even went on to blame television as a whole for an American cultural emphasis on appearances as opposed to essences. His condemnation continues: "Television is unjustly blamed for many wrongs in our culture, but this one [visual excess in recent opera, stage, and film design and architecture], I think, is deserved. It may be a long way from 'Wheel of Fortune' to the architecture of Helmut Jahn, but the connection is there. Eyes weaned on television are not accustomed to static things like traditional stage sets; they want movement, change and sparkle, which 'Starlight Express' gives them. They want things boiled down to their essence, made simple; they want, as I said before, logotypes, not essays" (34).

12. The glitter of the fetish is a symptom that draws "attention to a nodal point of vulnerability, whether within the psychic structure of an individual or the cultural structure of a social group," Mulvey reminds us in "Xala" (quoted in Shohat and Stam 275).

13. Pixar (*Toy Story*) will be joined by Pacific Data Images in the computer-graphic production of feature film.

14. Induction is, of course, a genre of liminality, a threshold state known to anthropologists from rites of passage, conveyed as movement. One might consider the initial letters in medieval manuscripts and early printed books as precursors of logo sequences if their function were held not only to be beauti-

ful, but to model induction into the text by making the letter into an image. This display invokes a psychic transformation of the text in the mind of the reader. That is, reading itself requires opaque symbols on the page to become transparent, revealing the image of a referent world to the mind.

Gary Hill's video "Incidence of Catastrophe" offers a striking visualization of the act of reading as a violent immersion in water, "a synesthesia of reading and dreamwork of the text." While both water and the heavens (associated with TV logos) can signify the mysterious other realm inside the text, they have quite different connotations, especially in relation to the body. "Literacy is seen as soul sickness; the final image of a drowned man before a wall of words expresses the abjection of the body in Western society's semantic culture" (*Electronic Arts Intermix* 109). The cosmos, on the other hand, seems not only to offer freedom from the earth but from the abject and the evolutionary stagnation of humanity.

15. Of course, all pixels are at the same zero-depth, on screen; even the most basic topological reality of in front and behind is completely fictional in television as opposed to say, painting, or even in terms of film emulsion.

16. The trip is a spoof of Jules Verne and thus willfully full of clichés and delightful absurdities. Times are based on the Kino Video release of *The Trip to the Moon* in *The Movies Begin 1*. In the z-axis move toward the moon (framed by clouds), at five seconds the moon is personified via lap dissolve with a human face. Méliès's narration adapted by Fabrice Zagury: "The gun is fired, and the shell disappears into space. The shell is coming closer every minute. The moon magnifies until finally it attains colossal proportions." There is a jump cut at thirteen seconds of the space vehicle stuck into the left side of the moon face. The space vehicle lands from frame left "on" the moon tableau at eighteen seconds. The same video compilation includes *Georgetown Loop* shown as a "phantom ride" in Hale's Tours cars, that is, as an extended z-axis subjective view of a train ride in the Colorado Rockies. Of course, phantom ride films are the nineteenth-century predecessor of contemporary ride film in virtual technology. See Huhtamo.

17. Howard Hughes is Virilio's example of the bedridden traveler in "The Third Window" 194, 196.

18. Use of zoom lenses became standard after the introduction of color television. See the lens explanation for constant zooming in Butler 222, though according to Barnouw 102, a Zoomar lens was used for the first time on television in a CBS telecast of a baseball game between the Brooklyn Dodgers and the Cincinnati Reds back in 1947. On a more subtle level, we can add zooming to the "endless, silken adjustments" that David Antin identified as television's "softening" conventions, by "a cameraman who is trained to act like an aircraft gunner . . . loosening up a bit here, tightening up there, gently panning and trucking in nearly imperceptible manner to keep the target on some imaginary pair of cross hairs" (160).

19. Direct cinema, for instance, made extended use of the investigative single camera to penetrate the backstage area of life, surprising private activities and conversations. This language of penetration and looting is borrowed from Melanie Klein's description of the boy child's presymbolic imagination, in which the space in question represents his mother's body (Klein 245). Klein is

perceptively applied in Skirrow 321–38, esp. 329. Some would speculate that the predominance of this trope of penetration in virtual reality has a relation to the military origin of virtual technologies.

20. Based on the remarks of Harry Marks at the 1985 Broadcast Industry Conference, San Francisco State University. Carl Rosendahl of Pacific Data Images was also a presenter. PDI and the few other high-end computer graphics firms deserve a more detailed treatment than is possible here.

The "Swiss look" refers to the designers who developed the "International Typographic Style" based on clarity and order (Meggs 379). Helvetica is the best-known expression of this ethos and used to identify the modern public sphere of transportation and government. See Savan.

21. In the famous tower sequence in Hitchcock's *Vertigo* (1958), Scotty's subjective point of view down into the tower is conveyed by similarly contradictory motions that convey a feeling of being pulled into a vortex of undecidable depth. Again, the background moves, suggesting a feeling not only of forces in contradiction but of unsteady ground. For comparison's sake, consider the symbol of a flat, spinning spiral that long signified a vortex, with connotations of a descent into madness or the unconscious in many films, from Ruttman's *Berlin—Symphony of a Great City* and Lang's *M*, to Duchamp's *Anemic Cinema*. The spiral also plays this role in Hitchcock's *Vertigo* along with the z-axis move. Today the spiral has camp connotations and it is hard to naturalize in the scene of a story-world, unlike the covert spiral of the tunnel.

22. A recent article by Janet Abrams on Trumbull's designs for Luxor Casino in Las Vegas and other "ridefilms" also explains that Trumbull's Slitscan method was inspired by descriptions of the experimental films of John Whitney (18). Merritt notes a BBC designer, Bernard Lodge, in connection with "streak-timing" and the "slit-scan" (10, 108–109). Trumbull describes various sources for the slit-scanned visuals: "patterns from Op Art books; strange grids out of *Scientific American* magazine; electron microscope photographs blown up high contrast and reversed; lots of things I drew. Very strange patterns, plus coloured gels, mounted together on a huge light table." Abrams notes the desire for spiritual transcendence implied by Trumbull's desire to produce altered states by means of particular experiences of motion (19).

23. The finished version of *powers of ten* of 1977 was $9\frac{1}{2}$". Snow's *Wavelength* explores, among other things, the hermeneutic effect of changing scale, especially as the camera arrives at its end point at the wall on the other side of the loft in an extreme close-up of a photograph of ocean waves. When the photo's frame is lost, the image pops into three dimensions and we see only disorienting waves, complementing the sound waves of white noise. A postmodern play on this zoom figure, *Cosmic Zoom*, was produced by the Pacific Data Images for their demonstration reel. In this comic piece, to be distinguished from the movie opener for Turner Broadcasting of the same name, a chain of goofy worlds, utterly hetereogeneous in composition and scale, is linked only by the apparent motion of the zoom.

24. The Luxor Pyramid in Las Vegas allows visitors to experience a simulation ride, visit a "live-seeming talk show" and then "a theatre of time" displaying four possible futures on a giant movie screen. See Baker 133–45. Note that virtual flight in a film such as the Lucas *Star Wars* trilogy allows the hero to

demonstrate mastery over technology, while the theme park ride allows the audience to enjoy the thrill of losing control on a journey with an inevitable happy end on solid ground.

25. Rivlin stresses the importance of flight simulation to the development of computer graphic conventions. What once required a camera and material objects, or techniques of digital film compositing and computer-controlled, rostrum cameras moving through miniature models could be entirely computer-generated. The flight simulator has a universe or database of objects in three dimensions; changes in shape and position of objects are computed by means of algorithms. The visual display of any particular flight path chosen by the "flier" could be computed in "real time," that is, immediately, in perspective on a monitor. The aspect of view was that of a pilot looking through an instrument panel and windshield.

26. Thus the "fourth wall" which normally governs and delimits fantasy is broken through by both the viewer's subjective move and the transitional figure of the host that can both occupy a fantasy world and engage in a discursive relation to the viewer—inviting us inside the playhouse too. Beyond his sweater and slippers ritual, "Mr. Roger's Neighborhood" uses a simple cut to transport the viewer into his model of a toy town, by showing the real-sized adults which people it, and which are, by the way, actually just inches tall on the screen no matter what size they are supposed to be in representation.

Another use of sinuous z-axis moves can be found in the dramatic semi-serial "ER." A direct-style handheld camera seems to make way for a gurney through the chaotic emergency halls and reception room. The gurney ride is accompanied by medical narration and usually culminates in an operation sequence that resembles a music video in its rhythmic use of voices and music. However, induction goes no further since the show is voyeuristic, not interactive, and it retains the fourth wall. We are not invited to view inside the bodies that are opened, for example. Breaking through the skin or violating the boundaries of the body is the fundamental assumption in the construction of virtual worlds, which are sometimes figured as journeys through the interior of a body.

27. The design for the Academy Awards Presentations in 1987, though not very well received, offered an inversion of back to front. The letters for "Hollywood" were shown from the back, anchored with barrels, reversed as if looking down on the city seen metaphorically from the point of view of the people backstage who make the movies.

28. One canonical filmic instance of such a pocket is the sequence in *Blade Runner* in which Decker analyzes replicant home snapshots on a monitor. As Decker uses a remote control to enlarge and enhance selected parts of a photo, he discovers the reflection on the edge of a convex mirror in the photo like the one in the famous 1434 Jan van Eyck painting *The Arnolfini Wedding*. A space beyond the edge of the photo is reflected, revealing a hidden member of a couple; unlike the secret of the murder gradually revealed through photographic enlargement in *Blowup*, the hidden pocket in this "photo" holds the secret of the replicant's capacity to love.

29. According to a statement at the Interactive Media Festival, Los Angeles, May 1995.

30. This piece is another statement of the tunnel-corridor trope that has also

had a history in fine art, where it has developed rich and largely dystopic connotations of constriction and disintegration, as opposed to its use in filmic narrative and theme park rides.

31. I mistook this move cutting through the body of a graphic form implicitly with the viewer's own body for a "slice" in my original paper. The slice is simply a way of cutting a layer off an extruded graphic form.

32. See Luce Irigaray: "Commodities among themselves are thus not equal, nor alike, nor different. They only become so when they are compared by and for man. The *prosopopoeia of the relation of commodities among themselves is a projection* through which producers-exchangers make them reenact before their eyes their operations of specula(riza)tion" (177, emphases in the original). While Irigaray is specifically concerned with the status of women as objects and not as subjects of exchange, her remarks on specularization are applicable here: the viewing subject and the network dance in their aerial relation as the two televisual commodities: airtime and audiences. The viewer on screen is a genderless vector, though otherwise, televisual subjectivity is quite gendered in its on-screen presenters and offscreen viewing practices. The logo symbol as a fetish is by definition an ambiguously gendered maternal phallus.

33. According to John Fiske, that equation is: "The Discourses of TV Quiz Shows or, School+Luck=Success+Sex." Note, however, that in this American game show, "school" plays a far lesser role in recognizing words in the equation than enculturation by television itself.

34. Zettl defines "graphication" as "the deliberate rendering of a television-mediated event as a two-dimensional, picture-like image that assumes the characteristics of a magazine illustration" (389). He interprets the function of this flattening in news reporting as a way of creating a distinction between first-order and second-order space on screen. First-order space (occupied by the host) allows for a higher degree of personification and verisimilitude than the second-order space of guests and news events (204–205).

35. The references of "magazine" include not only the journal in print, but the notion of storage displayed in layers and stacks, as well as the department store. The most familiar example of the magazine format would be the news-magazine show "60 Minutes." However, that show is a conservative example of the practice of segmentation, since each story remains an integral unit. The practice developed in print of segmenting the unit or journal issue and even the page into multiple topics, divided among various authors including editors and advertisers, and addressing multiple readerships. The magazine format on television can offer far more extreme examples of subdivision of segments into different spatial planes and of seriality or the distribution of narratives and discursive material over time.

36. Oddly enough, "graphic" is a word commonly applied to images of violence and sex that are evidently too candid, going beyond some tacit norm in showing gore and lust, thus foregrounding the image in a way that is all too stark and "real."

37. Morphing takes the place that juxtaposition and magical transformation play in print advertising in the transfer of value from an objective correlative to a product. See Williamson's *Decoding*.

4. An Ontology of Everyday Distraction

1. Rudolf Arnheim's mention of the "aeroplane" along with the "motor car" suggests another analog of television in the airport, in the experience of flying, and in the air transportation network (164, also quoted in Rath 199). This investigation is primarily concerned with consumption and everyday experience. Because flying is not as everyday an experience as driving and shopping and because it is imbricated directly in corporate as well as military and surveillance uses of images (for example, Paul Virilio's *War and Cinema*), the airplane as analog of television is left to exploration elsewhere.

The mass-circulation periodical which preceded television, the magazine in print, is another obvious and important analog of television. The magazine format and the "magazine concept" were discussed in the paper on which this chapter is based, given at the Conference on Television at the Center for Twentieth Century Studies in 1988.

2. Todd Gitlin's discussion of the iconographic function of the automobile in the program "Miami Vice" and its juxtaposed ads exemplifies this kind of analysis. For a general description of the iconography of automobiles, the title essay of Marshall McLuhan's *The Mechanical Bride* remains among the most insightful in making the link between technology and sexuality, the automobile and the female body as a love machine with replaceable parts. Stephen Bayley's *Sex, Drink, and Fast Cars* is a more recent monograph on the subject which notes pleasures of all kinds connected with the automobile, from kinesthetic/visceral and aesthetic to the sadomasochistic and death-driven. Bayley emphasizes the masculinity of that iconography. The difference between the two conceptions of automotive gender may be negotiated via the distinction between an interior womblike comfort zone versus the exterior, between driver and driven, the auto-woman as object of mastery and status display. Malls, on the other hand, are a predominantly female domain, as papers by Ann Friedberg and Meaghan Morris demonstrate and develop, while the gender of the television even in terms of the machine itself is divided in ways related to division of labor in the home and workforce.

3. The projects of synthesis drawn on here also have in common their work against the terror imposed by theory or intellectual discourse as well as the terror of the state. By returning to an earlier rich and highly validated cultural period at the cusp of the development of commodity culture, Benjamin's longterm view circumvents some of the immediate intellectual prejudices of his age which might foreclose the capacity to analyze cultural forms in the broadest sense. Bakhtin's appreciation of heterogeneity and the mixture of different voices in culture is designed to validate difference and make heard suppressed and otherwise voiceless parts of the social world. He developed the concept of the *chronotope* (see esp. the essay "Forms of Time and of the Chronotope in the Novel") in an age in which intellectuals sought tools for circumventing a closed discourse with concepts which reached into the manifestations of daily life in representation for reminders of what is not included in it. Compare other work which turns to the common, the everyday, and the "real" in the 1930s and 1940s in the context of economic failure and the exposure of discourses of the "word" as tools of institutional power. The relations of class to culture that Williams

studied formed the intellectual framework against and within which he articulated his ideas. Michel de Certeau's project of evasion and transformation of dominant and predetermined forms of everyday life can also be seen as an attempt to poke holes in a hermetic, structuralist notion of language as well as to find possibilities for liberation in the everyday.

4. E. Ann Kaplan cites Baudrillard's automobile metaphor in relation to a McLuhanian comparison of hot and cold media in *Rocking around the Clock* 50–51.

5. Brodsly is here writing of Los Angeles. The same dream is in force today, despite smog and congestion. "The sustaining dream of most Southern Californians is to not live in, or even near, a city. Just as when millions of young families flocked to the small farming town on the fringes of a burgeoning Los Angeles after World War II, today people are seeking economically and socially homogeneous suburban neighborhoods. In short, they're looking for a comfortable small-town atmosphere within commuting distance of a big city, an almost idyllic place to watch the kids, the grass, the real estate values and the equity grow while they pursue the American dream" (Sam Hall Kaplan 28). The author explains that today people who look at computer screens all day do not want tract housing, but rather accept higher density in order to attain a "village atmosphere." Despite what is sometimes considered an infrastructure nearing the point of defeat and random outbreaks of freeway frustration into violence, surveys of Los Angeles commuters suggest surprising equanimity and even satisfaction with their lot.

6. "On both sides of these passages, which obtain their light from above, there are arrayed the most elegant shops, so that such an arcade is a city, indeed a world, in miniature"—*Illustrated Paris Guide*, cited by Walter Benjamin in "Paris: Capital of the Nineteenth Century" (165).

7. Modeled directly on buildings in theme parks such as Disneyland, which was itself modeled on Disney's hometown of Marceline, Missouri. Kowinski 67, reviewing the work of Richard Francaviglia.

8. The typical layout of a mall includes two fully enclosed levels, a central court, and side courts, with one or more department stores or "anchors" at either end, and about one hundred shops, services, and eating places. The interior typically mixes elements associated with exterior and interior design. The Urban Land Institute defines a mall as "a group of architecturally unified commercial establishments built on a site which is planned, developed, owned and managed as an operating unit. . . . Design, temperature, lighting, merchandise, and events are all planned according to unifying principles" (see Kowinski 60).

9. The difference between the two is not merely size and ownership but every facet of public relations, marketing, and retailing (see DePalma 1).

10. Graham and Hurst note that corporate atriums are "parallel forms to the suburban shopping malls" which evidence the same tensions: "The urban corporate atrium is an attempt to smooth over contradictions between environmental decay and technological progress. As a miniutopian retreat from the stresses of city life it revokes the old notion of a 'garden' as an idealized landscape (the return to a preurban Eden), attempting to reconnect it to the idea of technology as an aid to man." The authors conclude that because these

atriums are largely separate from the fabric of the city, they represent exclusive enclaves which do not serve democratic values or the maintenance of community (71).

11. A recent application of the *chronotype* to film noir by Vivian Sobchack in "'Lounge Time'" suggests the importance of the semipublic *loungetime* as an idyllic contrast to the road for rootless postwar sexual-social relationships. Today's homeless and displaced people find public lounge space with difficulty, for it has been rededicated to driving and paying customers and linked to commercial sightlines.

12. For an interpretation of pleasure and the home reception of the news related to this very distancing from the world, see Stam 23–43.

13. Joshua Meyerowitz discusses displacement in the figurative sense as a loss of the sense of place in the social hierarchy in *No Sense of Place*. He argues that because televisual representation has provided a view of the "backstage" of adulthood and masculinity, as well as political power, the dominant positions in the social hierarchy have been essentially demystified for children, women, and the citizen. His observations about the "public-public" nature of events such as the press conference "that are carried beyond the time-space frame by electronic media, and therefore are accessible to almost anyone" (287), are plausible as applied to representation before it is mediated by the television apparatus. Here it is argued that the realm of controlled production and privatized reception as a framework within which such "public-publicness" is embedded has significant consequences not only for the representation itself but also for the metapsychology of its reception. Notions such as "nonspace" allow the imaginary aspects of Meyerowitz's unifying and leveling process to be conceptualized.

14. In many cities, the freeway once acted as a kind of container or beltway around the city, eventually to become surrounded by suburbia. However, wherever the freeway may be drawn on the map, it is not really "located" in the grid of streets over or under which it extends, nor is it accessible without specially designed transitions, which are, as Lynch pointed out, not always easy to locate from the street.

15. The effects of an imaginary unity are not restricted to "nationhood," but can extend to smaller and greater units. See, for instance, Rath on the counternational effect of the broadcast transmission area in German-speaking countries.

Andrew Ross describes how the weather acts as an ideology, a means of naturalizing the social, and a way of explaining "an otherwise apparently contingent world of events" ("Work" 123). Note that Ross is discussing the weather outside the venues discussed here—the world without comfort control beyond the window or glass. The "ideology" of the national weather inside is a more truly "lived relation" to the relations of production for most Americans. Meanwhile, the vagaries of traffic and the speed of travel to work, the beach, or the mall as impeded by accidents and contingencies, are most often considered and treated as if they were a force of nature like the weather "outside" of which Ross speaks.

16. Brian McHale provides an explanation of the *mise-en-abyme* and its impor-

tance for postmodernist literary fiction in expressions of ontological uncertainty (124–28).

17. The engaged utterance is a simulacrum of the situation of enunciation, that is, *discourse*. The disengaged utterance is story. Note that subject, space, and time can be engaged or disengaged separately rather than en masse.

18. "Flow" here is not the pure juxtaposition of unrelated segments that Raymond Williams found so fascinating in television. It is rather the result of proposing a model hierarchy among segments, in a way related to Nick Browne's notion of the "supertext," but conceived in terms of discourse and including other discursive material on a par with commercials. At some primary level, though, Williams's pure and unreconstructed flow undeniably plays a role in television reception. See also Turner in "Frame."

19. Kowinski, in "The Mall as City Suburban," describes the motivation for building the first mall as providing needed opportunities for face-to-face contact among the isolated environments of cars, housing, and office. Victor Gruen modeled the first covered mall in the United States, Southdale Center in Edina, Minnesota, on covered pedestrian arcades, especially the Galleria Vittorio Emanuel in Milan in 1956 (Kowinski 119). The large department stores of Europe were in turn modeled on the garden city in such ideal realizations as the Crystal Palace.

20. Public and private are complex and historically shifting notions. While Jürgen Habermas is the best-known contemporary philosopher of the disappearance of the public realm, this concern has a long tradition in the United States in the struggle between market forces and democratic values for dominance of areas of life. Hannah Arendt's *The Human Condition* traces the changing practices and concepts regarding *privacy* from the Greeks through the Romantic period and is the most generally helpful on the concept.

21. See Culver, whose enlightening link between Frank Baum's *Emerald City of Oz* and the growth of commodity display in shop windows is tied to a model of discrete fiction and identification rather than the utterly different disposition of the spectator "inside" the glass which characterizes the most sophisticated development of consumer culture. Culver's main question can guide any investigation of the institutions of consumption: why is it that Americans so willingly and apparently knowingly seek out and accept bogus substitutes, paper symbols, and commodity objects they know are inadequate to fulfill their needs, not to mention their desires? Culver presumes this occurs as an act of will—rather than in a state of distraction.

22. Spaulding Gray's "L.A., the Other" features a "real" story told by a woman who suddenly finds herself traveling in the opposite direction on the freeway miles from where she was last aware of her relative position. She interprets this lapse as an intervention in her life by beings from outer space. Such experiences of "spacing out" are viewed here as endemic rather than otherworldly.

23. I might add that this experience of motility and subjectivity is divided differently by gender, much as David Morley has described the power relations around the dial and the remote control around the family television—the wife and mother decides what to watch only when no one else is there. Just so, the

experience of driving is gendered. As his future bride said to Sonny Crockett in an episode of the 1987–88 season's "Miami Vice," "I'll bet no woman has driven your testosterone."

24. See the chapter "Speed" in Stephen Kern's *The Culture of Time and Space 1880–1918* for a discussion of the distinction between relative and absolute (subjectively intuited) motion. Note also that *nonspace* is not at all Kern's "empty space" or the void. Paul Virilio's meditations on the relation between speed and power of a coercive or military nature are only peripherally related to the "private" speed developed here.

25. See Freud on jokes and body responses to "too much" and "too little" in *Jokes and the Unconscious*.

26. The two local hosts of the show address the home viewer directly across the heads of nameless other people, as if they were in a bubble of space which could exchange talk and looks with our home-viewing space, while an objectively closer realm in front of them remains an otherwise distant and unrelated diegetic world. This bubble of subjectivity can also be found in other televisual genres such as logos and rock videos. What seems to be at stake are two things: the end of a "line" or fourth wall which divides representational realms, and the notion of a mobile rather than stationary or positioned spectator and/or presenter, able to roam and cross the barriers between multiple worlds at will. The constant alternation of static settings with "driving" segments in "Miami Vice" is an inverse example of the process embedded within story, marking the interiorized subjectivity or "true" self "under cover," also reflected in music and conversation.

27. "For the Navajo, walking was an important event in and of itself and not just a way of getting somewhere. We expected the filmmakers to cut out most of the walking footage—but they didn't. It was the least discarded footage" (Worth and Adair 146). "In reading the Navajo myths and stories later we were struck by how, in most Navajo myths, the narrator spends much of his time describing the walking, the landscape, and the places he passes, telling only briefly what to 'us' are plot lines" (147).

28. See 120–21 and 140–41, and generally his discussion of television. Ellis does not relate "segmentalization" to the development of spot advertising, whereas it could be argued that the struggle for control of the enunciation which led to spot advertising is served by segmentation, that is, an argument of consequences not from particular events but from techniques of power.

29. These include mixtures of pictorial systems, two- and three-dimensional images, symbols, and the written word in a single image as well as different planes of language. Worth and Adair considered it odd that the Navajos made photos with layouts of painted words to "try out ideas" and that they linked clips of symbolic events without concern for spatiotemporal continuity. However, layouts of painted words would be quite compatible with contemporary televisual representation.

30. Especially in regard to fiction films on television, such an alternation of story and discourse is perceived as interruption by all sorts of extraneous material and an incessant disruption of the psychological mechanism of disavowal that Beverly Houston explained in "Viewing Television."

Segmentation imposed on continuity editing is a mismatch of principles of coherence and dramatic unity of character, plot and setting, and editing, as well as conditions of viewing which promote fairly concentrated attention, and identification can only suffer thereby. What is interruption from the point of embedded fictions is more likely to be perceived as passage among segments and engagement with the viewer in discursive genres. Nonetheless, ads have retained the sense of being foreign bodies in flow at least since the advent of spot advertising in the mid-1950s, whereas when sponsors controlled programming the shift of subjects of discourse was smoother.

31. "It is hardly an exaggeration to call the freeway experience," as Joan Didion does, "the only secular communion Los Angeles has" (quoted in Brodsly 36–37).

32. The boulevard is discussed at length in Berman; street lighting in Schivelbusch.

33. Sachs goes on to explain how the symbolic value of the auto is undermined as soon as it becomes generally accessible and how it actually generates social inequalities.

34. See McHale, esp. 43–58. McHale proposes that the shift in dominance from epistemological to ontological questions is the primary distinguishing feature of postmodernism. The *zone* is a concept with a prior history in nineteenth-century Paris suburbs.

35. "In short, Dorothy loves the mechanism which turns display into a narrative of desire and enables her to experience the pastoral idyll vicariously.... She desires the figure that represents desire, recognizing in that image her own capacity for infinite desire" (Culver 112–13).

36. Kowinski stresses the chain of relationships: "The shopping mall completed the link between the highway and television; once the department stores and the national chains and franchises were inside, just about anything advertised on the tube could be found at the mall. The mall provided the perfect and complementary organization for the national replicated and uniform outlets of the Highway Comfort Culture. The mall, too, was national, and it was also replicated and uniform in management as well as appearance—the chains knew what to expect just about everywhere. They could slip easily into any mall; one size fits all" (51).

37. Denis Hollier calls Caillois's essay on the praying mantis in *Le myth et l'homme* the first to deal with the issue of simulation (76–77).

38. Duensing describes the technology patented by Jay Schiffman of Auto Vision Associates in Ferndale, Michigan. The virtual television is resisted for safety reasons, but its gradual acceptance is anticipated as a process comparable with the pioneering of the car radio by Bill Lear in 1929. What kind of programming the virtual television will display is discussed largely in terms of safety and attention. The process of looking at the virtual screen while driving is described in terms of "time sharing."

39. Avenues for images and voices which might represent subjects other than network representatives, advertisers, and celebrities, that is, members of a general public, or for that matter other private voices remain few: independent productions, the lowly public service announcement, cable community access programming, private networks for exchanging videocassettes, and computer networks. The growing segmentation of what was once broadcasting into cable

channels and superstations supported by satellite as well as the videocassette is an opportunity for heterogeneous voices to enter into representation—but only if the discursive practices developed in network television are themselves changed. Venues of "publicness" that range from PBS and C-SPAN to Paper Tiger and Captain Midnight merit separate discussion as to how each contributes as a model of entry into the realms of distraction.

5. What Do Cyborgs Eat?

1. Epigraph on a nineteenth-century human growth hormone from chapter 1 of Lewis Carroll's *Alice in Wonderland*. The outcome of the pill is revealed in chapter 2: "'Curiouser and curiouser!' cried Alice (she was so much surprised, that for the moment she quite forgot how to speak good English). 'Now I'm opening out like that largest telescope that ever was! Good-bye feet!'" Alice's early Wonderland adventures are largely culinary and like those of smart drug users, especially concerned with "fit."

2. Allucquère Roseanne Stone has nominated this attitude of "cyborg envy" (619). Her article "Virtual Systems" addresses the notion of "decoupling" (620) agency or subjectivity from the physical body and calls attention to the spiritual overtones in virtual worlds. Yet, she claims, "The 'original' body is the authenticating source for the refigured person in cyberspace: no 'persons' exist whose presence is not warranted by a physical body back in 'normal' space. But death in either normal space or cyberspace is real, in the sense that if the 'person' in cyberspace dies, the body in normal space dies, and vice versa" (604).

Manuel De Landa's *War in the Age of Intelligent Machines*, a history of technology from the machine point of view, implies not only a fundamental problem of incompatibility but ultimately of opposed interests of humans and machines. Of course, the discursive strategy of posing a subjectivized and empowered telos for machines is making humans aware of our own alienated and thus unchecked desires and actions.

3. Definition from *The American Heritage Dictionary*, cited in Schwab (80). Donna Haraway writes, "By the late twentieth century, our time, a mythic time, we are all chimeras, theorized and fabricated hybrids of machine and organism; in short, we are cyborgs. The cyborg is our ontology; it gives us our politics. The cyborg is a condensed image of both imagination and material reality, the two joined centres structuring any possibility of historical transformation" ("Cyborg Manifesto" 150). Haraway's "The Actors Are Cyborg" insists on the metalepsis of the cyborg as "monster" or "boundary creature" who speaks from within the belly of the monster.

Of course, Haraway's is but one of many formulations of the cyborg metaphor—from *Robocop* and *The Terminator* versus *Terminator 2* to the totalizing subject of the war machine to Haraway's own bad-girl hybrid in a local war against dualisms. Her rhetorical strategy is to displace a female subjectivity from (a feminist essentialist vision of) nature *into* the machine, as opposed to De Landa's radical exclusion of human subjectivity from the developmental logic of the machine.

Note that the "machine" metaphor applied to monastic life and other political and social organizations does not address the more literal problem of physical accommodation of the body and the electronic discussed here. However useful the cyborg as metaphor may be, it begs the question of fusion in the first place—or it is satisfied with making all tool users into cyborgs.

4. "Meat" is the human body as defined in *Mondo 2000*'s *A User's Guide to the New Edge*: "This expression communicates the frustration that people dealing with an infinitely expandable infosphere feel at the limitations imposed upon the wandering mind by the demands of the body" (170).

5. See Grosz for a lucid description of the difference between repudiation, negation, and disavowal as psychical defense mechanisms and an application of these categories strategically, rather than therapeutically, in cultural criticism. Grosz's article was brought to my attention by Patricia Mellencamp's *High Anxiety*.

6. The excerpt from Patterson's *Eating the "I"* continues: "I had always thought that one class of beings eats another; that all forms of life, gross and subtle were engaged in a kind of perpetual eating or, as Gurdjieff called it, 'reciprocal maintenance.' The different classes (the vertebrates, invertebrates, man and angels) are separated by what they eat, the air they breathe and in what medium they live. It had never occurred to me that within classes of beings the strong psychically feed on the weak. The waitress was 'food' for her boss" (284).

7. In *identification*, or mirroring and mimicry, one mistakes not-self (for instance, a mirror image) for the self. Thus, identification with a double or like demands distance (ultimately to be overlooked) and a slight difference in scale between a subject and an object (a difference to be ignored).

8. An oral typology of covering or engulfing/being covered or engulfed also plays a role in the logic of some video games and computer displays and interaction with, for instance, the Pac-Man or Macintosh Windows and interface.

9. The passage specifically refers to "the love-relationship to the mother." In some psychoanalytic thinking, orality is not restricted to an oral or primitive stage. Richard M. Gottlieb in "Rethinking Cannibalism" notes the pervasiveness of cannibalistic fantasy in contemporary culture. His remarks especially emphasize the theme of the body in pieces (much like food that is cut up, broken, and torn) as well as the theme of the resurrected or intact body. Gottlieb also suggests that digestion, decay, and decomposition are part of this body-as-food continuum, themes comparable to the terms of waste and abjection in this chapter.

10. For contrasting visual images of nonfood, see "Future Food," a glamour shot of gels and pills, steel worm/conduit, and rather menacing looking brussels sprouts (year 2010), styled by Erez and photographed by Joshua Ets-Hokin, in *Mondo 2000* 3 (Winter 1991): 102. A contrasting matte and ascetic simulation of an ad for a soup of supplements captioned, "Do you need a soup of supplements? . . . especially if you can't stand broccoli and brussels sprouts," appears in Toufexis 55.

11. Metaphor courtesy of St. Jude, *Mondo 2000*.

12. Durk Pearson and Sandy Shaw of Designer Foods™, however, emphasize

that "All ingredients [in their SMART Products] are recognized and utilized by the human body as a food" (*Intelli-Scope: The Newsletter of Designer Foods*™ *Network* 2 [Feb. 1993]: 4). Despite its name, the newsletter also disclaims that "Smart Drinks" will improve IQ, though they will increase well-being, energy, and clarity, especially for someone who is "feeling constantly tired, drained or stressed out."

13. Karl Abraham set the oral-sadistic stage concurrent with teething and the fantasy of being eaten or destroyed by the mother, whereas Melanie Klein placed infantile sadism throughout the oral stage. "The libidinal desire to suck is accompanied by the destructive aim of sucking out, scooping out, emptying, exhausting" (quoted in Laplanche and Pontalis 289).

14. Moravec and Sussman appear to entertain the questionable idea that there will still be an "I" and a "mind" capable of "thought" in this future union of brain and hardware.

15. Cited in the publicity for the exhibition *Ars Electronica 93: Genetic Art, Artificial Life* in Linz, Austria.

16. See the adventures of the homunculus in Goethe's *Faust II.*

17. See also Andreas Huyssen's reasoning in *The Great Divide* or Freud's explanation of the death drive in *Beyond the Pleasure Principle.*

18. For a perceptive application of Klein's psychoanalytic theories to video games, see Skirrow.

19. I am not unaware of the metaphor of oral sex as "eating," but here eating is not a metaphor, and sexuality reappears in terms of sadomasochistic affect— as pain and ecstasy. Flanagan "explores the effects of chronic illness on sexual identity, in particular, sadomasochism" in his installation "Visiting Hours" at the Santa Monica Museum of Art, LAX Festival 1992 (*Los Angeles Exhibition 92* catalogue 94).

20. SmartSkin™ is a new product introduced in the *Intelli-Scope* above. For a psychoanalytic elaboration of the concept of the skin ego (especially the second skin) with case histories, see Didier Anzieu's *The Skin Ego*, in particular the chapters on "The Second Muscular Skin," "The Envelope of Suffering," and "The Film of the Dream." Anzieu is also enlightening on the psychological significance of breaking the skin in sadomasochistic rituals. While *The Skin Ego* does not deal with electronic skin, it does treat film. To my memory, the most striking example of a written skin occurs in the *Hoichi, the Earless One of Kwaidan*, in which holy words protect the body against being eaten by ghosts.

21. As in "his eyes devoured her" (Sartre 390). Julia Kristeva's critique of the philosophy of "meaning as the act of the *transcendental ego*, cut off from its body, its unconscious, and also its history" ("System" 1249–50) refers to Klein and could as easily refer to virtual reality.

22. Deleuze and Guattari describe the development of "face" as a "white wall, black hole system" (see 167–91), a system that is implicitly racially determined, as Meaghan Morris has suggested in her essay, "Great Moments in Social Climbing."

23. Yet as malnutrition, hunger, and deficits have grown, disentitlement has become an increasingly respectable political option. Many different kinds of theorists, from anthropologists like Mary Douglas to political scientists and activists, suggest that hunger is most often a result of lack of legal entitlement and social inequities rather than of scarcity.

24. Dr. Robert Klesges put on a tape of the television dramedy *The Wonder Years* and measured the metabolic rate of thirty-two girls ranging from seven to twelve years old, half of them normal weight, half of them obese. All showed a drop in metabolic rate, but that of the obese children was especially striking, suggesting why heavy use of television and obesity go together. The study was cited by Brody.

25. One San Francisco ex-restauranteur and co-owner of the mail-order firm Smart Products says, "I don't eat breakfast anymore. I don't eat lunch; I drink smart drinks" that take one minute to stir and one to consume. He would welcome being able to abandon "real" food from depleted and (we might add, even toxic) soils entirely (Rennie, in "Smart Drugs" and in a personal telephone interview, 2 Apr. 1992).

26. The food ideologies of the "fast" and the "fresh" were analyzed at length in my unpublished paper "Telefood and Culinary Postmodernism" delivered at the Society for Cinema Studies in 1988 and described briefly in earlier publications of this essay. See Acknowledgments.

27. "The psychotic's hallucination is not the return of the repressed, that is, the return of a signifier, but the return of the Real that has never been signified— a foreclosed or scotomized perception, something falling on the subject's psychical blind spot. The subject's perception is not projected outward onto the external world. Rather, what is internally obliterated reappears for the subject as if it emanates from the Real, in hallucinatory rather than projective form. It confronts the subject from an independent, outside position" (Grosz 45–46).

28. See also Case "curled in his capsule in some coffin hotel, his hands clawed into the bedslab, temperfoam bunched between his fingers, trying to reach the console that wasn't there" (*Neuromancer* 5). And "Case sat in the loft with the dermatrodes strapped across his forehead. . . . Cowboys didn't get into simstim, he thought, because it was basically a meat toy. He knew that the trodes he used and the little plastic tiara dangling from a simstim deck were basically the same, and that the cyberspace matrix was actually a drastic simplification of the human sensorium, at least in terms of presentation, but simstim itself struck him as a gratuitous multiplication of flesh input" (137–38).

29. One study found 20 percent who ate chips with Olestra had gastro-intestinal problems. The Center for Science and the Public Interest has asked the FDA to ban Olestra. See Narisetti.

30. Woolley's conclusion: "One of the aims of this book has been to show that reality is still there, though not in the material realm of the physical universe where the modern era assumed it to be. In my attempt to distinguish between simulation and imitation, the virtual and the artificial, I have tried to provide a glimpse of where that reality may be, in the formal, abstract domain revealed by mathematics and computation. This is not to say that any mathematics can discover it. Rather, the computer has, through its simulative powers, provided what I regard as reassuring evidence that it is still there" (254). In a contrasting view, Paul Virilio in *The Machine of Vision* castigates the very will to mathematical power as the occasion for voluntarily blinding the horizon of sight and hearing. My page reference is the German translation of *La machine de vision, Die Sehmaschine* 171.

31. Naimark's "Nutrition" was made with students at the San Francisco Art Institute, 1990. A prior piece, *Eat* (1989), explores the absurdity of a virtual

restaurant, with video projection meals like "Jackson Pollock" and an "eat" button that can lead to surprising effects—like the Heimlich maneuver.

32. Disavowal allows two contradictory forms of defense to coexist without influencing each other: "It does not rely on the unconscious, but pre-dates it. Like repudiation, it involves a split in the ego, but does not involve a failure in representation. The child's acceptance and refusal of reality . . . generates the representational impulse to produce profuse significatory contexts and fantasy scenarios" (Grosz 46).

33. It is true that the virtual reality interfaces of glove, helmet, or suit map the physical body onto the virtual body—but not in a one-to-one correlation. The immersive illusion depends on kinesthetic sensations in the real body as it moves, but the machine tracking body coordinates allow for locomotion in a very circumscribed area in real space.

Descriptions of the body in virtual reality are contradictory, probably because there are at minimum two bodies—one virtual and one actual. The virtual body can be delegated to one or more figures in the artificial world or remain subjective. The actual body can reportedly feel "disembodied." Scott Fisher imagines a man in the year 2001 composing a model for a new pharmaceutical in virtual space: he is crawling on all fours, as if "miming a wrestling match with himself, or recapitulating his infancy" (423–24). Interfaces like the helmet and data suit which occlude impressions of the physical world are, according to Myron Krueger, a problem; in remarks made at the Cyberthon, he offered a simple solution—transparent lenses of virtual information beyond which the physical world may be viewed.

34. In terms of description of effects, Dean Ward, M.D., and John Morgenthaler, for instance, report that piracetam promotes the flow of information between the right and left hemispheres and "might increase the number of cholinergic receptors in the brain. Older mice were given piracetam for two weeks and then the density of the muscarinic cholinergic receptors in their frontal cortexes was measured. The researchers found that these older mice had 30–40% higher density of these receptors than before. Piracetam, unlike many other drugs, appears to have a regenerative effect on the nervous system" (44). Deprenyl is described by Morgenthaler 36.

Ross Pelton's *Mind Food and Smart Pills* and Pearson and Shaw's *Life Extension* and *The Life Extension Companion* offer more detailed explanations of these drugs and lengthier citations of references than does Ward and Morgenthaler's *Smart Drugs*. St. Jude's tongue-in-cheek article "Are You as Smart as Your Drugs?" is about smart drug addiction ("Let's just face it—nobody with any chemically evolved intelligence is going to be exactly chuffed about, sinking back into the primordial ooze, brain-wise"). St. Jude describes the efficacy of "800 mg of piracetam" in remembering "an obscure Japanese technical term—*kyogen*! that's the word—never noticing how all-out *unnatural* it is to recall stuff like *kyogen*" (38). In a telephone interview Jude, who is both knowledgeable and skeptical about mainstream medicine, revealed her past as a physician's assistant. Her pseudonym is an indication of the knowledge of the hopeless, yet nevertheless. . . .

35. Toufexis 56. In the sidebar to the *Time* piece we read, "Can You Survive by Pills Alone?"

36. Like Alice, the discourse of smart drugs and drinks is all about "too

much" and "too little." McKenna in *Food of the Gods* (to be distinguished from the H. G. Wells novel with the same main title) also posits a distinction between bad drugs (which include television) and good drugs (largely hallucinogenics) as one of "fit" fostered by coevolution of plants with shamanistic practices from archaic times.

37. Testimonials from Ward and Morgenthaler (179–84), and Morgenthaler, "Smart Drugs Update."

38. See especially Pearson and Shaw with Milhon, "Durk and Sandy," but this theme is universal.

39. *Abject Art: Repulsion and Desire in American Art*, catalog of an exhibition, June 23–August 29, 1993, Whitney Museum of American Art, argues a broader case for abjection in art than is proposed here.

40. Christine Tamblyn treats the abject in the work of feminist performance artists like Karen Finley in "The River of Swill" (10–13).

41. Helms sought to amend Public Law 101–121 of 1989 banning the NEA from funding obscene art to include the depiction or description of sexual or excretory activities or organs "in a patently offensive way," a prohibition that one Senator, Tim Wirth (D-Col.), noted medically includes the human skin. According to Helms, much of the art sanctioned by the NEA "turns the stomach of any normal person" (*New York Times* 20 Sept. 1991: C3). In the words of Eric Planin of the *Washington Post* (20 Sept. 1991: B1–2): "Seemingly unimpressed by the NEA's get tough policy in denying grants to artists who, for instance, smear chocolate on their nude bodies or urinate on stage, the Senate voted 68 to 28 to adopt the amendment." This Senate stand was later abandoned in a "Corn for Porn" swap, that is, the maintenance of cheap grazing rights on public lands. Subsequent events—the charges of "blasphemy" by Pat Buchanan's presidential primary campaign ad attacking Marlon Riggs's *Tongues Untied* (a lyrical documentary on black homosexual identity politics), as well as the reportedly forced resignation of John Frohnmeyer, NEA Chair, resulting from the pressure of the Buchanan presidential campaign on President George Bush—support the role of "excretory art" as site of struggle over cultural change.

42. Barry chose two models who bore an uncanny resemblance to each other. The photographic results were digitally combined, as well as manipulated in other ways: since the fit between a human head, the severity of a cube, and the aspect ratio (length in relation to width) of a video screen is not ideal, judicious computerized stretching of the digital image was required, especially around the hairline, to make the head fit the cube to the corners. The result is the restoration of at least part of the body to art *as* minimalist sculpture.

43. Charles Hagen compares *Imagination Dead Imagine*, "With its blend of the sensual and the repulsive," explicitly with "Andres Serrano's photography combining religious symbols and bodily fluids" in his 25 Oct. 1991 review in the *New York Times* (C5). Barry cites other literary inspirations—for instance, J. G. Ballard's "The Impossible Room" includes the following description: "A perfect cube, its walls and ceilings were formed by what seemed to be a series of cinema screens. Projected on to them in close-up was the face of Nurse Nagamatzu, her mouth, three feet across" (33).

44. Words which embody or enact what they mean are in fact calligrams—except that "calli" means beautiful. Michel Foucault wrote on the phenomenon in "Ceci n'est pas une pipe" (9–10).

6. The Body, the Image, and the Space-in-Between

1. I saw it at a retrospective at the Long Beach Museum in 1988. The piece is discussed in detail in Kraus (24) and in my "Closed Circuits and Fragmented Egos," given at the Society for Photographic Education, Rochester, 1989.

2. To clarify, naturally all of the elements that make up a video installation, such as sculptural objects and the videotapes themselves, are art, too—they are not yet an installation. Another practical consideration for artists is that what is left over when the space-in-between is removed may, however, be of considerable bulk. Thus installation artists have in common their storage problems, sometimes solved by living amid the sculptural remains of up to two decades of work. As a consequence, some artists have been exploring smaller, more compact forms that do not enclose the visitor. Shigeko Kubota has always considered her work sculptural and self-contained—so the change in her most recent work is largely in scale. Rita Myers is exploring a type of Duchampian peephole-on-a-scene in future work.

3. However, there is such a thing as performance video, which may have sets and the presence of a "live artist," as well as electronics.

4. The fact that space-time can be rented to the installation visitor (via a museum fee) suggests a relation to popular kinds of rental institutions such as movie theaters or funhouses, to which Ken Feingold compared the form in a conversation with me. Yet what the installation visitor rents is not so much a seat as the right of passage. One might find the popular shadow of this art form in an experience somewhere between the didacticism of a multimedia display and the bodily experience offered by a funhouse. See the discussion of the exhibition form by Judith Barry.

5. Not that installation art today is not for sale—the artists cited in this chapter figure in American and European museum, corporate, and private collections. Although some respected artists of the installation form have yet to realize income from their work, others, including Nauman, Graham, and Paik, are among the superstars of the art world. After a period when the art market turned its attention to neotraditional art forms, the 1990s has seen a resurgence of collector interest in electronic and performance arts, including media installation.

6. Film installations are rare. One example is Roger Welch's simulation of the drive-in movie apparatus, "Drive-In: Second Feature," installed at the Whitney Museum, 1982. However, there are video installations that use filmic constructions of space within the monitor image. Marie-Jo Lafontaine's "Victoria" installed at the Shainman Gallery, 1989, is one example. Slides with inserts of other (sometimes moving) image material are a more common reference to our frozen image culture, reminiscent of billboards, posters, and walls. See my "Architecture" for a detailed interpretation of two installations in this medium.

7. Dara Birnbaum's work has been the most directly related to the reworking and critique of the televisual representational forms per se, in such installations as "P M Magazine." See Buchloh's *Dara Birnbaum*. In a very different vein, Judith Barry's "Maelstrom" places the body of the visitor within a new construction of spatial representation seen primarily on television, the forced perspectival space of motion control and image processing.

8. Language here is used in an inclusive sense to encompass all forms of expression, including the nonverbal and artistic. Émile Benveniste theorizes about these two planes in *Problems*. Gérard Genette extends this distinction to literary genres in "Frontiers." In subsequent writing on the subject, Genette has stressed that these planes of language are not either/or distinctions, but rather coexist in subtle shifts even within a narrative form. These planes in art, undoubtedly as complex and copresent, are presented here in global form for the sake of introducing the distinction between them.

9. Ann-Marie Duguet treats video installation at the end of the 1960s and during the early 1970s as a period in which the apparatuses of representation since the Renaissance were systematically explored and critiqued. She views the closed-circuit installation form of video as the privileged tool of this exploration, as it models representation itself.

10. The deconstruction of presence and identity is also the project of post-structuralist philosophy (Derrida and Foucault) and psychoanalysis (Lacan) as well. I discuss the notion of the fiction of discourse as it operates in American broadcast television in chapters 1 and 2. In my view, installation video deconstructs rather than furthers this fiction.

11. The description of the sculpture as surrogate person and Smith's ride on the New Jersey Turnpike are also addressed by Fried.

12. My analyses of television representation show that it is discursive in this way as well, but not self-consciously or in a way that questions its own process. I have addressed the multiple levels of discourse in particular videos in several places: "Video Mom," "Cyclones," and reviews of AFI Video Festivals of 1987 and 1988.

13. The world created via interaction can be digitized on a computer screen, but it is not one that a visitor can enter bodily. Unless there is charged space outside the screen or a passage for the body, we have left the realm of installation art per se. To questions about how interactive interactive video actually is, again the analysis of experiential subjects is illuminating: the visitor interacts with what or whom? Is the interaction dialogic (that is, between two subjects) or does it amount to a range of choices within a system of organization (who is the subject then)?

14. A theme that continues in, for example, her installation "Asylum, a Romance" (1986). See my "Mary Lucier."

15. A plywood construction with mirror, two five-inch TV sets, and five thirteen-inch TV sets. The four channels were a Grand Canyon helicopter trip; a drive on Echo Cliff, Arizona; a Taos sunset and mirage; and a Teton sunset. See the description in *Shigeko Kubota* 37, 39.

16. Described in detail in *Bill Viola: Survey of a Decade* (Houston: Contemporary Arts Museum, 1988) and discussed in my "Interiors."

17. The piece had six to seven video and audio channels and from nineteen to twenty-three monitors on pedestals, plus a video camera when presented at the Kitchen Museum (1974) and the Whitney Museum (1977).

18. Such was the hardware needed to make the serial comparison: to an audio loop add three half-inch reel-to-reel VHS recorders comprising two for prerecorded playback and one live channel of input from a black-and-white camera, time delayed and displayed every four seconds. The live image appeared on

the center screen alternating with four seconds of live broadcast TV. The switcher constantly changed the placement of the other channels of time-delayed, live images and prerecorded playback (four of each) on the eight screens surrounding the center. Today, multiple-monitor, multiple-channel installations are commonly as complex.

19. Shown on three monitors set in a shallow 122° curve about two-and-a-half feet apart.

20. See the reproduction of her score in the description of the piece in *Video Art*, edited by Schneider and Korot. Her subsequent installation, "Text and Commentary" (1977), made this weaving metaphor explicit. "Dachau" was one of the three pieces in the Long Beach retrospective of 1988 and was also included in the retrospective in Cologne (1989).

21. The retrospective *American Landscape Video*, comprising three of the seven installations—Mary Lucier's "Wilderness" (1986), with its strong narrative dimension, Doug Hall's "The Terrible Uncertainty of the Thing Described" (1987), and Steina Vasulka's "The West" (1983)—exploited these poetic possibilities in very different ways. See my "Interiors."

22. William D. Judson emphasizes the contribution of Rosalind Krauss's 1976 critique of this strand of work with feedback of the artist's own image in displacing the application of modernist aesthetic criteria to video (Judson). Krauss's first example for the narcissism thesis, Vito Acconci's "Centers" (1971), would seem to support her diagnosis of capture in a parenthesis between the camera and the monitor. The artist points into a camera lens, adjusting his position by looking at a monitor: as a result, the image of Acconci's finger points out of the center of the monitor. "I'm looking straight out by looking straight in" (EAI, 12). Of course, since the camera would have to be above or at the side of the monitor, centering himself required constant readjustment and recalculations in what is a slightly asymmetrical configuration. The monitor is not a mirror and the replicant image is not a reflection—the production of "Centers" is decentered, if the image is not. Pointing at the viewer is also an exaggeration of the use of virtual address typical of commercial television or the news. Similarly, to interact with one's own monitor image, e.g., to kiss it, requires prior taping or a temporal delay in order to create the impression of simultaneity. Krauss exempts "Boomerang," Campus's installations, and Joan Jonas's "Vertical Roll" from her critique of narcissism through their strategies of media critique from within, physical assault on the mechanism, and the sculptural qualities of installation per se. However, the overall equation of monitor and mirror is problematic.

7. Cyberscapes, Control, and Transcendence

1. Gibson was using a typewriter at the time he wrote *Neuromancer* and his fantasy of the space on the other side of the monitor was based on little knowledge of the state of computing. See Scott Rosenberg. Timothy Binkley carefully distinguishes these levels in "Refiguring Culture."

2. N. Katherine Hayles's distinctions between absence/presence and randomness/pattern, made in "The Seductions of Cyberspace," might be con-

ceived as different stages of information (which have different psychic roots and subject-effects) that coexist rather than that succeed each other in a developed information society (173–90, esp. 186–87).

3. Allucquère Roseanne Stone emphasizes opacity of computer packaging in "Sex, Death and Architecture." For Friedrich Kittler, the myth of user-friendly software generates a dangerous ignorance of machine language, which is in any case, a "Protected Mode."

4. Virtuality compares to what Sigmund Freud described as "uncanny," evoking both a strange and familiar feeling that recalls the moment of the discovery of sexual difference or the sight of a corpse.

5. See chapter 1, especially the citation from "A Conversation between Peter Weibel and Friedrich Kittler."

6. Bogard's *The Simulation of Surveillance: Hypercontrol in Telematic Societies* came out too late to take account of in writing this chapter. It offers a model of surveillance similar to one of the possibilities discussed here under "control" and in chapter 3 as "telematic danger." However, Bogard uses a narrower definition of simulation (as pastness not as the simulation of presence) and treats virtualization and hyperrealization as equivalents of surveillance. Hence its model of surveillance is different in that it is narrower, yet more all-encompassing.

Julia Scher has explored the psychical and cultural implications of electronic and computer surveillance in work spanning over a decade, including her 1993 installation, "Predictive Engineering," at the San Francisco Museum of Modern Art, mixing live and recorded video on two chiastically arranged and elegantly situated surveillance camera and monitor set-ups.

7. Marsha Kinder developed the discomfiting gender implications of the killing moves and the arcade milieu of "Mortal Kombat" in a paper delivered at the Console-ing Passions Conference in Tucson in April 1994.

8. Allucquère Roseanne Stone discusses the notion of warrant and the "fiduciary subject" in "Sex, Death and Architecture" and other places.

9. Wolfgang Schivelbusch deals with the history of street lighting and its social and cultural ramifications in *Disenchanted Night*. The advent of electric light was the beginning of suburbanization. Edison's carbon-filament incandescent light was patented in 1880. The census of 1880 didn't mention use of electric power in industry but by 1900 it was equal with steam. Edison invented illumination by electricity in 1876, and by 1879–80, cities were lighting streets with arc lamps. The electric trolley was developed in 1887, permitting the first suburb, Tuxedo, New York, to come into existence. See Hession and Sardy.

10. An appreciation of the acculturation of the machine to the human appears in my "Judith Barry." A discussion of the mixture of the physical and the projected appears in my "Muntadas' Media-Architectural Installations."

11. Those who want to "fill" cyberspace have been charged with the sin of neocolonialism on occasion. However, indigenous people are not "in" cyberspace to be conquered and colonized, but in the realm outside that has been obscured by virtualities. Here is rather another instance of discursive struggle—whose legacy and whose culture will occupy those virtual spaces? At best one can fill cyberspace with many voices and traditions.

12. While this piece was a collaboration in every phase, Toni Dove was

primarily responsible for the visual realizations of this virtual world and Michael Mackenzie for its plot(s) and interactive design. In addition, a team of programmers and computer-based designers, along with a large mainframe computer, contributed to this very labor-intensive project. As Mackenzie pointed out, while dramatic productions have a well-known division of labor and a general sense of the time necessary to complete each task, this is a new area in which the very production structures and practices must themselves be improvised. Toni Dove described the end result as an armature without the beta testing one would do from inside, much as Mackenzie sees it as a kind of drama that has been constructed and presented without the fine-tuning of a rehearsal process. Yet far from being an orphan, each sees this piece as an important part of the trajectory of his or her work.

13. The passage continues: "There were no signs directing your gaze, no coin-operated binoculars, and no brochures answering your unasked questions about local flora, geology or the history of the land. . . . By the mid-twentieth century, it seemed, nature had to be explained to its human inhabitants; it was not enough to just try to experience it. As a result, conflicting information about the natural world blankets out visual and aural environments. Much of this information is promotional—that is to say, often misleading, mystifying, or simply irrelevant" (53).

14. MacCannell proposes that the loss of authenticity in everyday life fuels the tourist's search for authentic nature and community, thereby producing the simulation of both and the recedence of the physical world under superimposed signs and images.

15. Tourism and its practices have been the object of cautionary and de-mystifying sociological and ethnographic studies and semiotic analyses for at least two decades. (It is amazing how relatively few positive values are accorded to the romance and the revenue involved.) For instance, the "self-destruct theory" of mass tourism puts ostensibly harmless activities such as sight-seeing in the context of a slow death of a cultural landscape, while "Doxey's index of irration" charts the phases of the host population's reaction to guests, from initial euphoria to antagonism. Shaw and Williams review many of these theories and models.

16. Pinney questions whether surrogate travel is travel at all if it doesn't leave the spot. However, this understanding of the virtual environment does not take into account that the display and interactive devices do indeed act as frame and that virtual motion is travel in effect, if not actually. The distinction between actual and virtual travel becomes less telling once we recognize that "depth" in the narrational journey is already a metaphor—therefore, why can't movement through the space of an embodied metaphor be as effective (or not) as movement through physical space?

17. Elizabeth Grosz's "Bodies-Cities" deals with the city *and* the body (not city as body). Susan Stewart's *On Longing* is useful on the imaginary social body as one gigantic individual. In a particular example of the pathetic fallacy, the landscape in Ernest Hemingway's "Hills Like White Elephants" evokes the pregnant body of the protagonist. The city as skeleton or corpse evokes the symbolic or "unfilled" nature of cyberspace, though it may also be a bleak view of contemporary cities.

Works Cited

Abrams, Janet. "Escape from Gravity." *Sight and Sound* 5, no. 5 (1995): 14–19.

Allen, Jeanne. "The Social Matrix of Television: Invention in the United States." In E. Ann Kaplan, ed., *Regarding Television*, 109–19.

Antin, David. "Video: The Distinctive Features of the Medium." *Video Culture: A Critical Investigation*, 147–66. Ed. John G. Hanhardt. Rochester: Visual Studies Workshop, 1990.

Anzieu, Didier. *The Skin Ego: A Psychoanalytic Approach to the Self*. Trans. Chris Turner. New Haven: Yale UP, 1989.

Arendt, Hannah. *The Human Condition*. Chicago: U of Chicago P, 1974.

Arnheim, Rudolf. *Rundfunk als Hörkunst*. Munich: Hanser, 1979.

Artaud, Antonin. "All Writing Is Pigshit." *Artaud Anthology*, 38–40. Ed. Jack Hirschmann. Trans. David Rattray. San Francisco: City Lights, 1965.

Austin, J. L. *How to Do Things with Words*. 2nd ed. Cambridge: Harvard UP, 1975.

Bachelard, Gaston. *The Poetics of Space*. Trans. Maria Jolas. Boston: Beacon, 1969.

Baker, Christopher W. *How Did They Do It? Computer Illusion in Film & Television*. Indianapolis: Alpha, 1994.

Bakhtin, Mikhail. *The Dialogic Imagination: Four Essays*. Ed. Michael Holquist. Trans. Caryl Emerson and Michael Holquist. Austin: U of Texas P, 1981.

Ballard, J. G. "Project for a Glossary of the Twentieth Century." In Crary and Kwinter 268–79.

———. "The Impossible Room." *The Atrocity Exhibition*, 33. San Francisco: Re/Search, 1990.

Barnouw, Eric. *Tube of Plenty: The Evolution of American Television*. London and New York: Oxford, 1975.

Barrett, Marvin. *Rich News, Poor News*. New York: Crowell, 1978.

Barry, Judith. "Designed Aesthetic: Exhibition Design and the Independent Group." *Modern Dreams: The Rise and Fall and Rise of Pop*, 41–45. Ed. Lawrence Alloway et al. Cambridge, Mass. and London: MIT P, 1988.

Barthes, Roland. "Historical Discourse." *Structuralism: A Reader*, 145–55. Ed. Michael Lane. London: Jonathan Cape, 1970.

———. "Le Discours de l'histoire." *Social Science Information* 6, no. 4 (1967): 66–75.

————. *Mythologies*. Trans. Annette Lavers. New York: Hill, 1972.

————. "Rhetoric of the Image." *Image, Music, Text*, 32–44. Ed. and trans. Stephen Heath. New York: Hill and Wang, 1977.

Baudrillard, Jean. "The Ecstasy of Communication." *The Anti-aesthetic: Essays on Postmodern Culture*, 126–34. Ed. Hal Foster. Port Townsend, Wash.: Bay P, 1983.

————. *Simulacra and Simulation*. Trans. Sheila Faria Glaser. Ann Arbor: University of Michigan Press, 1994.

Baum, Geraldine. "D.C.'s Deflated Ego: Historical events have made sky-high headlines, but left Washington feeling like a lead balloon." *Los Angeles Times* 19 Mar. 1990: E1.

Bayley, Stephen. *Sex, Drink, and Fast Cars: The Creation and Consumption of Images*. London: Boston Faber, 1986.

Beckett, Samuel. *Imagination Dead Imagine*. London: Calder, 1965.

Benjamin, Walter. *Das Passagen-Werk*. Ed. Rolf Tiedemann. Frankfurt am Main: Suhrkamp, 1983.

————. *Paris, capitale du XIXe siecle: Le livre des passages*. Trans. Jean Lacoste. Paris: Editions du Cerf, 1989.

————. "Paris: Capital of the Nineteenth Century." In *Illuminations*. Ed. Hannah Arendt. Trans. H. Zohn. New York: Shocken, 1969.

Benveniste, Émile. *Problems of General Linguistics*. Trans. Mary Elizabeth Meek. Miami: U of Miami P, 1971.

Berger, Peter, and Thomas Luckmann. *The Social Construction of Reality*. New York: Anchor-Doubleday, 1967.

Berman, Marshall. *All That is Solid Melts into Air: The Experience of Modernity*. New York: Simon, 1982.

Bernstein, Richard. "Will the Gulf War Produce Enduring Art?" *New York Times* 9 June 1991: H22.

Bhabha, Homi. "Interrogating Identity." In *Identity*. Ed. Homi Bhaba. London: Institute of Contemporary Arts, 1987.

Bill Viola: Survey of a Decade. Houston: Contemporary Arts Museum, 1988.

Binkley, Timothy. "Refiguring Culture." In *Future Visions: New Technologies of the Screen*, 92–122. Ed. Philip Hayward and Tana Wollen. London: BFI, 1993.

Boeke, Kees. *Cosmic View: The Universe in Forty Jumps*. New York: John Day, 1973.

Bogard, William. *The Simulation of Surveillance: Hypercontrol in Telematic Societies*. Cambridge: Cambridge UP, 1996.

Bolter, Jay David. *Writing Space: The Computer, Hypertext and the History of Writing*. Hillsdale, NJ: Lawrence Erlbaum Assoc., 1991.

Boorstein, Daniel. *The Image: A Guide to Pseudo-Events in America*. New York: Atheneum, 1977.

Brodsly, David. *L. A. Freeway: An Appreciative Essay*. Berkeley: U of California P, 1981.

Brody, Jane E. "Literally Entranced by Television, Children Metabolize More Slowly." *New York Times* 1 Apr. 1992: B7.

Browne, Nick. "The Political Economy of the Television (Super) Text." *Quarterly Review of Film Studies* 9 (1984): 174–82.

Buber, Martin. *I and Thou*. Trans. Ronald Gregor Smith. New York: Scribner, 1958.

Buchloh, Benjamin, ed. *Dara Birnbaum: Rough Edits: Popular Image Video.* Pamphlets: Nova Scotia College of Art and Design, 1987.

Butler, Jeremy G. *Television: Critical Methods and Applications.* Belmont, Calif.: Wadsworth, 1994.

Caldwell, John Thornton. *Televisuality: Style, Crisis, and Authority in American Television.* New Brunswick, N.J.: Rutgers UP, 1995.

Caillois, Roger. *Le mythe et l'homme.* [c.1938] Paris: Gallimard, 1972.

Canetti, Elias. *Crowds and Power.* New York: Viking, 1973.

Carey, James W. "Why and How? The Dark Continent of American Journalism." In Manoff and Schudson 195–96.

Carey, John, and Pat O'Hara. "Interactive Television." In d'Agostino and Tafler 219–34.

Carman, John. "NBC Learns ABCs of News." *San Francisco Chronicle* 23 Jan. 1997: E1, 9.

Carroll, Lewis. *Through the Looking Glass and What Alice Found There.* London: Macmillan and Co., 1872.

Center for Media and Public Affairs, "Drawing Back the Iron Curtain: TV News Coverage of Eastern Europe in 1989." *Media Monitor* 4, no. 3 (1990): 1.

Chatman, Seymour. *Story and Discourse: Narrative Structure in Fiction and Film.* Ithaca and London: Cornell UP, 1978.

Cohen, Stanley, and Laurie Taylor. *Escape Attempts: The Theory and Practice of Resistance to Everyday Life.* London: Penguin, 1978.

Computer Basics. New York: Time-Life, 1989.

Comstock, George. *Television in America.* Beverly Hills: Sage Publications, 1980.

Cornwell, Regina. "Where is the Window? Virtual Reality Technologies Now." *Artscribe* (Jan-Feb. 1991): 52–55

Crary, Jonathan. "Critical Reflections." *Art Forum* 32 (1994): 58–59+.

Crary, Jonathan, and Sanford Kwinter, eds. *Incorporations.* New York: Zone, 1992.

Cullen, Robert. "Report from Romania." *The New Yorker* 2 Apr. 1990: 94–112.

Culver, Stuart. "What Manikins Want: *The Wonder World of Oz* and *The Art of Decorating Dry Goods Windows.*" *Representations* 21 (1988): 97–116.

d'Agostino, Peter, and David Tafler, eds. *Transmission: Toward a Post-Television Culture.* Thousand Oaks, Calif.: SAGE, 1995.

Dayan, Daniel, and Elihu Katz. *Media Events: The Live Broadcasting of History.* Cambridge: Harvard UP, 1992.

de Certeau, Michel. *The Practice of Everyday Life.* Trans. Steven F. Rendall. Berkeley and Los Angeles: U of California P, 1984.

De Landa, Manuel. *War in the Age of Intelligent Machines.* New York: Zone, 1991.

Deleuze, Gilles, and Félix Guattari. *A Thousand Plateaus: Capitalism and Schizophrenia.* Trans. Brian Massumi. Minneapolis: U of Minnesota P, 1987.

Denton, Richard. "Imaging in the Persian Gulf War." *Advanced Imaging* 6, no. 4 (1991): 58.

DePalma, Anthony. "The Malling of Main Street." *The New York Times* 19 Apr. 1987: Business 1.

Derrida, Jacques. *Limited Inc.* Trans. Samuel Weber. Evanston: Northwestern UP, 1988.

Diamond, Edwin. *Sign Off: The Last Days of Television.* Cambridge: MIT P, 1982.

Dibbell, Julian. "A Rape in Cyberspace." *The Village Voice* 21 (Dec. 1993): 36–42.

Doane, Mary Ann. "Information, Crisis, Catastrophe." In Mellencamp, *Logics* 222–29.

Doty, Alexander. *Making Things Perfectly Queer: Interpreting Mass Culture.* Minneapolis: U of Minnesota P, 1993.

Douglas, Mary. "Standard Social Uses of Food: Introduction." *Food in the Social Order: Studies of Food and Festivities in Three American Communities*, 1–39. Ed. Mary Douglas. New York: Russell Sage Foundation, 1984.

Du Brow, Rick. "TV News Too Trivial to See the Big Picture." *Los Angeles Times* 10 Feb. 1990: F1, 6.

Duensing, Edward S. "Television on the Move: In-Car Video Screen Small but Critics Question Safety." *Los Angeles Times* 11 Sept. 1989: II-3.

Duguet, Ann-Marie. "Dispositifs." *Communications: Video* 48 (1988): 221–42.

Dyer, Richard. *Stars.* London: British Film Institute, 1979.

Electronic Arts Intermix: Video, a Catalogue of the Artists' Videotape Distribution Service of EAI. Ed. Lori Zippay. New York: Electronic Arts Intermix, 1991.

Ellis, John. "Television as Working Through." In the series *Media Knowledge and the Role of Television.* Ed. Jostein Gripsrud. *Rhetoric - Knowledge - Mediation Working Paper 2*, 47–73. Bergen: University of Bergen, 1996.

———. *Visible Fictions: Cinema, Television, Video.* London: Routledge and Kegan Paul, 1982.

Emmeche, Claus. *The Garden in the Machine: The Emerging Science of Artifical Life.* Princeton: Princeton UP, 1994.

Farocki, Harun. "The Industrialization of Thought." Trans. Peter Wilson. *Discourse* 15, no. 3 (1993): 76–77.

Felman, Shoshona. *The Literary Speech Act: Don Juan with J. L. Austin, or Seduction in Two Languages.* Ithaca: Cornell UP, 1983.

Feuer, Jane. "The Concept of Live Television: Ontology as Ideology." In E. Ann Kaplan, ed., *Regarding Television*, 12–22.

Fisher, Scott S. "Virtual Interface Environments." *The Art of Human-Computer Interface Design*, 423–24. Ed. Brenda Laurel. Reading, Mass.: Addison-Wesley, 1990.

Fiske, John. "The Discourses of TV Quiz Shows or, School+Luck=Success+ Sex." *Central States Speech Journal* 334 (Fall 1983): 139–50. (Rpt. in *Television Criticism: Approaches and Applications*, 445–62. Ed. Leah R. Vande Berg and Lawrence A. Wenner. New York: Longman, 1991.)

Fiske, John, and John Hartley. *Reading Television.* London and New York: Methuen, 1978.

Fjermedal, Grant. *The Tomorrow Makers.* New York: Macmillan, 1986.

Flitterman, Sandy. "Psychoanalysis, Film, and Television." *Channels of Discourse*, 200. Ed. Robert Allen. Chapel Hill: U of North Carolina P, 1987.

Foucault, Michel. "Ceci n'est pas une pipe." Trans. Richard Howard. *October* 1 (1976): 6–19.

———. *Discipline and Punish: The Birth of the Prison.* Trans. Alan Sheridan. New York: Vintage, 1979.

Freeman, Michael. "Murder by television? 'Jenny'-related shooting has raised concern over talk-show content." *Mediaweek* 20 (Mar. 1995): 9–10.

Freud, Sigmund. *Beyond the Pleasure Principle* (1920). Vol. 18, *The Standard*

Edition of the Complete Psychological Works of Sigmund Freud, 3–64. Ed. and trans. James Strachey. London: Hogarth, 1955.

———. *Jokes and the Unconscious.* Trans. James Strachey. New York: Norton, 1963.

———. *The Interpretation of Dreams.* Trans. James Strachey. New York: Norton, 1963.

Fried, Michael. "Art and Objecthood." *Minimal Art: A Critical Anthology*, 116–47. Ed. Gregory Battcock. New York: Dutton, 1968.

Gamson, Joshua. *Claims to Fame: Celebrity in Contemporary America.* Berkeley and Los Angeles: University of California Press, 1994.

Gardner, Howard. "Cracking the Codes of Television: The Child as Anthropologist." *Transmission: Theory and Practice for a New Televison Aesthetics*, 93–102. Ed. Peter d'Agostino. New York: Tanam P, 1985.

Genette, Gérard. "Boundaries of the Narrative." *New Literary History* 8, no. 1 (1976): 1–15.

———. "Frontiers of Narrative." *Figures of Literary Discourse*, 127–44. Trans. Alan Sheridan. New York: Columbia UP, 1981.

Gibson, William. *Neuromancer.* New York: Ace, 1984.

Gilmore, Tom. "A Strange Mix of Football and War News." *San Francisco Chronicle* 21 Jan. 1991: D5.

Gitlin, Todd. "Car Commercials and *Miami Vice*: 'We Build Excitement.'" *Watching Television: A Pantheon Guide to Popular Culture*, 136–61. Ed. Todd Gitlin. New York: Pantheon, 1986.

Goethals, Gregor T. *The TV Ritual: Worship at the Video Altar.* Boston: Beacon P, 1981.

Goffman, Erving. *On the Presentation of Self in Everyday Life.* New York: Anchor, 1959.

Goldberger, Paul. "Design: The Risks of Razzle-Dazzle." *New York Times* 12 Apr. 1987, sec. 2: 1, 34.

Gottlieb, Richard M. "Rethinking Cannibalism." Unpublished paper given at New York University, 18 Aug. 1992.

Graham, Dan, and Robin Hurst. "Corporate Arcadias." *Artforum* (Dec. 1987): 68–74.

Greenfield, Jeff. Interview. "Lead Story: The News on Networks." *Inside Story.* PBS, 23 Apr. 1982.

Greimas, A. J., and J. Courtés. *Semiotics and Language: An Analytical Dictionary.* Trans. Larry Christ et al. Bloomington: Indiana UP, 1982.

Grosz, Elizabeth A. "Lesbian Fetishism." *differences* 3, no. 2 (1991): 39–54.

———. "Bodies-Cities." *Sexuality and Space*, 241–53. Princeton: Princeton U School of Architecture, 1992.

Hackett, Robert A. "Bias and Objectivity in News Media Studies." *Critical Studies in Mass Communications* 1, no. 3 (1984): 229–59.

Hall, Jane. "AIDS activists barge in on CBS, 'MacNeil/Lehrer' Show." *Los Angeles Times* 23 Jan. 1991: A16.

Hallin, Daniel. *We Keep America On Top of the World: Television Journalism and the Public Sphere.* London and New York: Routledge, 1994.

———. "Where? Cartography, Community and the Cold War." In Manoff and Schudson 109–145.

Hanhardt, John G. "Décollage/Collage: Notes toward a Reexamination of the

Origins of Video Art." In *Illuminating Video: An Essential Guide to Video Art*, 51–69, 498. Ed. Doug Hall and Sally Fifer. New York: Aperture; San Francisco: BAVC, 1991.

Haraway, Donna J. "A Cyborg Manifesto: Science, Technology and Socialist Feminism in the Late Twentieth Century." In *Simians, Cyborgs and Women: The Reinvention of Nature*, 149–81. New York: Routledge, 1991.

———. "The Actors Are Cyborg, Nature Is Coyote, and the Geography Is Elsewhere: Postscript to 'Cyborgs at Large.'" In *Technoculture*, 21–26. Ed. Constance Penley and Andrew Ross. Minneapolis: U of Minnesota P, 1991.

Hardison, O. B. *Disappearing through the Skylight: Culture and Technology in the Twentieth Century.* New York: Viking, 1989 and Penguin, 1990.

Harrison, Harry, and Marvin Minsky. *The Turing Option.* New York: Warner, 1992.

Hartley, John. *Understanding News.* London and New York: Methuen, 1982.

Hayles, N. Katherine. "Narratives of Artificial Life." *Future Natural: Nature/ Science/ Culture*, 146–164. Ed. George Robertson et al. London and New York: Routledge, 1996.

———. "The Seductions of Cyberspace." In *Rethinking Technology,* 173–90. Ed. Verena Andermatt Conley. Minneapolis: U of Minnesota P, 1993.

Hemingway, Ernest. "Hills Like White Elephants." In *Men without Women*, 50–55. New York: Scribner, 1997.

Herdeg, Walter. *Film and TV Graphics.* Zürich: Graphis, 1967.

Hess, Dick, and Marion Muller. *Dorfsman and CBS.* New York: American Showcase, 1987.

Hession, Charles H., and Hyman Sardy. *Ascent to Affluence: A History of American Economic Development.* Boston: Allyn and Bacon, 1969.

Hobbs, Robert. "Introduction." *Robert Smithson: Sculpture.* Ithaca: Cornell UP, 1981.

Hollier, Denis. "The Word of God: 'I am Dead.'" *October* 44 (1988): 76–77.

Houston, Beverly. "The Metapsychology of Endless Consumption." *Quarterly Review of Film Studies* 9, no. 3 (1984): 183–95.

Huhtamo, Erkki. "Encapsulated Bodies in Motion: Simulators and the Quest for Total Immersion." In *Critical Issues in Electronic Media*, 159–86. Ed. Simon Penny. Albany: SUNY P, 1995.

Hurrell, Ron. *Van Nostrand Reinhold Manual of Television Graphics.* New York: Van Nostrand Reinhold, 1973.

Huyssen, Andreas. *The Great Divide: Modernism, Mass Culture, Postmodernism.* Bloomington: Indiana UP, 1986.

Irigaray, Luce. *This Sex Which Is Not One.* Trans. Catherine Porter. Ithaca: Cornell UP, 1985.

James, Caryn. "Looking Back on the Oracle as Everyman." *New York Times* 5 January 1997: H37.

Jeffords, Susan, and Lauren Rabinovitz, eds. *Seeing Through the Media: The Persian Gulf War.* New Brunswick: Rutgers UP, 1994.

Judson, William. *Points of Departure. Origins in Video: Peter Campus, Beryl Korot, Bruce Nauman, William Wegman.* Exhibition catalogue, 4–18. Ed. William Judson. Pittsburgh: The Carnegie Museum of Art, 1990.

Kaplan, E. Ann. *Rocking around the Clock: Music, Television, Postmodernism and Consumer Culture.* New York: Methuen, 1987.

————, ed. *Regarding Television: Critical Approaches — an Anthology.* Frederick, Md.: University Publications of America; Los Angeles: AFI, 1983.

Kaplan, Sam Hall. "The New Suburbia." *Los Angeles Times Magazine* 16 Sept. 1988: 28.

Kern, Stephen. *The Culture of Time and Space 1880–1918.* Cambridge: Harvard UP, 1983.

Kinder, Marsha. "Gendered Violence in Video Games." Paper delivered at the conference "Console-ing Passions," Tucson, April 1984. Published as part of "Contextualizing Video Game Violence: From Teenage Mutant Ninja Turtles I to Mortal Kombat II." In *Interacting with Video*, 25–37. Ed. Patricia M. Greenfield and Rodney R. Cocking. Norwood, N.J.: Ablex Publishing Corp., 1996.

Kittler, Friedrich. "A Conversation between Peter Weibel and Friedrich Kittler." In *On Justifying the Hypothetical Nature of Art and the Non-Identicality within the Object World*, 149–177. Ed. Peter Weibel. Trans. Jörg von Stein. Frankfurt: Städelschule-Institut für Neue Medien; Cologne: Buchhandlung Walther König, 1992.

————. "Protected Mode." In *Computer als Medium*, 209–220. Ed. Norbert Bolz, Friedrich Kittler, and Christoph Tholen. Munich: Fink Verlag, 1994.

Klein, Melanie. *Writings II.* London: Hogarth, 1980.

Kowinski, William Severini. *The Malling of America: An Inside Look at the Great Consumer Paradise.* New York: William Morrow, 1985.

Kozel, Susan. "Spacemaker: Experiences of the Virtual Body." *Dance Theater Journal* 11, no. 3 (1994): 12–13, 31, 46–47.

Krauss, Rosalind. *Passages in Modern Sculpture.* Cambridge: MIT P, 1981.

————. "Sculpture in the Expanded Field." In *The Anti-Aesthetic: Essays on Postmodern Culture*, 31–33. Ed. Hal Foster. Port Townsend, Wash.: Bay P, 1983.

————. "Video: The Aesthetics of Narcissism," *October* 1 (Spring 1976): 50–64. Rpt. in *Video Culture: A Critical Investigation*, 179–191. Ed. John Hanhardt. Rochester: Visual Studies Workshop, 1990.

Kristeva, Julia. *Powers of Horror: An Essay on Abjection.* Trans. Leon S. Roudiez. New York: Columbia UP, 1982.

————. "The System and the Speaking Subject." *Times Literary Supplement* (12 Oct. 1973): 1249–50.

Lacan, Jacques. "The Mirror Stage as Formative of the Function of the I." *Écrits: A Selection*, 1–7. Trans. Alan Sheridan. New York: Norton, 1977.

Laplanche, Jean, and J.-B. Pontalis. *The Language of Psychoanalysis.* Trans. Donald Nicholson-Smith. New York: Norton, 1973.

Laughton, Roy. *TV Graphics.* New York: Reinhold, 1966.

Levy, Mark R. "Watching TV News as Para-Social Interaction." *Journal of Broadcasting* 1, no. 1 (1979): 72.

Levy, Stephen. *Artificial Life: The Quest for a New Creation.* New York: Pantheon, 1992.

Longworth, R. C. "Access to TV revolutionizes Eastern Europe." *San Francisco Chronicle* 7 Jan. 1990: A12.

Lovink, Geert. "Aesthetics of the Video Document: The Romanian Tele-revolution according to Farocki and Ujica." *N5M* (1993): 59–60.

MacArthur, John R. *Second Front: Censorship and Propaganda in the Gulf War.* New York: Hill and Wang, 1992.

MacCannell, Dean. *The Tourist: A New Theory of the Leisure Class.* New York: Schocken, 1976.

Macgregor, Brent. "International television coverage of the bombing of the Baghdad 'bunker,' 13 February 1991." *Historical Journal of Film, Radio and Television* 14, no. 3 (August 1994): 241–69.

Mannoni, Octave. *Cléfs pur l'imaginaire: ou l'autre scène.* Paris: Éditions du Seuil, 1969.

Manoff, Robert Karl, and Michael Schudson, eds. *Reading the News.* New York: Pantheon, 1986.

Marin, Louis. *Portrait of the King.* Minneapolis: U of Minnesota P, 1988.

McHale, Brian. *Postmodernist Fiction.* New York: Methuen, 1987.

McKenna, Terence. *Food of the Gods: The Search for the Original Tree of Knowledge, a Radical History of Plants, Drugs, and Human Evolution.* New York: Bantam, 1992.

McKie, Robin. "Intel chief shuns 'superhighway'" (on Andy Grove). *San Francisco Examiner* 20 Mar. 1994: C5–6.

McLuhan, Marshall. *The Mechanical Bride: Folklore of Industrial Man.* Boston: Beacon, 1967.

Meehan, Eileen. "Why We Don't Count: The Commodity Audience." In Mellencamp, *Logics* 117–37.

Meggs, Philip B. *A History of Graphic Design.* New York: Van Nostrand Reinhold, 1983.

Mellencamp, Patricia. "Excursions in Catastrophe: Power and Contradiction in the Philippines" (review of Steve Fagin's "The Machine That Killed Bad People"). *Afterimage* (Apr. 1990): 8–11.

———. *High Anxiety: Catastrophe, Scandal, Age, and Comedy.* Bloomington: Indiana UP, 1992.

Mellencamp, Patricia, ed. *Logics of Television.* Bloomington: Indiana UP, 1990.

Merritt, Douglas. *Graphic Design in Television.* Oxford: Focal Press, 1993.

———. *Television Graphics—from Pencil to Pixel.* London: Trefoil, 1987.

Metz, Christian. *Film Language.* Trans. Michael Taylor. New York: Oxford UP, 1974. Rpt. Chicago, U of Chicago P, 1991.

———. "Story/Discourse (A Note on Two Kinds of Voyeurism)." *The Imaginary Signifer: Psychoanalysis and the Cinema,* 91–98. Trans. Celia Britton. Bloomington: Indiana UP, 1982.

Meyerowitz, Joshua. *No Sense of Place: The Impact of Electronic Media on Social Behavior.* New York: Oxford UP, 1985.

Mitchell, William J. *The Reconfigured Eye: Visual Truth in the Post-Photographic Era.* Cambridge: MIT P, 1992.

Moores, Shaun. "'The Box on the Dresser': Memories of Early Radio and Everyday Life." *Media Culture and Society* 10 (1988): 23.

Moravec, Hans. *Mind Children: The Future of Robot and Human Intelligence.* Cambridge: Harvard UP, 1988.

———. "The Universal Robot." In *Out of Control: Ars Electronica 1991*, 13–28. Ed. Gottfried Hattinger and Peter Weibel. Linz: Landesverlag, 1991.

Morgenthaler, John. "Smart Drugs Update." *Mondo 2000* 5: 36–37.

Morris, Meaghan. "Great Moments in Social Climbing: King Kong and the Human Fly." In *Sexuality and Space*, 1–51. Ed. Beatriz Colomina. New York: Princeton Architectural P, 1992.

Morrison, Philip, and Phylis Morrison. *Powers of Ten* (1982). New York: Scientific American Library, 1994.

Morse, Margaret. "The Architecture of Representation: Video Works by Judith Barry." *Afterimage* (Oct. 1987): 1, 8–11.

———. "Art in Cyberspace: Interacting with Machines as Art at Siggraph's 'Machine-Culture—The Virtual Frontier,'" *Video Networks* 17, no. 5 (1993): 19–23.

———. "¿Ciberia o comunidad virtual? Arte y ciberespacio." (Cyberia or the virtual community: art in cyberspace) *Revista de Occidente* 193, trans. Mariano Antolín Rato (1994): 73–90.

———. "Closed Circuits and Fragmented Egos." Rochester: Society for Photographic Education, 1989.

———. "Cyclones from Oz: On George Kuchar's Weather Diary 1." *Framework* (Apr. 1989): 24–30.

———. "The End of the Television Receiver." In *From Receiver to Remote Control: The TV Set*, 139–41. Ed. Reese Williams and Matthew Geller. New York: New Museum of Contemporary Art, 1990.

———. "Interiors: A Review of *The American Landscape Video*," *Video Networks* 13 nos. 1/2 (February/March 1989): 15–19.

———. "Judith Barry: The Body in Space." *Art in America* (Apr. 1993): 116–21, 143.

———. "Mary Lucier: Burning and Shining." *Video Networks* 5 (1986): 1–6 and 6/7 (1986): 3–7.

———. "Muntadas' Media-Architectural Installations." *Muntadas: Trabajos Recientes*, 7–16, 112–17. Valencia, Spain: IVAM Centre Julio Gonzalez, 1992.

———. "Rock Video: Synchronizing Rock Music and Television." In *Television Criticism: Approaches and Applications*," 289–312. Ed. Leah R. Vande Berg and Lawrence A. Wenner. White Plains, N.Y.: Longman, 1991.

———. "The Shifting Media Landscape: New Video Venues and Postmodern Media Mixes," *Video Networks* 12, nos. 6/7/8 (Summer 1988): 11–13.

———. "Talk, Talk, Talk: The Space of Discourse in TV News, Sportcasts, Talk Shows & Advertising." *Screen* 26, no. 2 (March-Apr. 1985): 1–11.

———. "The Television News Personality and Credibility: Reflections on the News in Transition." *Working Paper No. 5* (Fall 1985). Center for Twentieth Century Studies, University of Wisconsin; in *Studies in Entertainment: Critical Approaches to Mass Culture*, 55–79. Ed. Tania Modleski. Bloomington: Indiana UP, 1986.

———. "Video at the Crossroads: The AFI Video Festival 1988." *Video Networks* 13, nos. 3/4 (April/May 1989): 21–23.

———. "Video Mom: Reflections on a Cultural Obsession." *East/West Film Journal* (June 1989): 53–72.

Mueller, John. *Policy and Opinion in the Gulf War*. Chicago: U of Chicago P, 1994.

Multimediale 3. Karlsruhe: Zentrum für Kunst und Medientechnologie, 1993.

Mulvey, Laura. "Visual Pleasure and Narrative Cinema." *Screen* 16, no. 3 (1975): 6–18.

———. "'Xala', Sembene, Ousmane (1974), the Carapace that Failed." Rpt. from *Third Text* 16/17 (Autumn/Winter 1991) in *Camera Obscura* 31 (Jan.– May 1993): 48–71.

Naimark, Michael. "Frame Rate." *Elements of Realspace Imaging*, 34–35. San Francisco: Apple Multimedia Lab, 1991.

Nam June Paik. New York: Norton and Whitney Museum, 1982.

Narisetti, Raju. "Anatomy of a food fight: The Olestra debate. (Center for Science in the Public Interest urges Food and Drug Administration to ban Olestra by focusing negative campaign against Procter & Gamble Co. and Frito-Lay Co.) *Wall Street Journal* Wed., July 31, 1996: B1(W), B1(E).

Newcomb, Horace, and Paul M. Hirsch. "Television as a Cultural Forum." In *Television: The Critical View*, 5th ed., 503–515. Ed. Horace Newcomb. New York, Oxford: Oxford UP, 1994.

Nichols, Bill. "The Work of Culture in the Age of Cybernetic Systems." *Screen* 29 (1988): 22–46.

Oreskes, Michael. "America's Politics Loses Way as Its Vision Changes World." *New York Times* 18 Mar. 1990: 1, 16.

———. "Political Failures Are Creating a New Constituency for Change: Rules on Television Ads and Fund Raising Sought." *New York Times* 21 Mar. 1990: 1.

Patterson, William Patrick. *Eating the "I": In Search of the Self*. San Anselmo, Calif.: Arete, 1992.

Pearson, Durk, and Sandy Shaw. *Intelli-Scope: The Newsletter of Designer Foods Network*. Ed. Mark Rennie. Feb. 1993.

———. *Life Extension: A Practical Scientific Approach*. New York: Warner, 1983.

———. *The Life Extension Companion*. New York: Warner, 1984.

Pearson, Durk, and Sandy Shaw, with Jude Milhon. "Durk and Sandy Explain It All for You." *Mondo 2000* 3: 32–34.

Pelton, Ross. *Mind Food and Smart Pills*. New York: Doubleday, 1989.

Pinney, Christopher. "Future Travel." In *Visualizing Theory: Selected Essays from Visual Anthropology Review 1990–94*, 409–428. Ed. Lucien Taylor. New York and London: Routledge, 1994.

Plato. "The Simile of the Cave." *Symposium*.

Plunkett, John. "The Subtle Art of Bespoke Type." *Wired* 3, no. 8 (1995): 126–27.

Popcorn, Faith. *The Popcorn Report*. New York: Bantam, 1991.

Powers, Ron. *The Newscasters*. New York: St. Martin's P, 1977.

Rath, Claus-Dieter. "The Invisible Network: Television as an Institution in Everyday Life." In *Television in Transition: Papers from the First International Television Studies Conference*, 199–204. Ed. Phillip Drummond and Richard Paterson. London: British Film Institute, 1985.

Reich, Robert B. *The Work of Nations: Preparing Ourselves for 21st-Century Capitalism*. New York: Vintage, 1992.

Rennie, Mark. "Smart Drugs' True Believers: Highly Developed Thoughts on These Additives for the Psyche." *San Francisco Chronicle* 4 Mar. 1992: D3.

Rheingold, Howard. *The Virtual Community: Homesteading on the Electronic Frontier.* Reading, Mass.: Addison-Wesley, 1993.

Rifkin, Jeremy. *Biosphere Politics: A New Consciousness for a New Century.* New York: Crown, 1991.

Rivlin, Robert. *The Algorithmic Image: Graphic Visions of the Computer Age.* Redmond, Wash.: Microsoft, 1986.

Rosen, Jay. "From Slogan to Spectacle: How the Media and the Left Lost the War." *Tikkun* (May/June 1991): 22–26.

Rosenberg, Howard. "Title." *The Media and the Gulf: A Closer Look.* Proc. of a Conference at the Graduate School of Journalism, UC Berkeley. 3–4 May 1991. Berkeley: UC Berkeley, 1991.

Rosenberg, Scott. "Cybervisonary." *San Francisco Examiner* 7 Aug. 1994: C15.

Rosler, Martha. "Video: Shedding the Utopian Moment." In *Illuminating Video: An Essential Guide to Video Art*, 31–50. Ed. Doug Hall and Sally Fifer. New York: Aperture and the Bay Area Video Coalition, 1991.

Ross, Andrew. "The Work of Nature in the Age of Electronic Emission." *Social Text* 18 (1987–88): 116–28.

Roszak, Theodore. *The Cult of Information: The Folklore of Computers and the Fine Art of Thinking.* New York: Pantheon, 1986.

Rucker, Randy, R. U. Sirius, and Queen Mu. *Mondo 2000's User's Guide to the New Edge: Cyberpunk, Virtual Reality, Wetware, Designer Aphrodisiacs, Artificial Life, Techno-Erotic Paganism, and More.* New York: HarperCollins, 1992.

Rutledge, Virginia. "Reality by Other Means." *Art in America* 84 no. 6 (June 1996): 38–39.

Sachs, Wolfgang. "Are Energy-Intensive Life-Images Fading? The Cultural Meaning of the Automobile in Transition." Unpublished.

Safire, William. "Don't Be Afraid, Americans, Join the Parade." *San Francisco Chronicle* 11 June 1991: A19.

Sartre, Jean-Paul. "Intentionality" (1939). Trans. Martin Joughin. Rpt. in Crary and Kwinter 387–91.

Savan, Leslie. "This Typeface is Changing Your Life." In *Media Culture: Television, Radio, Records, Books, Magazines, Newspapers, Movies*, 223–234. Ed. James Monaco. New York: Dell, 1978.

Scarry, Elaine. "Watching and Authorizing the Gulf War." In *Media Spectacles*, 57–73. Ed. Marjorie Garber, Jann Matlock, and Rebecca L. Walkowitz. London and New York: Routledge, 1993.

Schier, Jeff. "Lee Harrison." *Eigenwelt der Apparate-Welt: Pioneers of Electronic Art*, 92–95. Artistic director, Peter Weibel; curators Woody Vasulka and Steina Vasulka; editor David Dunn. Linz: ars electronica, 1992.

Schivelbusch, Wolfgang. *Disenchanted Night: The Industrialization of Light in the Nineteenth Century.* Trans. Angela Davies. Berkeley: U of California P, 1988.

———. "The Policing of Street Lighting." *Yale French Studies: Everyday Life* 73 (1987): 61–74.

Schmidt, William E. "In U.S., Timid Hope on a New World." *New York Times* 11 Mar. 1990: 1.

Schmitt, Eric. "Bad Computer Hobbled Defense Against Scud That Killed GIs." *San Francisco Chronicle* 20 May 1991: A9.

Schneider, Ira, and Beryl Korot, eds. *Video Art: An Anthology*. New York: Harcourt Brace Jovanovich, 1976.

Schulz, Jeff. "Virtu-Real Space: Information Technologies and the Politics of Consciousness." *Computer Graphics: Visual Proceedings*, 159–163. ACM Siggraph, Annual Conference Series, 1993.

Schwab, Gabriele. "Cyborgs: Postmodern Phantasms of Body and Mind." *Discourse* 9 (Spring-Summer 1987): 64–84.

Searle, John R., and Daniel Vanderveken. *Foundations of Illocutionary Logic.* London: Cambridge UP, 1985.

Shaw, Gareth, and Allan M. Williams. *Critical Issues in Tourism: A Geographical Perspective*. Oxford and Cambridge, Mass.: Blackwell, 1993.

Shigeko Kubota: Video Sculptures. Essen: Museum Folkwang, 1982.

Shohat, Ella, and Robert Stam, eds. *Unthinking Eurocentrism*. New York and London: Routledge, 1994.

Silverman, Kaja. *The Subject of Semiotics*. New York and Oxford: Oxford UP, 1983.

Skirrow, Gillian. "Hellivision: An Analysis of Video Games." In *High Theory/Low Culture*. Ed. Colin MacCabe. Manchester: Manchester UP, 1986. (Rpt. in *The Media Reader*, 320–38. Ed. Manuel Alvarado and John O. Thompson. London: BFI, 1990.)

Sobchack, Vivian. "'Lounge Time': Post-war Crises and the Chronotope of Film Noir." *Refiguring American Film Genres: History and Theory.* Ed. Nick Browne. Berkeley: University of California P, forthcoming.

Sorkin, Michael. "Scenes from the Electronic City." *I.D.* (May/June 1992): 70–77.

Sorlin, Pierre. Unpublished paper, Conference on "Cinema and Television: Cain and Abel." Cinemateek Haags Filmhuis, The Netherlands, November 1993.

Spivak, Gayatri Chakravorty. "Subaltern Studies: Deconstructing Historiography." *In Other Worlds* (New York: Routledge, 1988), 197–221.

St. Jude. "Are You as Smart as Your Drugs? A Paranoid Rant by St. Jude." *Mondo 2000* 5: 38.

Stam, Robert. "Television News and Its Spectator." In *Regarding Television,* 23–43. Ed. E. Ann Kaplan.

Stewart, Susan. *On Longing: Narratives of the Miniature, the Gigantic, the Souvenir, the Collection.* Baltimore: Johns Hopkins UP, 1984.

Stone, Allucquère Roseanne. "Sex, Death and Architecture." *any 3: Electrotecture: Architecture and Electronic Culture* (Nov./Dec. 1993): 34–39.

———. "Virtual Systems." In Crary and Kwinter 609–21.

Sutherland, Ivan. "The Ultimate Display." *Proceedings of the IFIP Congress*, 506–508. Information Processing Techniques Office, ARPA, OSD. 1965.

Swartz, Jon. "The Second Coming of Television." *San Francisco Chronicle* 28 Jan. 1997: C4.

Tafler, David. "Boundaries and Frontiers: Interactivity and Participant Experience—Building New Models and Formats." In d'Agostino and Tafler 235–67.

Tamblyn, Christine. "The River of Swill: Feminist Art, Sexual Codes and Censorship." *Afterimage* 18, no. 3 (1990): 10–13.

Terry, Don. "Decades of Rage Created Crucible of Violence." *New York Times* 3 May 1992: 1, 17.

The Luminous Image. Stedelikjk Museum, Amsterdam. 1984.

The Situated Image. Curator: Chip Lord. Mandeville Gallery, San Diego. 1987.

Todorov, Tzvetan. *The Conquest of America.* Trans. Richard Howard. New York: Harper & Row, 1985.

———. "Enunciation." *Encyclopedic Dictionary of the Sciences of Language.* Ed. Oswald Ducrot and Tzvetan Todorov. Baltimore and London: Johns Hopkins UP, 1979.

Toufexis, Anastasia. "Health: The New Scoop on Vitamins." *Time* (6 Apr. 1991): 54–59.

Trilling, Lionel. *Sincerity and Authenticity.* Cambridge: Harvard UP, 1972. Rpt. New York: Harcourt Brace Jovanovich, 1980.

Turkle, Sherry. *The Second Self: Computers and the Human Spirit.* New York: Simon & Schuster, 1984.

Turner, Victor. "Frame, Flow and Reflection: Ritual and Drama as Public Liminality." In *Performance in Postmodern Culture,* 33–55. Ed. Michel Benamou and Charles Caramello. Madison: Coda, 1977.

———. *From Ritual to Theater: The Human Seriousness of Play.* New York: Performing Arts Journal, 1982.

Urban, Greg. "The 'I' of Discourse." In *Semiotics, Self and Society,* 27–51. Ed. Benjamin Lee and Greg Urban. Berlin and New York: Mouton de Gruyter, 1989.

Venturi, Robert, Denise Scott Brown, and Steven Izenour. *Learning from Las Vegas: The Forgotten Symbolism of Architectural Form.* Cambridge: MIT P, 1972, 1977.

Virilio, Paul. "The Third Window: An Interview with Paul Virilio." Trans. Yvonne Shafir. In *Global Television,* 185–97, 194, 196. Ed. Cynthia Schneider and Brian Wallis. Cambridge: MIT P, 1988.

———. The *Vision Machine.* Bloomington: Indiana UP, 1994.

———. *War and Cinema: The Logistics of Perception.* London: Verso, 1989.

Ward, Dean, and John Morgenthaler. *Smart Drugs and Nutrients: How to Improve Your Memory and Increase Your Intelligence Using the Latest Discoveries in Neuroscience.* Santa Cruz, Calif.: B&J, 1990.

Weinbren, Grahame. "Film Space: An Outline Study." *Millennium Film Journal* 16/17/18 (1987): 328–35.

White, Mimi. "Site Unseen: An Analysis of CNN's War in the Gulf." In Jeffords and Rabinovitz 121–141.

Wiener, Norbert. *Cybernetics: Or, Control and Communication in the Animal and the Machine.* 2nd ed. Cambridge, Mass.: MIT P, 1969.

Willemen, Paul. *Looks and Frictions: Essays in Cultural Studies and Film Theory.* Bloomington: Indiana UP, 1994.

Williams, Raymond. *Television: Technology and Cultural Form.* New York: Shocken, 1975; Rpt. Hanover, NH: UP of New England, 1992.

Williamson, Judith. *Decoding Advertisements: Ideology and Meaning in Advertising.* London: Marion Boyars, 1978.

Wilson, Alexander. *The Culture of Nature: North American Landscape from Disney to the Exxon Valdez.* Oxford and Cambridge, Mass.: Blackwell, 1992.

Winograd, Terry, and Fernando Flores. *Understanding Computers and Cognition: A New Foundation for Design.* Reading, Mass.: Addison Wesley, 1986.

Woodward, Bob. *The Commanders.* New York: Simon & Schuster, 1991.

Woolley, Benjamin. *Virtual Worlds: A Journey in Hype and Hyperreality.* Oxford: Blackwell, 1992.

Worth, Sol, and John Adair. *Through Navajo Eyes: An Exploration in Film Communication and Anthropology.* Bloomington: Indiana UP, 1975.

Wren, Christopher S. *The End of the Line: The Failure of Communism in the Soviet Union and China.* New York: Simon and Schuster, 1990.

Zettl, Herbert. "Graphication." In *Television Studies: Textual Analysis*, 137–163. Ed. Gary Burns and Robert J. Thompson. New York: Praeger, 1989.

———. *Sight, Sound, Motion: Applied Media Aesthetics.* 2nd ed. Belmont, Calif.: Wadsworth, 1990.

Zielinski, Sigfried. "Medien/Krieg. Ein kybernetischer Kurzschluss." *Medien Journal: Medien im Krieg* 15, no. 1 (1991) (citation trans. Morse): 18.

Zukin, Sharon. "Gentrification, Cuisine, and the Critical Infrastructure: Power and Centrality Downtown." *Landscapes of Power: From Detroit to Disney World*, 179–215. Berkeley: U of California P, 1991.

Index

Abjection: body fluids, corpses, 148; simulated, 150; between death and resurrection, 151

Alice in Wonderland, drugs and fit, 232

Analogs of television: in built environment, 99; airport as, 226

Anchors: as shifters, 38–40; and credibility, 42–43; as representing collective subject, 43; struggle for position; 43–44; graphics as, 94

Antin, David, on televisual reframing, 115

Arcades, of Milan as model for mall, 109

Art pieces: "The Golden Calf," 26, (illus) 27; "Telematic Dreaming" (illus) 31, 97; *Prime Time in the Camps,* 37; *Videogramme einer Revolution,* 60; *2001, A Space Odyssey,* 82; *A rough sketch,* 82; *Wavelength,* 83; "Royal Road," 88, (illus) 89; "Telematic Vision," 97, (illus) frontispiece; "Virtuality, Inc.," 141, (illus) 142; "Imagination Dead Imagine," 149, (illus) 150; "Live Taped Corridor," 155, (illus) 156; "Dachau," 167, 168; "haute CULTURE," 168; "Exposicion," 169; "Left Side Right Side," 172, (illus) 173; "Three Transitions," 172, (illus) 175; "Interface," (illus) 174; "mem," (illus) 174; "Boomerang," "Opposing Mirrors and Video Monitors on Time Delay," 176; "Handsight," (illus) 186; "A Very Nervous System," 193; "Faraday's Garden," 193, (illus) 194; "Adelbrecht," 194; "Family Portrait," 194; "Archeology of a Mother Tongue," 199, 200, 205, (illus) 206–207; "See Banff!," 180, 203, (illus) 204; "The Fileroom," 188, (illus) 189; "Revolution," 190; "Televirtual Fruit Machine," 190, (illus) 191; "The Flock," 193; "Osmose," 208, (illus) 209

Art, excremental, and contamination strategies, 147

Art as cognitive and aesthetic experimentation, 34

Artaud, Antonin, "All Writing is Pigshit," 151

Artificial life as metaphor for dynamic interrelation, 22; and emergent social behavior, 210; to model biodiversity, 214

Artists: Shaw, Jeffrey, 26, 27, 88; Sermon, Paul, 31, 97; Marker, Chris, 37; Farocki, Harun, and Andrei Ujica, 60; Méliès, Georges, 81; Eames, Charles, and Ray Eames, 82; Snow, Michael, 83; Naimark, Michael, 141, 142; Barry, Judith, 149, 150; Nauman, Bruce, 155, 156; Lucier, Mary, 164; Korot, Beryl, 167, 168; Jonas, Joan, 172, 173; Campus, Peter, 172, 174, 175; Graham, Dan, 176; Serra, Richard, 176; Hegedüs, Agnes, 186, 190, 191; Hoberman, Perry, 193, 194; Courchesne, Luc, 194; Dove, Toni, and Michael Mackenzie, 199, 200, 205, 206, 207; Sommerer, Christa, and Laurent Mignonneau, 210; Davies, Char, 208, 209

Artists, mention of: Rita Myers, Joan Jonas, Mary Lucier, Ken Feingold, Muntadas, Dieter Froese, Francesc Torres, 163; Wolf Vostell, Nam June Paik, Ant Farm, Mary Lucier, 165; Nam June Paik, Shigeko Kubota, Mary Lucier, 166; Ira Schneider, Frank Gillette, 167; Curt Royston, 168; Muntadas, 168–69, 188–89; Bruce Nauman, Peter Campus, Dan

Graham, 171; Joan Jonas, Vito Acconci, 172; Laura Kurgan, Robert Kyr, Toni Dove, 180; Naimark, Michael, 180, 203, 204; Shaw, Jeffrey, 190, 197; Jeff Schulz, 192; Rinaldo, Kenneth, and Mark Grossman, David Rokeby, 193; Martin Spanjaard, 194; Ken Goldberg, 210; Catherine Richards, 211
Austin, J. S., and infelicities, 13
Authenticity and tourism, 242
Automobile: as metaphor of postmodernity, 103; interior as idyll, 107, 111; as metaphor for myth, 111; and gender, 226

Bachelard, Gaston, 81
Back side or backstage: as pocket of fiction, 87; in Academy Awards, 224; and television, 228
Bakhtin, Mikhail, and the chronotope, 101
Ballard, J. G., on food as eating self, 128
Barry, Judith, "Imagination Dead Imagine," 149, (illus) 150, 151
Barthes, Roland: "having been there," 11; automobile and myth, 111; "Operation Margarine" on denial and inoculation, 140; cenesthesia, 145
Baudrillard, Jean: simulation and automobile and postmodernity, 103
Beckett, Samuel, *Imagination Dead Imagine,* 149
Benjamin, Walter: *Passagenwerk,* 100; metapsychology of privatization, 108; phantasmagoria of the interior, 109; film and invisible technology, 134
Benveniste, Émile, 9
Berger, Peter, and Thomas Luckmann, *The Social Construction of Reality,* 9
Blade Runner and van Eyck's *Arnolfini Wedding,* 224
Blinding of Iraqi infrastructure, 29
Blindness and technology: and virtual reality, 25, 26, 183; in telematics, 26, 143; Winograd and Flores on, 26; in Gulf War, 28; machine vision and, 29–30; psychotic hallucination, 235
Body fluids, waste, simulated, 149–50; as mortality symbols, 151
Body and food loathing, 126–27, 148
Body, physical and virtual contrasted, 125, 236
Body-image split in "Live Taped Corridor," 155

Bolter, David J., on artificial intelligence and magic, 7
Bosnia, PBS reporting on, 47
Brecht, Bertolt, on culinary theater, 134
Brodsly, David: local vs. metropolitan, 104; freeway vector, 106; segmentation of experience, 107
Bubble: of virtual space, 112; of subjectivity, 230
Buber, Martin, and "I-Thou," 10
Built environment as protocyberspace, 17
Bush, President George: Gulf War and Los Angeles rebellion addresses, 44

Calligram, 237
Camcorder footage: democracy and surveillance from below, 59; in "Nightline" on Romania, 59; long takes in, 60; oppositional vs. precious commodity, 60; offscreen space and enunciative context in, 60–61
Camera-induced performance: simulated skirmishes, 62; testimony, 46, 61–62
Campus, Peter: "Interface," (illus) 174; "mem," 166, (illus) 174; "Three Transitions," 172, (illus) 175
Canetti, Elias, *Crowds and Power,* 105
Cannibalism, psychic, 127
Cannibalistic fantasy: fragmenting and resurrecting the body, 128; and Melanie Klein, 131; and envelopment, 134; and cultural distress, 135, 233
Castration symbols, worms as, 131
Catastrophe coverage, 219
CBS graphic style: William Golden and Louis Dorfsman, 75
CBS Tuesday Movie Opener (illus) 79, 85; legibility and monumentality, 86
Ceauşescu's corpse on screen, and disputed video record, 54
Certeau, Michel de, *The Practice of Everyday Life* on space vs. place, 101
Change, cultural strategies of, 122–24
Character generator, 74
Chronotopes: as units of space/time, 101, 226; street, arcade, mall, 105; road, 123; lounge, 228
Cinematic apparatus, presentational plane of, 160
City and/as body, 205, 242
Civil rights news and "wall within," 63
Closed-circuit installation and critique of representation, 239

CNN open newsroom: the process as the story, 57–58

CNN reporting: on cruise missile, 28; on free speech in Romania, 40; from hotel in Baghdad, 214

Cold War's end: as victory or challenge, 48–49; negative response to, 218

Condensation: in engaged television segments, 114; and automobile windshield, 115; and stacks, 115

Consumers vs. subjects of discourse, 122

Contamination strategies and excremental art, 147

Convergence: of social institutions and media, 9; of executive power and media in Romania, 53; of media in cyberculture, 65; of television, mall, and freeway, 121

Corporate atriums, 227

Corruption, reports on in Romania, 218

"Cosmic Zoom," 223

Courchesne, Luc, "Family Portrait," 194

Credibility based on referential or enunciative fallacy, 12

Crowd movements: on networks, 187; in film, 190; in virtual space, 192; in artificial life, 210

Culinary discourse of information society, 125

Cultural glue, advertising and entertainment as, 47

Cyberculture: and television, 3; in inverse relation to information society, 4–6; as no less authentic, 10, 14; and feedback, 14–15; impoverishment of, 196

Cyberization: of material artifacts and space, 7; uneven distribution of, 8; of toys, 97; of money, 192; and surrogate travel, 202–203

Cyberspace: composed of metaphors, 17, 178–79; interactivity and immersion in, 17, 182; genres of, 179; entertainment versus art in, 181; negative or shadow of, 188

Cyborg: eating habits of, 125, 126; creation by mechanics vs. incorporation, 126; in video installation, 150; as metaphor, 232; envy of, 232; production of a, 237

Davies, Char, "Osmose," 208, (illus) 209

Death and virtuality, 211

Defense mechanisms, postculinary: negation, repudiation, denial, diavowal,

and nonfood, 126; symbolic use of in cultural distress, 138

Denial and simulated fat, 139, 140, 141

Derrida, Jacques, and the deconstruction of presence, 13

Dibbell, Julian, on performative speech-acts as incantations, 8

Direct cinema techniques and Melanie Klein, 222

Disavowal: of the camera/monitor, 15, 16; in anchor's virtual address, 18; and celebrity, 19; and smart food and drugs, 143; in virtual reality, 141; in telematics, 143; defined, 236

Discourse and story as passage and segmentation, 100

Discourse: pronouns, shifters, and reversibility in, 9

Disengagement: and impersonal forms, 12; as primordial rupture or break, 12; internal and narrative dereferentialization, 108

Dislocation of mass media, 107

Displacement: and nonspace, 103; of body-screen relation, 171

Dissimulation: and enunciative fallacy, 13; and on-screen power, 51;

Distraction: copresence of discourse and story, 99; as semifiction effect, 100; and enunciative and referential fallacies, 101; as detached involvement, 110; and habitual automatisms, 118; recognition and control of, 122

Distress, post–Cold War, and nonfood, 135

Dorfsman, Louis, and CBS corporate design, 75

Dove, Toni, and Michael Mackenzie, "Archeology of a Mother Tongue," 199–200, 205, (illus) 206–207

Downloading consciousness: Moravec on, 129–30; Harry Harrison and Marvin Minsky, Larry Yeager and Gerald Jay Sussman on, 130

Durán, Diego, on flaying in Aztec ceremony, 132

Duration: in hearings and trials, 23; Marcos deposed in, 36; and televisual events, 49

Eames, Charles, and Ray Eames: *A rough sketch for a proposed film dealing with the powers of ten and the relative size of things in the universe*, 82; simulated zoom and immensity, 83

Eating/being eaten as dialectic, 128

Ellis, John: and working through, 64; double distance of television viewer to world, 106; on segment, 114

Empathy and cyberspace, 210

Enchantment of everyday life, risks of, 180–81

Enculturation: and modes of narration, 4, 5; and "the process," 65; and surrogate or actual travel, 202

Endoscopic eye, 186

Engagement: simulates enunciation in utterance, 11, 12; after primordial disengagement, 12

Enunciative fallacy: speech-act equated with its simulation, 11; and television news, 12, 38; when crowd sees its image, 52

Exchange across ontological boundaries: in communication and transportation, 99; through television, 115, 119

Excretory art, 127, 237

Experience, modes of: kinesthetic insight, 156

Farocki, Harun, and Andrei Ujica, *Videogramme einer Revolution,* 60, 61

Fast food: and information society, 136; and television/microwave, 137; social cost of, 137; barbecue potato chips, 144

Fatness, class, and information society, 136

Fattening, television watching as, 136

FDA's schedule one, 144

Feedback: and interactivity, 15; and closed-circuit installation, 176

Felman, Shoshona, on promising, 13

Felt body, 210

Fetishism and glitter, 221

Fiction: as disavowal, 18; liminal function of, 18–19; filmic vs. virtual, 19–20; safety vs. immersion in, 20; televisual, as engaged, 19–20

Fictions of presence: and soft social control, 8; virtual relations and, 17; deconstructed by video installation, 160

Finley, Karen, and excretory art, 148

Fit, between virtual and material, 204

Flanagan, Bob, *Happiness in Slavery,* 131

Flaying and mutilation in Bosnia, 133

Flight simulation and computer graphics, 224

Flight, fantasy of weightless, 91

Flitterman, Sandy, and soap opera framing, 115

Flocking algorithms, 193

Flow, 229

Food ideologies, failure of, 127

Food: and mediation of self and other, 135; junk, 140; virtual, 141

Formats: news, simulation by Bosnian refugees, 36; Bosnian "room stories," 37; news, hierarchy, and disparities in power, 38–40; news, window, and wallpaper, 41; of tabloid daytime talk, 45; of news magazine tabloid, 46; degrees of condensation and "processing" in news, 55, 56; catastrophe and crisis news, 57–58, 63–64; "Nightline" challenged in South Central L.A., 63; vs. local and heterogeneous values, 123; of talk, 216

Foucault, Michel, on execution spectacle and shift of sympathy, 54

Fourth wall, 224

Freeway: passage and idyll, 107; and mobile subjectivity, 111

Freeze-frame as mask, 55

Fresh food ideology: and word processing, 137; elitism as social failure of, 137

Freud, Sigmund, and childhood fantasy of weightless flight, 91

Fried, Michael, on minimal sculpture and theatricality, 162

Games with celebrity and the democratic process, 213

Gibson, William: coiner of *cyberspace,* 17; *Neuromancer,* and body parking, 139; death in, 185, 205

Glass, disengagement, and regression, 110

Golden, William, and CBS eye logo design, 73

Graham, Dan, "Opposing Mirrors and Video Monitors on Time Delay," 176

Graphic images, 225

Graphication vs. realism, 94

Graphics defined, 219

Greimas, Algirdas Julien, on simulation and enunciation, 11, 12

Grosz, Elizabeth, on psychic defense mechanisms, 138

Gulf War: computer and television graphics in, 24; machine vision and displays in, 25

Hallin, Dan: on sound bites, 37, 45; compares Italy and U.S. television, 39; on television screen as barrier, 40; on tabloids, 46

Hardison, O. B., *Disappearing through the Skylight* and incorporation into machine, 130

Harrison, John, programmer of "Osmose," 209

Harrison, Lee, and Animac analog animation, 75

Having been there then vs. being here now, 15

Hegedüs, Agnes, "Handsight," (illus) 186; "Televirtual Fruit Machine," 190, (illus) 191

Hitchcock's *Vertigo* and contradictory motion choreography, 223

Hoberman, Perry, "Faraday's Garden," 193, (illus) 194

Holliday, George, and Rodney King beating video, 64

Hudson, Walter: and immobility, 137; and induction, 141

Humiliation: of "real people" on television, 46; of Ceauşescu, 52; with simulated waste, 149

"Hype," and cyberspace, 183

Identification: vs. introjection, 127; defined, 233

Image-surround as raw material for computer processing, 165

Images, engaged, as space of events, 21

Imaginary: and paramount reality, 10; defined, 213

Immediacy and the postsymbolic, 134

Immersion: and cyberculture, 4; and cyberspace, 17; transcendence and inorganic rebirth, 130; in the womb and Melanie Klein, 131; of cyborg in simulated waste, 149, 150; in language and symbols, 181, 210; spiritual values in, 185; and deep-sea diving metaphor, 208

Incorporation as range of subjective processes, 135

Indexical vs. digital image, 11

Induction: as vortex into television space, 71; archaic origin and liminal function of, 80; and z-axis moves, 81; in textual miniatures, 81, 222

Infelicities: in J. S. Austin, 13; in Felman, 14

Information: society and exchange-value, 4; decontextualized, 5; superhighway, 17; access to vs. invisibility, 35; and innovation vs. revolution, 67

Installation: film in, 238; as commodity and critique, 238

Intelligence, carbon- vs. silicon-based, 125

Interactivity: as virtual relationship, 4; and engagement, 5, 16; and sound media, 6; and cyberspace, 17; vs. intersubjectivity, 21–22, 29; and image as agency, 23; as machine feedback, 193; art as metacommentary on, 194; human standards apply to, 194; degrees of, 239

Interface devices: link to responsive symbolic world, 18; in virtual reality, 181; in "Archeology," 205; balance-sensor motion capture, 208

Internal engagement and disengagement, 108

Internet: historical comparisons of, with amateur radio, 66, with precinematic period, 66, 67; television as structuring metaphor, 67; compared with Panofsky's analysis of Gothic cathedral, 187

Intersubjectivity: vs. interactivity, 22; and news formats, 37; and dialogue, 39; public desire for, 46; art as metacommentary on, 195

Introjection: vs. identification, 127; Laplanche and Pontalis on, 128; nearness, the imaginary and, 133

Invertibility of two and three dimensions, 121

Jonas, Joan, "Left Side Right Side," 172

Killing symbols as mastery in cyberspace, 184

Kinesthetic insight as learning with body, 156, 161

Kinetoscope simulation, 203

King, Rodney, video and Gulf War, 215

Kinks in the road and monumentality, 120, 121

Klein, Melanie, and immersion, 131

Knowing as eating, Sartre on, 134

Korot, Beryl, "Dachau," 167–68

Kowinski, William Severini, *The Malling of America,* 103

Kozel, Susan, performance in "Telematic Dreaming," 31–32

Krauss, Rosalind, and narcissism thesis, 171, 176

Kristeva, Julia, *Powers of Horror* and abjection, 147–48

Krueger, Myron, and artificial reality sans blindness, 214

Kubrick, Stanley, *2001, A Space Odyssey,* 82

Lacan, Jacques, and the imaginary, 10

Language, planes of, 239

Lévi-Strauss, Claude, on food and myth, 134

Levy, Mark, and parasocial behavior, 18

Liminality: cultural function of, 19; in virtual environments, 180; defined, 221

Liquidity: of exchange across ontological boundaries, 100; resistance to, 119, 169; secret of commodity culture, 121

Liveness: and cultural maintenance, 15; and video installation, 159

Logic of alternation on z-axis in television, 115

Logos, network and station IDs: and 3-D motion choreography, 71; as corporate bodies, 72; induction, immersion, and weightless flight in, 73; animation as subjectivity in, 73; as shifters, 73; and network differentiation, 74; as cultural indicators, 76; and visual excess, 77; signs of exchange, 92, 225

Look that kills and tourism, 203

Los Angeles and the American dream, 227

Lost objects as mass-produced, 106

Lucas, George, *Star Wars,* 85

Lucier, Mary: "Ohio at Giverny," (illus) 164; "Untitled Display System," (illus) 164

Lynch, Kevin, on freeways, 104

MacCannell, Dean, *The Tourist,* 201

Machine vision: rewrites the map, 28–29; and synthetic viewpoint, 29

Machines: as subjects and narrators, 6; and automation of enculturation, 8–9; developmental logic of, 232; as metaphors, 233

Magazine as analog of television, 226

Magazine format, 225

Magic, sympathetic and apotropaic, and smartness, 147

Mall: surveillance and privatized idyll, 105; defined, 227; history of, 229

Malnutrition and social inequity, 234

Mantegna's *Dead Christ,* 205

Marker, Chris: *Prime Time in the Camps,* 37; edits Ceauşescus' trial, 55

Marketplace of ideas vs. ideas in marketplace, 122

Marks, Harry, and flight simulator conventions for television graphics, 78, 85

Mathematics and the real, 235

McHale, Brian: on opalescence and uncertain reality status, 180

McKenna, Terence, *Food of the Gods* and psychoactive drugs in mental evolution, 146

McLuhan, Marshall, on media prostheses, 126

Meat, 127, 131, 139, 141, 151, 233

Media events and televisual events, 50

Media interrelated, 23

Méliès, Georges, *A Trip to the Moon,* 81

Metaphors as buses in Athens, 101

Metz, Christian: and the imaginary, 10; filmic fiction as *histoire* (disengaged), 19, 20

Miniatures: and malls, 104; Bachelard on mastery and, 120; of mall and television, 119; Stewart on feminization and, 120; arcades as, 227

Mirror image versus video replicant, 172

Mise-en-abyme, 44, 107, 176, 228

Mitchell, William J., on "postphotography" and digital, 11, 12

Mobile privatization: and distraction, 100; as liberty, 117, 118

Mobility: from escape to commodity, 101; as virtual travel, 111–13

Monumentality, tall vs. long and low, 120

Moravec, Hans, *Mind Children* and being eaten, 129, 130

Morphing: transformation vs. spatial transit, 74; mechanical vs. magical, 96; and juxtaposition, 225

Mortality: and food and waste, 126; of television set, 165

Motion choreography: in exchange and ontological transformation, 92, 95; conveying subjectivity, 96

MTV logo designs, 76

MUD/MOO, 187

Muntadas: haute CULTURE and noncontiguous space, 168; "Exposicion," 169; "The Fileroom: An Interactive Computer Project Addressing Cultural Censorship," 188, (illus) 189

Museum as megainstallation, 171

Index

Museumization, of video installation and commodification, 170
Myth as experience of continuous elsewhere, 111

Naimark, Michael: nutrition in "Virtuality, Inc.," 141, (illus) 142; "See Banff!," 180, 203, (illus) 204; "Panoramic and Movie-Map Studies in Computer 3-Space," 197; "Field Recording Study #1," (illus) 198
Narcissism in video art, 171, 176, 240
Narrative in video art, 162
National Endowment for the Arts, 148, 237
Nauman, Bruce, "Live Taped Corridor," 155, (illus) 156, 171
NBC: radical alteration of news format toward tabloid, 41, 42; IDs and graphic styles, 76; openers and Las Vegas style, 85, choreographic complexity and repeatability, 87
NBC Network ID, Pacific Data Images, (illus) 78
Negative space in print and cosmos, 84
Neocolonialism and cyberspace, 241
Networks and distributed space, 187
News as cause of events, 15
"Nightline," "Revolution in a Box," and television democracy, 49, 58
Noncommodity arts and process, 157–58
Nonfood: purification and health, 127; foodceuticals as, 129; Olestra, 140; smart like computer, 145–46; as future food, 233
Nonspace: and cyberspace, 17; displacement as, 103, 104; condensation as, 104; dislocation as, 106; and mobile subjectivity, 112; links television, freeway, and mall, 116; of the mind, 178; protocyberspace, 192; vs. the void, 230
Nootropics and raves, 144

Oceanic feeling and self-annihilation, 132
Opalescence and ontological uncertainty in cyberspace, 180, 203
Oral logic: and scale, 128; incorporation, 126, 134
Oral sadism, 128, 234
Oz and commodity fetishism, 229

Pacific Data Images, "Globo Fantastico," (illus) 77, 78, 79, 85; morphing from automobile into Exxon tiger, (illus) 89; production strategy of, 221

Paradox: of personalized impersonality, 5; of mobility in stasis, 112; of massification and isolation, 117; of mobility and homogeneity, 118; of virtual travel, 199
Paralinguistic cues, 6
Paramount reality: social construction of, 9; face-to-face, 10; unreality of, 10
Parasocial behavior, 18
Parking the body, 139, 235
Passage: and segmentation, 113–14, 230–31; from conceptual to material, 158; between 2- and 3-D images, 161
Pastness, produced by enclosure, 109
"Pee-wee's Playhouse" and variable motion design, 86
Performance art and personal pronouns, 161
Performative speech acts, 8, 121
Phantasmagoria of the interior and distraction, 100
Phantom ride in Hale's Tours, 222
Pinney, Christopher, virtual travel as self-fragmentation, 202
Plato's cave: and proscenium arts, 160; and learning with the body, 169
Postculinary discourse and Alice in Wonderland, 138
Posthuman oedipal journey, 205
Postmodernism and derealization, 161
Postsymbolic and hidden apparatus, 134
Power, disparity of in telematics, 143; walking, 102
Precinematic devices in art, 219
Presence, critique of: in philosophy, 13; in art, 32, 33, 34, 239
Presentational arts: vs. representational arts, 158, 160–61; recognition of, 171
Privacy, history of, 229
Privatization, metapsychological effects of, 108, 109; and massification after WW II, 117
"Process" and "working through," 64
Projection and immersion, 98
Propriocentric and kinetic senses, 29
Proxemics, 6
Psychotropics and FDA, 144
Public access, 187, 231, 232
Public sphere, impoverishment of, 44, 46, 47
Purification strategies: vs. contamination, 127; repudiation, 138; denial, 139; smart drugs, 129; negation and nonfood, 135

Railway vs. liberty of automobile, 117–18
Real time: and computer graphics, 22; as unreal, 23; vs. duration, 23
Recriprocity, need for in discourse, 14
Referential fallacy: world equated with its representation, 11; in photography, 12; in print, 38
Reich, Robert, and symbolic analysts, 137
Remoteness: actual and metaphoric, 25
Renaissance space and virtual reality, 182
Representation vs. presentation, 20
Repudiation and cyberpunk, 138, 139
Resolution, photographic, desire for, 184–85
Retail drama, 105
Rinaldo, Kenneth, and Mark Grossman, "The Flock," 193
Rokeby, David, "A Very Nervous System," 193
Romanian Revolution / Coup: reports compared, 51, 55; crowd as studio tableau, 53; and Panamanian invasion, 56–57; "Nightline" critiques Romanians, 58, 59; camcorders behind the scenes, 61

Scale: as mental construct, 88; relation to frame and monumentality, 90
Scarry, Elaine, and the "mimesis of deliberation," 45
Schorr, Daniel, on Bosnia, 47
Schwarzkopf, General Norman: war not Nintendo, 25; the luckiest man in Kuwait, 30; as anchor, 44
Second skins: and automobile, 112; and other, 132; in virtual reality, 141
Sermon, Paul, "Telematic Dreaming," 31, (illus) frontispiece, 97; "Telematic Vision," 97
Serra, Richard: "Boomerang," 176
Serrano, Andres, and excretory art, 148
Shaw, Jeffrey, "Royal Road," 88, (illus) 89; "The Golden Calf," 26, (illus) 27; "Revolution," 190
Shifters: pronouns as, 9; and engagement, 11; television graphics as, e.g., squeezeframe, 94
Shock: doubling effect when crowd sees itself on television, 52, 54; of passage between local and metropolitan, 104
Simulation: Greimas on, 11; and authenticity, 14; not used pejoratively, 213
Simulator sickness and lag, 182
Simultaneity in visual field, 114

Sincerity and authenticity, 13
Skin egos: second skin and self-transformation, 132; muscular, symbolic, electronic, 133; examples of, 234
Slice defined, 225
Smart food and drugs: and information flow, 128; introjected phalluses, 143; bad-tasting, 145; learning and fit, 146, 235–36
Smartness: and agency of object world, 128; and skin, 133; drugs and data, 144; performance and, 146–47
Smith, Tony, on suburbia, 102, 161
Smithson, Robert, on vicariousness, 102–103
Snow, Michael, and zoom duration in *Wavelength*, 83
Social justice and cultural forms, 34
Sociality, impoverished image of, 35
Society of massacre vs. sacrifice, 133
Sommerer, Christa, and Laurent Mignonneau: "Interactive Plant Growing," "Phototropy," 210
Sorkin, Michael, on Walter Hudson and immobility, 136
Sound bites, length of, 37
Space: television, composed of stacks, 16; vs. place, 101; derealized nonspace, 102; idyll in front of television, 113; as interactive agency, 183
Space-in-between: in video installation, 155–57; and artifacts, 238
Spacing out, 100, 110, 229
Spanjaard, Martin, "Adelbrecht," 194
Spatial figure: magazine metaphor, 95; stack on z-axis, 95; inversion of inside / outside, 166
Spatial motif / spatial figure / tropes of motion defined, 73
Spatial motifs: outer space vs. West, 84; self-referential, 84
Spatial tropes: of forced perspective, 82; of moving toward as understanding, 88; of extreme nearness as "touch," 90; of inverted horizon, 90; *Top Gun* and Pepsi, 91; hanging box insert as balloon, 94; stacks at different ontological levels, 114
Spectacle, Ceaușescu's and public privation, 51
Speech-acts, perlocutionary force of, 13
Stone, Allucquère, on cyberspace, 138
Street lighting, 241

Street vs. the mall, 105
Subjectivity and reciprocity, 9–10;
Surgical bombing and disengagement, 28
Surveillance: as corollary of interactivity, 7; vs. habitual, distracted exercise of values, 117; in cyberspace and social control, 183
Sutherland, Ivan, and the "ultimate display," 184
Suture, interactivity as, 16
Symbolic acts and trauma, 30–32, 209

Talk show virginity, 46
Telematics: and power, 23, 29; disengagement and ethics, 23; vision machines and remoteness, 25; realism vs. agency, 26; brain surgery, bombing and, 143
Telepresence. *See* Telematics
Television: need for after WW II, 3; mastery of "we" and virtual "you," 4, 6–7; anticipation of cyberculture, 8; membrane between, and everyday life, 18; restricted subjects of, 38–41, 45; simulation of discourse, 48; parallel justice system, 65; virtual, 231; viewing and metabolism, 235
Television and democracy, 216
Television apparatus: dominant in image-surround, 158; as primordial video installation, 159, 163, 165
Television as modeling exchange, 100
Television democracy: Italy and U.S. compared, 39; in question, 40; democratic access, 47; Cold War victory or failure of, 49; vs. Internet, 66
Television graphics: before and after computer, 74; and analog animation, 75; and PDI, 76; standardized for local production, 80; spatial and hermeneutic transformation of, 86; periodization and categories of, 220; and excess, 221
Television news and "working through," 64–65
Television screen as barrier, 39–40
Television space of stacked levels, 41
Televisual events: between on- and off-screen space, 49; Marcos and Ceauşescu in, 50–51; and dissimulation in Timisoara, 52; crowd takes over television studio, 53; protest squashed in Bucharest and Tiananmen Square, 55
Televisuality, 219
Temporality: cyclic repetition, 109; dura-

tion as viewing time and banishment of decay, 109; pastness, 109; reruns, 110; of viewing installation vs. single image, 170
Terror: and partial visibility, 51; and unframed virtual space, 98
Theatricality: performance art distinguished from traditional, 161
Tin Man of Oz as organic displacement, 126
Todorov, Tzvetan, on flaying in Aztec ceremony, 132
Too much and too little: as culinary metaphors, 136; in jokes, 230; and smart drugs, 236
Tourism: and desire for otherness, 201; self-destruct theory of, 242
Transformation: motion vs. mechanical or magical metamorphosis, 96
Translating: culture from mechanical to virtual media, 196; images between 2 and 3 dimensions, and panoramic space, 197; z-axis and lateral motion, 199
Travel: from actual to surrogate, 182, 202, 242; and romantic construction of identity, 201
Trumbell, Douglas: *2001* and the Slitscan process, 82; and Las Vegas theme park design, 85; and Luxor Casino, 223
Turkle, Sherry, computer a second self, 15
Turning, the: at the end of the Cold War, 48; on- to offscreen power reversal, 48; changing camera point of view, 50, 51; and post–Cold War ideological crisis, 56–57

Ultimate display, death and enunciative fallacy, 184
Uncanny in information society, 205
Uncertainty of outcome: in video installation, 158; in virtual space, 211
Urban, Greg, on enculturation, 5

Vasulka, Woody, and Steina Vasulka on synthesizers, 220–21
Venturi, Robert, *Learning from Las Vegas,* on monumentality, 120
Victimization on television, 47
Video installation: site and ephemerality of, 157; vs. performance and proscenium arts, 158; closed-circuit video and recorded- vs. single-channel video art, 162; protointeractivity and immersion

in, 162–63; poetics of, 167–68; subject matter of, 169–70; vs. exhibition, 169; cyclical time in, 170; critique of mass consumer culture and impression of presence, 177

Viola, Bill: "Room for St. John of the Cross," 166, 167

Virilio, Paul: *War and Cinema*, 23, 28

Virtual, uncertain reality status of, 180

Virtual address of television, 15, 16

Virtual agents, autonomy in, 196

Virtual envelope of viewer and television, 113

Virtual flight in VRML on WWW, 80

Virtual images projected or wrapped vs. boxed or contained, 98

Virtual reality: a subset of cyberspace, 17; and second skin, 18; inversion of Renaissance space, 25; and blindness, 25, 26; closure of and ethics, 29; and disavowal of body, 141; blindness and diet in, 141; regression and vulnerability in, 143

Virtual relationship: and engagement, 4; to machines and images, 6

"Virtual Seattle" by VPL Labs: flight in, 181; void in, 196

Virtual space: unframed, 97; editing improvised in, 199; uncertain timing of interactivity in, 200; division of labor in, 242

Virtualities: bubble of, 7; as a species of fiction, 10; vs. simulation in ordinary language, 15; ontologically uncertain and insufficiently marked, 19, 23–25, 32; as fiction of presence, 20; immersion in and interaction with images, 21; and symbolic events, 21; and Borges map/territory relation, 28; distribution of, 29; disembodiment in as myth, 30; and symbolic events, 30; and tracking cultural shifts, 34; overview of, 33–35

Virtualized. *See* Cyberization

Wald, Richard, president of CBS vs. anchor omniscience, 42

Waste, simulated, as art medium, 148

Weather and ideology, 228

Weightlessness vs. vertical axis in Cloud City, 91

Wheel of Fortune letters and exchange of symbolic values, 92

Wiener, Norbert, and *cyber*, 14

Willemen, Paul, the "fourth look," 217

Williams, Raymond: and mobile privatization, 3, 100; on television and dramatic simulation, 14; on flow, 114

Wilson, Alexander, on landscape, 201

Wired typeface, 220

Womb and immersion, 131

Woolley, Benjamin, *Virtual Worlds*, denial and mathematics, 140

Word: as metonymy of body in writing and print, 72; fetish, and magical contagion in "Pee-wee's Playhouse," 93; secret, in Groucho Marx's "You Bet Your Life," 93

"Working through" as steadying the symbolic order, 64

Worth, Sol, and John Adair, walking in Navajo film, 113

WWW compared to mall, 67

Z-axis moves: and interactivity, 16; exchange between viewer and screen, 72; shifts of scale as ontological transformations, 81; cinematic, 82; impression of speed and time compression, 83; Death Star fly through, 85; transitions between databases in *T-Vision*, 87–88; as shish kebab, 199

Zettl, Herbert, and graphication, 94

Zones: Kansas and Oz, 119; history of, 231

Zoom: as virtual motion, 81; immensity vs. duration in, 83; lenses, 222